To Ja...

Best Wishes

Fred *(signature)*

50 CHILDREN

ALSO BY STEVEN PRESSMAN
Outrageous Betrayal

50
CHILDREN

One Ordinary American Couple's Extraordinary
Rescue Mission into the Heart of Nazi Germany

STEVEN PRESSMAN

With an Afterword by Paul Shapiro,
United States Holocaust Memorial Museum

HARPER PERENNIAL

NEW YORK • LONDON • TORONTO • SYDNEY • NEW DELHI • AUCKLAND

HARPER PERENNIAL

FIRST HARPER PERENNIAL EDITION PUBLISHED 2015.

Designed by Renato Stanisic

Library of Congress Cataloging-in-Publication Data has been applied for.

ISBN 978-0-06-223748-4 (pbk.)

18 19 OV/LSC 10 9 8 7 6 5 4 3

For Liz,
who always knew

Whoever saves a life, it is considered as if he has saved the entire world.

—THE TALMUD

Contents

Introduction

The inch-thick stack of yellowing onionskin paper rested in a brown cardboard binder held together by a rusting metal clasp. For years my wife, Liz, had kept it tucked away, half forgotten, in a desk drawer in our home in San Francisco, mixed in with the usual assortment of bank statements, medical records, and other household documents. But there was nothing even remotely mundane about the astonishing tale that had been carefully typed out on those brittle pages decades earlier. The contents of a small plastic bag, wedged between the manila file folders in the same desk drawer, added graphic drama to the pages in the binder: more than a dozen German passports, each stamped with a menacing Nazi swastika and bearing the name and photograph of a young girl or boy.

The broad outline of what Gil and Eleanor Kraus, my wife's maternal grandparents, had accomplished in the spring of 1939 was not exactly a secret. Family members had long been aware of the couple's daring voyage into Nazi Germany on the eve of the Holocaust and their return to the United States with fifty Jewish children in their care. For the rest of their lives, however, neither of them spoke in any detail with family or friends about their unlikely adventure. They certainly offered no clues that explained how—or why—a Jewish couple from Philadelphia wound up in Nazi-controlled Vienna determined to rescue children whose lives were at stake.

Eleanor, however, had written it all down. At some point she typed out a richly detailed account of a seemingly far-fetched plan that began with a simple discussion between her husband, Gil, and his friend Louis Levine, the head of a national Jewish fraternal organization called Brith Sholom. At first glance, the typewritten pages read like an improbable, if not impossible, product of a vivid imagination.

Incredibly, the rescue mission took place precisely as Eleanor described it. In fact, its full historical significance extended well beyond her own account. The fifty boys and girls whose lives were saved by Gil and Eleanor Kraus comprised the largest single known group of children, traveling without their parents, who were legally admitted into the United States during the Holocaust.

I first learned of Eleanor's private manuscript not long after Liz and I met in the summer of 2000. But it took another decade before I was able to give it my full attention and dig more deeply into this fascinating episode that for years had remained hidden in plain sight. It quickly became clear that this was much more than just another Holocaust rescue story. Research into Gil and Eleanor's unheralded exploits led to a greater understanding of the obstacles that stood in their way as they valiantly (and in Gil's case, single-mindedly) carried out their mission. The rescue project took place within the context of a profoundly hostile social and political environment in the United States that made their achievement all the more stunning— and, sadly, all the more singular. Moreover, the Krauses embarked on their journey during a brief window of time when the Nazis, determined to rid the Third Reich of all Jews, were allowing—in fact, pressuring—them to leave. Tragically, the greater challenge was finding countries that would take them in.

Gil and Eleanor Kraus never set out to be heroes. They were ordinary people who did something extraordinary and whose courageous deeds came very close to being lost to history. The stack of Eleanor's pages, ever more fragile to the touch, has been carefully placed back in the desk drawer. At long last I am proud to bring the dramatic story of their quiet heroism out of the darkness.

PART ONE

THE PLAN

CHAPTER 1

No one in his right mind would go to Germany now. It's not safe,
especially for Jews. I'd be too scared to put a foot into that country,
assuming the storm troopers would even let us in.

—ELEANOR KRAUS

PHILADELPHIA
JANUARY 1939

Eleanor Kraus glanced around the dining room of her spacious
three-story brick home on Cypress Street, in Philadelphia's
well-heeled Fitler Square neighborhood. The dinner hour was approaching, and Eleanor wanted to be sure that the table had been
set properly. Although her husband, Gil, had not yet arrived home
from his downtown law office, Eleanor had already dressed for the
evening, choosing a silk dress and a pair of T-strap pumps. A double
strand of pearls, set off against a new pair of matching earrings

and a deep-red coat of lacquered nail polish, completed the look. Carlotta Greenfield, one of Gil's nieces, was bringing her fiancé to dinner, and Eleanor, as always, wanted everything to shine.

When Gil walked through the front door a few minutes after six o'clock, Eleanor greeted him with a quick kiss on the cheek and reminded him that their guests were due to arrive any moment. Gil smiled knowingly at his wife, removed his overcoat, and set down his worn leather briefcase. As Eleanor was turning to dash back into the kitchen to check with the family cook on the dinner preparations, Gil caught her eye. "There is something that I need to discuss with you. Come into the bathroom while I shave. We can talk in there and while I'm getting dressed."

Eleanor followed him upstairs and into the bathroom that adjoined the couple's bedroom. Gil undid his necktie and pulled off his starched white dress shirt, leaving on a sleeveless undershirt as he prepared to shave. He was forty-two years old, and he and Eleanor had been married for more than fourteen years. But as he stood there in the bathroom, filling the sink with steaming hot water and then carefully scraping the straight edge razor across his face, it struck Eleanor just how fit and handsome he still was. With his broad shoulders and muscular torso, Gil had retained his physique of more than twenty years earlier, when he had competed on both the varsity wrestling and football teams during his undergraduate days at the University of Pennsylvania.

While Eleanor perched on the edge of the bathtub, Gil mentioned that his good friend Louis Levine had dropped by earlier that day. Levine was a successful real estate man in New York, but his visit to Gil's office had nothing to do with business matters. He had come in his capacity as the grand master of Brith Sholom, a national Jewish fraternal organization to which Gil also belonged.

The two men had talked all that afternoon about a seemingly impossible idea—whether there might be a chance to help save Jewish children trapped inside Nazi Germany. Both Gil and Levine were only too aware of the worsening conditions for Jews living inside Hitler's Reich, and they discussed the possibility that Brith Sholom might be able to sponsor some kind of rescue effort. Levine reminded Gil that the group had recently built a children's summer camp along the banks of Perkiomen Creek in Collegeville, a semirural area about an hour outside of Philadelphia. On the other side of the camp, Brith Sholom had also constructed a large stone house that included twenty-five bedrooms. The house, intended for possible use as an old-age home, at the moment was standing completely empty.

Gil had enormous respect for Levine, and he listened closely as his friend spoke passionately about the ever-increasing dangers that were confronting Jews—adults and children alike—living in Nazi Germany. As the afternoon wore on, Levine finally got to the real point of his visit. He knew all about Gil's reputation as a tough-minded lawyer who seemed able to solve just about any challenge put before him. Levine bluntly asked if Gil himself would be willing to take on the children's rescue project.

Reacting almost instinctively, Gil surprised himself by immediately agreeing. Of course, he was aware of the difficult—perhaps insurmountable—obstacles that would stand in the way of such a project ever succeeding. Would the Nazis consider letting children leave Germany? And even if they would, America's rigid immigration laws presented another imposing barrier. But Levine knew his friend well: Gil had a strong sense of justice, of right and wrong, and the rescue idea was right. Coincidentally three prominent Philadelphia Quakers—Rufus Jones, Robert Yarnall, and George Walton, all of whom Gil knew quite well—had traveled on their own to Berlin only a few weeks earlier in an effort to help Jews get out of Germany. Quaker groups in the United States, organized under the banner of the American Friends Service Committee, had become active in a variety of Jewish rescue efforts ever since Hitler had come to power in 1933. The Philadelphia trio had set out in hopes of meeting with high-ranking Nazi officials—perhaps even with Hitler himself—and arguing the case for making it easier for Jewish families to leave the Reich. But the high-minded mission was rebuffed. "Germans Ridicule Visiting Friends" read the headline in the December 9 edition of the Philadelphia *Evening Bulletin*. The accompanying article, an Associated Press dispatch from Berlin, reported that a German newspaper controlled by Nazi Propaganda Minister Joseph Goebbels "declared today that 'we must laugh' at the Quaker delegation, which is coming from the United States to investigate the condition of Jews and other minorities in Germany."

Other groups, including several leading Jewish organizations, had been trying since 1934—within a year of Hitler becoming Germany's chancellor—to bring Jewish children to safety in the United States. Such efforts had yielded very little success, resulting in the rescue of only a small handful of children before bumping up against America's stringent immigration regulations. No one could figure out a way to bring in larger numbers of children. By the time that Louis Levine left Gil's office on that January afternoon, Gil knew that he could not possibly turn down the challenge that others had been unable to meet.

Eleanor listened patiently while Gil recounted the conversation with Levine. Drying his face with a small cotton towel she handed him, he told her that Levine was confident that Brith Sholom's members would readily agree to raise all the money necessary for bringing children over to the United States. Gil glanced at the mirror and then turned toward Eleanor. Levine had asked if he would be willing to take on the project, he said. It would be a very complicated undertaking, of course, but he had promised his friend that he would certainly think it over. For the moment at least, Gil decided not to tell his wife that he had made up his mind on the spot.

Finally, it was Eleanor's turn to talk. "Gil, this is really crazy!" she exclaimed. "No one in his right mind would go into Nazi Germany right now. It's not safe, especially for Jews. I'm not sure you could stand it for even twenty-four hours. I'd be too scared to put a foot into that country, assuming the storm troopers would even let us in." Gil was quiet as he stepped into the bedroom, where he began to dress for dinner. He certainly was not surprised by her reaction. He was fully aware of the risks involved in moving ahead with the rescue plan. Traveling to Nazi Germany held little appeal for a Jew—even one traveling with the protection of an American passport. Gil also knew that the project would almost certainly require him to spend several weeks or even months in Europe. And even then, there was no way of knowing if the plan had any chance of succeeding.

IN THE WEEKS and months leading up to Gil and Eleanor's conversation, the newspapers had been filled with articles that described in grim detail the progressively brutal measures directed against hundreds of thousands of Jews living in Germany and Austria. On January 2, an Associated Press dispatch, which appeared in newspapers throughout the United States and Canada, reported on a New Year's message from Joseph Goebbels that demanded an international solution to the world's "Jew problem." "Germany's Jews . . . started the new year in dire circumstances," wrote the AP's Berlin correspondent. "Emigration, in the face of the Nazi aim to drive all but elderly Hebrews from the Reich, has bogged down in a jam of applications at consulates and in the problem of financing the exodus." A week later, on January 9, newspapers published a United Press report, also from Berlin, disclosing that hundreds of Jews had recently been brought into Gestapo headquarters, where they were forced to sign pledges to leave Germany or face imprisonment. "Similar pledges were exacted from Jews released from Nazi concentration camps in recent weeks," the wire service reported, "even though it was impossible for many to obtain foreign visas or enough money to get out of the country."

Ten months earlier, Hitler's storm troopers had streamed into neighboring Austria to carry out the Anschluss—Austria's annexation into the Third Reich. With only token opposition to Hitler's plan to fold the country into a Greater Germany, the German troops had been warmly embraced—in fact, eagerly welcomed. More than a million cheering citizens of Vienna lined the streets to greet Hitler with flowers, outstretched arm salutes, and thundering shouts of "*Sieg Heil!*" when he triumphantly motorcaded into the city in the late afternoon of Monday, March 14. The following morning, Hitler appeared on a balcony overlooking the vast Heldenplatz, where tens of thousands had gathered to hear him speak. He did not disappoint them. "In this hour I can report to the German people the greatest accomplishment of my life," Hitler proclaimed. "As Führer and chancellor of the German nation and the Reich, I can announce before history the entry of my homeland into the German Reich."

The Nazis wasted no time in subjecting Vienna's 185,000 Jews to the harsh measures that had been directed much more gradually against the 600,000 Jews who lived in Germany. There was nothing secret about these actions, all of which were widely reported in American newspapers. "Adolf Hitler has left behind him in Austria an anti-Semitism that is blossoming far more rapidly than ever it did in Germany," the *New York Times* reported on March 16, two days after Hitler's celebrated arrival. "All Jewish executives at Vienna's largest department store were arrested immediately after Hitler's arrival, the business being 'taken over' by Nazis. Shops, cafés and restaurants were raided and large numbers of Jews were arrested." Two weeks later, on April 3, a lengthy article in the *Times* described the terrifying new landscape for the Jews of Vienna. "In Austria, overnight, Vienna's Jews were made free game for mobs, despoiled of their property, deprived of police protection, ejected from employment and barred from sources of relief," the newspaper informed its readers. "The frontiers were hermetically sealed against their escape." Within six weeks of the Anschluss, Austria's new Nazi leaders announced their intention to rid Vienna of all of its Jews within four years. " 'By 1942, Jewish elements must be eradicated from Vienna and must disappear,'" the *Times* reported on April 27 in an article that quoted from an editorial published in Hitler's official newspaper. "'By that time no business, no factory should be allowed to remain in Jewish hands. No Jews should have an opportunity to earn a living . . . Jews! Abandon all hope. There is only one possibility for you: Emigrate—if someone will accept you.'"

The situation for Jews trapped inside Germany and Austria became even more desperate in the weeks that led up to Louis Levine's meeting with Gil. The November pogrom known as Kristallnacht had completely erased what slim doubts still remained about the Nazis' aims. Anyone reading the newspapers in America knew exactly what was going on in Europe.

As she pored over these chilling stories, Eleanor had also sensed the dangers that might greet anyone who hoped to do something in response to these tragic events, and she said as much to her husband as they walked downstairs to await their guests. Gil offered little to calm his wife's anxieties. Instead he frankly explained to Eleanor just how difficult it would be to bring Jewish refugees—even children—into the United States. Labor Department regulations made it impossible for any organization to bring children, unaccompanied by parents, into the country. This meant that Brith Sholom officially could neither sponsor the children's rescue nor legally act on its own to bring them to America. Although the group might be allowed to house and care for the children once they were here, there was still the challenge of complying with the nation's strict labor and immigration laws. Gil knew he would have to find another way to bring in children without running afoul of these laws.

Gil spoke with a growing resolve in his voice, which Eleanor recognized. It signaled her husband's steadfast determination to proceed, regardless of any obstacles that might stand in his way. She shot a wary glance at him, but he cut her off before she could say anything further. She was not surprised when Gil added that he and Levine had already made plans to travel to Washington early the following week in order to meet with officials at the State and Labor departments.

Carlotta Greenfield and her fiancé were due to arrive any moment. Eleanor could hardly imagine how she would make it through the evening with her head spinning with all this talk about Nazi Germany and rescuing Jewish children. Gil, meanwhile, had one more startling piece of information for his wife. If the rescue plan had any shot at succeeding, he would need to round up fifty individual sponsors— one for each child that he hoped to bring back to the United States. Each sponsor would have to fill out an extensive affidavit required by the government to ensure that they would provide sufficient financial support for any immigrant entering the United States. "How would you like to work on this with me?" he asked Eleanor in a voice that was at once both calm and insistent. "It will mean asking our friends and others we know for help. Are you game for that?" Gil figured that it would take several weeks both to find enough people in Philadelphia who would be willing to sponsor the children and to submit the detailed affidavits required by the government. Although he was anxious to begin at once, he told his wife they should wait until he was able to talk to officials at the State Department. "It might all come to nothing," said Gil. "It may all be impossible."

BY THE MORNING after the dinner party, Gil seemed even more determined to move ahead. "He said there must be some legal way to bring children into the United States," Eleanor jotted down in a diary that, years later, she would turn into a private written account about the rescue project. Eleanor knew how much confidence Gil had in his own abilities as a lawyer and also how resourceful he could be when it came to tackling tough problems. Still she tried to avoid becoming too enthusiastic about her own potential role in the mission. "I told myself this going-to-Germany idea was out," she wrote. "No one, not even Gil, could consider this a practical idea."

Other considerations stood in the way of Eleanor's enthusiasm. Only a few weeks earlier, she had talked a friend into offering her a part-time job in the advertising office at the Blum department store on Chestnut Street, not far from the equally fashionable Bonwit Teller and Lord & Taylor stores. Eleanor did not have to work. Gil's law practice was thriving, and he was more than capable of providing for his wife and two children while keeping the family in upper-middle-class comfort. Eleanor, for her part, embraced the lifestyle that came with the couple's elevated social standing in Jewish Philadelphia. She was a beautiful woman who rarely hesitated to remind others of her great looks. Having married into the socially prominent Kraus family, she was also mindful of the societal obligations that went along with being Gil's wife. She was in charge of the couple's social engagements, while also making sure that the family household ran smoothly. Her dinner parties were always elegant affairs, and she filled their busy schedule with evenings at the symphony, trips to art museums, and leisurely summer weekends at their oceanfront house on New Jersey's Long Beach Island. Her children attended Friends Select, Philadelphia's prestigious Quaker school that traced its beginnings back to 1689. Above all else, Eleanor was truly happy being a woman of her time.

Yet as a devotee of fine clothes, jewelry, and fashion, Eleanor was excited about working at the department store and hated the thought of having to give up her brand-new job before it had even started. After Gil's initial conversation about the plan, she knew, however, that she would almost certainly play a part. She explained to the friend who had offered the job that she might have to leave on short notice in order to help her husband with his work. Although she did not offer details, Eleanor casually mentioned that it might involve travel to Washington and, possibly, to Germany. In the end, the department store job fell by the wayside.

The more Eleanor thought about the project, the more she had to admit that it sounded like something she and her husband should do together. But she also kept reminding herself what an unlikely adventure it would be. "To think of being able to help even a handful of children is a beautiful thought. It is a luxurious dream but most impractical," she wrote. "After all, we are living a most serene existence in our pretty house on Cypress Street. My own two children seem most secure. Gil is very busy, and his work is going well."

Over dinner a few nights later, Gil showed Eleanor a couple of affidavit forms he had brought home from his office. The idea of having to ask anyone—let alone her closest friends—to fill out a document with such an exhaustive list of detailed financial questions made her deeply uncomfortable. The affidavits required the applicant to reveal intensely personal information about their income, bank accounts, stock holdings, life insurance policies. Eleanor preferred not to talk about money, and in fact considered the topic virtually off-limits. She rarely even spoke to Gil about the couple's own finances. How on earth could she even think of asking friends and casual acquaintances to reveal intimate financial details that would almost certainly embarrass them all?

Realizing how awkward this would be for his wife, Gil suggested that she begin by working on his own affidavit. Louis Levine would provide the second one. Once Eleanor grew more comfortable with the process, Gil would give her the names of four or five of his close friends from the Locust Club, the private establishment that served as a social gathering spot for Philadelphia's most prominent Jewish business, civic, and political leaders. "I don't think we're going to have too much trouble finding fifty sponsors," Gil assured Eleanor. "Everybody wants to help."

Even as he spoke, Eleanor realized that it was simply a matter of convincing herself—and her circle of friends—that saving children's lives was more important than concerns about violating social proprieties. Above all else, Eleanor knew that she had to help. It was simply the right thing to do.

CHAPTER 2

Miss Eleanor Shirley Jacobs, daughter of Mr. and Mrs. Harris D. Jacobs, was married to Gilbert J. Kraus today at the home of a brother of the bride.

—Evening Public Ledger

PHILADELPHIA
BEFORE 1939

Although Eleanor had plenty of persuasive reasons to avoid involving herself in the rescue project, her husband never hesitated for a moment. If he harbored any doubts about his ability to succeed where others had not, he never expressed them to anyone, including his wife. Above all, Gil Kraus was a strong-willed man with a resolute sense of what was right. And he would pursue that no matter what anyone else thought of him.

Gil's almost bullheaded conviction for doing the right thing did not come out of nowhere. His father, Solomon Kraus, had devoted years of his life to a wide variety of social, charitable, and philanthropic organizations and causes. Gil belonged to a German Jewish family that by the 1930s had long been an integral part of Philadelphia's Jewish society. He certainly shared his father's passion for championing the rights of those far less fortunate than himself. A long-shot effort to save the lives of imperiled children threatened by Hitler's campaign against Jews no doubt struck in Gil the same empathetic chord that Solomon had responded to in earlier years.

All four of Gil's grandparents made their way to the United States as part of the great migration of German Jews that took place during the 1840s and 1850s. His paternal grandparents, Leopold and Charlotte Kraus, immigrated to America in 1859, a few years after they were married. Their two oldest children, Fannie and Herman, were born in Austria, while two younger sons, Solomon and Milton, were born in Philadelphia. Leopold earned a middle-class living as a merchant—the 1880 U.S. census listed his occupation as a purveyor of "gents' furnishings and goods." Solomon, however, had bigger ambitions, and after a brief stint in the dry-goods business, he began a successful career as a Philadelphia real estate broker. In 1893, he married Eva Mayer, whose parents had come from Germany and settled in the small town of Tamaqua, Pennsylvania, where Eva was born. By the time she married Solomon, he was both a prominent businessman and an active participant in Philadelphia's rough-and-tumble Democratic politics. In 1892 he was chosen to cast a vote in the electoral college for Grover Cleveland, the successful Democratic presidential candidate that year. A few years later, Solomon ran for a judicial magistrate's position, competing in a raucous citywide political convention that was held to select the Democratic slate of local candidates. The gathering turned into "an unparalleled scene of disorder lasting for nearly five hours," reported the *Philadelphia Inquirer,* and culminated in fistfights on the convention floor. "Just before the close of the proceedings it became necessary to call in the police to clear the stage. Chairs were broken, several blows exchanged, and a handsome piano was treated in a manner that robbed it of its beauty."

Solomon's would-be career as an elected official soon came to an end after he decided to focus on business rather than politics. But he continued to cultivate valuable political as well as business contacts that served him—and later his son Gil—quite well. Chief among these useful contacts was Albert Greenfield, a scrappy young Russian immigrant who eventually would preside over a vast real estate and financial empire in Philadelphia comprising department stores, hotels, and a highly profitable mortgage banking company that helped to finance his various commercial enterprises. The two men seemed destined to be business partners when, in 1906, a precocious nineteen-year-old Greenfield first proposed a modest real estate deal with Kraus, who was twenty years his senior. "Greenfield and Kraus had similar personalities—aggressive, competitive, overbearing, tempestuous—and thus they took an instant dislike to each other," a Philadelphia journalist wrote about the two men. "Each liked to be in charge of whatever he did, so the two did not work well together. On the other hand, as businessmen, each recognized the benefits to be gained from working with the other."

In 1914, business ties turned into family ties when Greenfield proposed to Solomon's oldest daughter, Edna. Solomon's critical personal opinion of Greenfield had not changed simply because the blustery would-be mogul had been courting Kraus's attractive, blue-eyed daughter. But Solomon was nothing if not a pragmatist, and he recognized a good deal when he saw one. The marriage would be socially advantageous and also good for business. And it would certainly be much easier to deal with Greenfield as a son-in-law than as a potential business rival. Solomon swiftly consented to the marriage. By the time that Gil began his own career as a corporate lawyer in the early 1920s, the Greenfield-Kraus enterprise controlled more than two dozen building and loan associations spread across

Philadelphia, with assets approaching $35 million. The Russian immigrant and the son of German Jews also formed a highly profitable mortgage company that, soon enough, extended the reach of their business ties to New York City.

Solomon, along with many other German Jews, was avowedly nonreligious, espousing instead a highly secular form of Judaism that placed little stock in traditional religious practices. Although the Krauses were members of Keneseth Israel, Philadelphia's most prominent Reform synagogue (which at the time eschewed—as most Reform congregations did—bar mitzvahs for thirteen-year-old boys), they embraced social assimilation, celebrating what they felt were true American holidays like Christmas and Easter. When he turned sixteen, Gil participated in a religious confirmation ceremony at the synagogue but, like the rest of his family, otherwise paid little attention to Jewish rituals.

But the Jewish spirit of social service and *tikkun olam*—the Hebrew phrase meaning "healing the world"—remained an integral part of life for the city's Jewish community leaders, including Solomon Kraus. In the early decades of the twentieth century, even as assimilation threaded through the social fabric of upper-class German Jewish life, Jews were still Jews. There were Jewish social clubs, Jewish charities, and an abundance of Jewish philanthropy. In 1905, a group of forty-four prominent Philadelphia Jews formed a fraternal organization, which they named Brith Sholom—Hebrew for "Covenant of Peace." The group pledged itself to providing an array of social services for newly arrived immigrants—primarily poor Jews who had been arriving in increasingly large numbers in the wake of pogroms in Russia and other Eastern European countries. By the time of Brith Sholom's second convention, which took place in June 1906, Solomon had been chosen to be chairman of the group's Committee on Charity.

Three years later, his commitment to public service resulted in the establishment of the Philadelphia Jewish Sanatorium for Consumptives—a hospital for patients suffering from tuberculosis. Solomon played a leading role in the project by making the financial arrangements to purchase farmland in Eagleville—a rural area thirty miles west of Philadelphia—that became the site of the hospital. He also offered the farm owner one hundred dollars out of his own pocket as a down payment on the land, which was purchased for a total of $6,500. Barely eight months after Solomon and others began discussing the hospital project, the facility opened its doors to its first four tuberculosis patients. In the years that followed, Solomon played prominent roles in several other Jewish organizations, serving as vice president of the American Jewish Congress, vice president of the Zionist Organization of America, and, in 1927, chairman of the United Palestine Appeal campaign in Philadelphia. By then, he had also been elected as Brith Sholom's grand master.

As Solomon's only son—Gil was sandwiched between his older sister, Edna, and his younger sister, Lillian—it was expected that he would follow in his father's footsteps. Solomon cast a long shadow, and Gil wanted his father's respect. Gil, in turn, was all Solomon could ask for in a son. Tall, ruggedly handsome, and determinedly athletic, he had sailed through the University of Pennsylvania, completing his undergraduate degree during the waning days of World War I. Along with several other classmates from Penn, Gil enlisted in the army even as the war was ending in the fall of 1918. He underwent a quick round of basic training at Camp Gordon in Georgia, which led to his continued assignment there as a bayonet instructor. His brief military career concluded in December, just weeks after the armistice silenced the guns in Europe and brought an end to the War to End All Wars. After returning home to Philadelphia, Gil, along with three army buddies, enrolled at Penn's law school and wound up racing through the normal three-year course of studies in two years. Without obtaining a formal diploma, Gil was officially admitted to the bar in October 1921, sworn in by a prominent Philadelphia judge whose son had been one of Gil's friends from the army.

At the age of twenty-three, he began his legal career in a small Jewish-owned firm, where he spent most of his time handling routine business matters—lease negotiations, small property disputes, simple bankruptcies—for the firm's most prominent client, Albert Greenfield's company. It was hardly glamorous or particularly interesting work. "Will you write to Miss Margaret Andrews, threatening foreclosure proceedings, as she has failed to pay her taxes for 1922," Greenfield's corporate secretary instructed Gil in one typical transaction. "Give her about a week or ten days to pay it, and if she doesn't produce the receipted tax bill, I will then send you the papers to commence foreclosure proceedings."

Patience was never Gil's strong point, and he quickly grew eager to make his own mark both in the law and in society. Within a few years of starting his career, he formed his own small firm with two other attorneys while continuing to handle legal and business matters for his brother-in-law Greenfield, which guaranteed a steady stream of work. Gil by now was living in an apartment in Philadelphia's stately Hotel Majestic, located only a short distance from his law office. The Majestic also happened to be just a quick trolley ride away from Baker Bowl and Shibe Park, Philadelphia's two baseball stadiums that were home to the National League Phillies and the American League Athletics, respectively. Given its location, the Majestic was the preferred hotel for many of baseball's top stars in the 1920s, including Rogers Hornsby and Babe Ruth. The prestigious address certainly would have appealed to Gil, who proudly relished his own athletic career at Penn.

It was during these early days of Gil's legal career that he began courting Eleanor Jacobs, the beautiful young daughter—one of six children—of Harris and Rosa Jacobs. Eleanor's parents had immigrated to the United States from Latvia and settled in New Jersey several years before Eleanor was born, in Philadelphia, in 1903. Precisely how and when Gil and Eleanor first met is not known, but it is unlikely that their families would have been close or even known each other, given the significant disparity in their social standings.

Whatever the circumstances of their meeting, however, it is hardly surprising that Gil and Eleanor, despite a six-year age difference, were attracted to each other. A photograph accompanying a newspaper announcement of his appointment as an assistant city attorney in February 1924 revealed a young man with a full head of dark wavy hair and a strong jawline. The handsome lawyer also happened to be witty, intelligent, urbane, and ambitious—in other words, quite a catch. But in Eleanor Jacobs he had met his equal: with her soft doe eyes, porcelain skin, keen sense of fashion, and a charming wit of her own, she immediately enchanted all those around her. She certainly proved enchanting to Gil.

That summer he traveled alone on the SS *Paris* steamship, which sailed from New York City to Le Havre, France. From there, Gil journeyed to Germany and Austria during an extensive European tour that apparently did not interfere with his obligations back home in Philadelphia. He must have done quite a bit of thinking about the petite brunette he had been seeing while he was away. Not long after his return from Europe, he and Eleanor were married in a small ceremony held at the Philadelphia home of Eleanor's brother Frank. Presiding over the ceremony, which took place on October 9, 1924, was Rabbi William Fineshriber, who had arrived in town only a few weeks earlier to take up his new position as chief rabbi at Keneseth Israel. At the time of the wedding, Eleanor had not yet turned twenty-one, which meant that her father had to sign a legal form—"Consent to the Marriage of a Child or Ward"—that gave permission for his daughter to marry.

Four years later, in July 1928, Gil's father died suddenly in Atlantic City, where he and his wife had recently taken up residence in an apartment at the Ritz-Carlton Hotel. Solomon was sixty-two years old and had retired only a few years earlier from his position as vice president of Albert Greenfield's real estate and finance company. A memorial service, which took place at Keneseth Israel, attracted an overflow crowd of more than three thousand people and was attended by Philadelphia's mayor, district attorney, and scores of other political, civic, and business leaders. At the time of his death, Solomon was still serving as grand master of Brith Sholom, and he was lauded by many for his years of service and commitment to the organization and its goals. "To work for his people was his great passion," Rabbi Max Klein, the spiritual leader of the city's Adath Jeshurun synagogue, wrote in a memorial tribute. "And to help make their dreams come true was the joy of his life."

Seven months later, Eva Kraus passed away in Philadelphia at the age of fifty-four. In sharp contrast with the publicity that accompanied her husband's death, Eva's obituary was limited to a three-paragraph item in the *Jewish Exponent,* one of Philadelphia's two Jewish newspapers. A private funeral service was held at the home of her daughter Edna. She was buried next to her husband in a Jewish cemetery in Northeast Philadelphia. Gil, barely into his thirties, now found himself heir to the Kraus legacy even as he continued to thrive professionally and socially.

By the early 1930s, Gil and Eleanor had two young children—Steven, born in 1926, and Ellen, who arrived four years later. Although the Great Depression was wreaking havoc on the economy and creating misery for millions of Americans, it did not appear to have much effect, if any, on the Kraus household. Gil's law practice continued to grow in size and prominence, and by the late 1930s he had formed a new partnership with Edward Weyl, who was related to Eleanor through marriage. Gil and Eleanor themselves had become part of a prominent Jewish world in Philadelphia that was cultured and affluent, trimmed with all the social niceties that accompanied that stratum of society. It was, as Eleanor later wrote, a truly "serene existence" and idyllic life that the couple enjoyed.

And a well-connected one, too. Gil's law partner had a brother, Charles Weyl, who together with his wife, Ollie, were close friends of the Krauses. Charles was a pioneering professor of electrical engineering at Penn, who also happened to be keenly interested in classical music. During the 1930s, Weyl collaborated with Leopold Stokowski, the acclaimed conductor of the Philadelphia Orchestra, on new techniques in sound engineering that resulted in technologically advanced recordings by the highly regarded ensemble. "Stokowski pioneered what later became a standard recording practice," the *New York Times* reported decades later. "But in the early 1930s, the Philadelphia recordings were unmatched for fidelity." The overlapping relationships among Gil, Eleanor, the Weyls, and Stokowski eventually led to rumors, which were never confirmed, of a romantic fling between Eleanor and the maestro, who was more than twenty years older. Rumor, of course, frequently followed glamour—and Eleanor's beauty attracted a lot of attention.

Throughout this same period, Gil became increasingly active in Brith Sholom and its various philanthropic efforts. At its height earlier in the century, the Jewish organization boasted more than fifty thousand members around the country. By the 1930s, the group's membership had fallen to about half that number, but the organization itself, divided up into smaller lodges, remained a vital one. The largest Brith Sholom lodge in Philadelphia had been renamed in Solomon's memory, and Gil had expanded his own visible presence in the city's circle of Jewish business and civic leaders.

Not everything went smoothly. A potentially awkward family rupture occurred in 1935, when Gil's emotionally volatile sister, Edna, abruptly flew off to Tijuana in order to obtain a quickie divorce from Albert Greenfield, leaving him to care for the couple's five children. Despite the uncomfortable marital break between the Krauses and the Greenfields, Gil and his now ex-brother-in-law managed to maintain a good and prosperous relationship.

Gil also recognized how fortunate his family was to remain unaffected by the country's economic woes. At the same time, he was becoming aware of a very different set of challenges faced by Jews and others in far-off Europe. For the moment, however, Gil had no way of knowing where that awareness would lead.

CHAPTER 3

Up until the time that the Nazis marched in, our family was living a very nice and comfortable life.

—Paul Beller

Vienna
Before the Anschluss

Robert Braun's family could trace its Viennese roots back some six hundred years. The blue-eyed, dark-haired youngster's ancestors had lived in Vienna during the time of the Ottoman Empire's siege of the city in 1529, when Suleiman the Magnificent first attempted to conquer the Austrian capital. Centuries later, Robert's father, Max, proudly served in the Austrian emperor's army in the early 1890s, during a time when soldiers, many of them sporting broad and bushy mustaches, still wore gaudily colorful uniforms that looked as if they came straight out of a Gilbert and Sullivan production. "My father always felt one hundred percent Viennese, and he thought of himself as an Austrian patriot," recalled Robert. "As a matter of fact, I would describe him as a super patriot."

Jews had long been extremely loyal to the Habsburg monarchy, which had endeared itself to them by opposing anti-Semitism and relaxing a series of laws that had historically oppressed the empire's Jewish population for centuries. Men like Max Braun had been more than happy to fight for Austria both before and during World War I. Those who survived the battlefields later wore their medals and ribbons with immense pride, sharing Max's patriotic feelings for the Fatherland that, at least during this period, did not discriminate against them because of their religion.

Max and his brother later went into the wine business, buying a small vineyard near Baden, a spa town twenty-five kilometers south of Vienna. Along with growing their own grapes, the Braun brothers also purchased wine from neighboring grape growers and stored it in the cellar of a building in Vienna's First District, at No. 2 Schulof.

As a young child, Robert would sometimes descend with his father into the cool damp darkness of the wine cellar, which had originally been carved out of part of Vienna's ancient catacombs. "The building had a steep stairway, and I remember going down there with my father, and the aroma of wine would permeate everything." Robert naturally assumed that he might take over his father's wine business when he grew older.

Robert had been born in 1928, the youngest of Max and Karoline Braun's three children. The family, which also included two daughters, Martha and Johanna, lived in a comfortable apartment at No. 22 Porzellangasse, in Vienna's heavily Jewish Ninth District. They lived on the second floor, and Robert loved to hang his head out of the bedroom window, which overlooked a sidewalk café directly beneath their apartment. Through creeping vines that grew around a string of wires supporting a canopy above the café, the young boy would watch the men playing chess, drinking strong Viennese coffee *mit schlag,* reading the newspapers, arguing endlessly about issues of the day. The apartment building was right around the corner from the Schubert Schule, the grammar school that Robert and his sisters attended. The school had been named for Franz Schubert, the beloved Vienna-born composer who had taught at the school as a young man.

Max Braun came from a Jewish family, but his wife, who grew up in a small village in Bohemia (which later became part of Czechoslovakia), had been raised as a Catholic. At the time of their marriage, shortly after World War I, Austrian law did not permit marriages among couples from different religious faiths. Karoline, without giving the matter much thought, agreed to convert to Judaism. "But we were not religious at all," recalled Robert. "Once a year my father would go to a large hall for a Yom Kippur service, and he would drag me along with him. I didn't like it at all, mostly because there were a lot of older men there with horrible breath because they hadn't eaten for twenty-four hours. That was about the extent of my Jewish upbringing."

In the summertime, the close-knit Braun family rented two rooms on the second floor of a farmhouse in Piesting, a little village located about twenty-five miles south of Vienna. During the week, Max would remain in the city to tend to his wine business and then take the train down to Piesting, where he savored the lazy summer weekends with his wife and children. "My sisters and I would spend the summer going barefoot and playing with the farm kids. I remember walking in the morning with the cows up into the hills, where they would graze during the day, and then riding them back down with their bells clanging," remembered Robert. "Altogether, I had an extremely happy childhood."

. . . .

SLENDER, BLOND, AND energetically precocious, Henny Wenkart, like Robert Braun, was born in Vienna in 1928. Her father, Hermann, had been born and raised in Galicia, which later became part of Poland but at the time was still part of the sprawling Austro-Hungarian Empire, in the waning glory days before it splintered into pieces in the aftermath of World War I. Hermann's parents had made their way to Vienna when he was six years old, and he grew up in a peaceful city presided over by Emperor Franz Josef, who was endearingly known as "The Old Gentleman."

Like the Brauns, the Wenkarts were Viennese to the core. They were also Jewish. But in Vienna, that didn't seem to matter. Life within the Wenkart household blossomed amid a robust atmosphere of social and cultural sophistication. Henny's mother, Ruchele—who, like her husband, originally came from Galicia—enjoyed the comforts of being a lawyer's wife, spending her days at the city's French and English clubs and her evenings at the opera or the symphony. For much of her childhood, Henny was an only child; she was nine when her younger sister, Eleonore, was born. She was particularly close to her father. "He was supposed to take me to nursery school when I was very young, and I would cry and cry and cry to the point that he wouldn't want to leave me there," Henny remembered years later. Instead, Hermann would bring his daughter to his law office inside a magnificent baroque-style building on Franz-Josefskai, a wide street filled with commercial and office buildings directly across from the Danube Canal. "He would set me down in his office and let me type away on his typewriter. Then he would try to read what I had typed." From the time she was very young, Henny immersed herself in piano lessons, English studies, and Hebrew instruction with teachers who came to the splendid Wenkart apartment at No. 5 Ferstelgasse for private sessions with the young girl. Saturday mornings were spent at her father's side at a nearby synagogue, and the major Jewish holidays were celebrated with grandparents and other relatives. "During the holiday of Simchat Torah, we'd all go up into the rabbi's apartment, which was a tiny place," Henny recalled. "The women would be in the bedroom and the men would be in another room, dancing around the table with the Torahs. And we'd all be singing and clapping with them."

The weekly Sunday outings to the Vienna Woods, where Henny and her father would speak in reverent whispers, helped to forge an inseparable bond between them. During the summers, the family would sometimes take short vacations to the Austrian Alps or to nearby Czechoslovakia. Like the Braun family, the Wenkarts would also rent modestly priced summer quarters in the country as a welcome retreat from the humid hustle and bustle of city life. "Daddy would spend the week at work, but he would come out Friday afternoon on an early train," according to Henny. "He was always the father who came out earliest on Fridays and then he wouldn't leave until Monday morning. I would hear my parents whispering and then he would leave, and I would go back to sleep because I didn't want to wake up into a morning when he wasn't there."

EMIL WEISZ SHARED Hermann Wenkart's love of the Vienna Woods but for very different reasons. Weisz was an avid horticulturist who loved to spend his spare time grafting trees and grapevines on a small plot of land in the woods that had been handed down through several generations in the family. He pored over landscaping and gardening books, sharpening his green-thumb skills, which greatly benefited all of his friends and acquaintances who relied on him to help culture their own crops and grapes for making wine and other products. Along with two sisters, Emil owned a stall in Vienna's bustling Fleischmarkt, where he sold sausages, smoked meats, chickens, eggs, cheeses, and other dairy products.

From the time she could first read, Emil's shy daughter Helga loved to memorize the Latin names for the flowers and plants she found in her father's gardening books. She also reaped the rewards from Emil's hobby of making children's toys out of pieces of scrap wood and other odd bits of material lying around the house. "He once made an electric play oven, and I also remember a wonderful dollhouse and a firehouse that he had put together," recalled Helga, who was born in 1930. "I really lacked for nothing, and I was certainly loaded with toys."

Helga's mother, Rosa, had been a nurse during World War I and later found work as a midwife. But after she and Emil got married, Rosa—as was the custom for most married Viennese women, Jewish or otherwise—did not work outside the home. She loved to sing, however, and would often take Helga to one of the local cinemas, where the little girl always clamored to see the latest Shirley Temple film from America. Helga began singing herself at an early age and was known around the neighborhood—the Weisz family lived at No. 6 Krongasse—as Mopsi because her dark brunette curls made her look like a mophead.

Helga attended local public schools, which at the time were operated by the Catholic Church. Classes were held six days a week, with Sundays the only day off for the students, who were expected to attend church services that day. Jewish students, however, were often excused from Saturday classes, particularly if they came from Orthodox families that observed the Jewish Sabbath. But the Weisz family was not that religious, and Helga's parents chose not to have her excused from Saturday classes. Still, there was a nod to the family's Judaism. While Catholic students received regular instruction in catechism and other Catholic rituals, students from other faiths—usually Protestant—would be taken to another room at the school for a different set of lessons. Helga's mother sent in a note confirming that Helga would be attending Hebrew lessons rather than join in with the Catholic students.

. . . .

LIKE THOUSANDS OF other Jewish families in Vienna, Kurt
Herman's family lived in Leopoldstadt, the city's teeming Second
District carved out of an island formed by the Danube Canal to the
west and the much wider Danube River that ran along the district's
eastern edge. His father, Heinrich, had been born in Poland but grew
up in Vienna and, as an adult, ran a fabric business with Kurt's grandfather. Kurt's mother, Martha, was born in the eastern German town
of Görlitz, just across the border with Poland. As a youngster—Kurt
was born in 1930—the round-faced boy with oversize ears and an
impish smile remembered the joyous experience of accompanying his
father to one of Vienna's public bathhouses, not far from the family's
apartment at No. 8 Lilienbrunngasse. "Little kids were always bathed
in the sink in the apartment building where my family lived, so it was
a thrill for me whenever I could go to the bathhouse with my dad," he
said. "We would either walk or take one of the trams. My uncle was
a traveling salesman and was also the only person in the family who
owned an automobile. So a really big thrill was to go to my uncle's
house on Sunday for a ride in the car."

FOR GENERATIONS, THE residents of Leopoldstadt—Jews and
non-Jews alike—had enjoyed the green and leafy surroundings of
the Wiener Prater, the former imperial hunting grounds that had
been transformed into a large public park during the eighteenth century. At the edge of the Prater stood the gargantuan Wiener Riesen-
rad, the famous Vienna Ferris wheel that was built in 1897 to celebrate the golden jubilee of Emperor Franz Josef I. Such was life in
the late 1920s and early 1930s for the tens of thousands of Jewish
boys and girls growing up across Vienna. Erwin Tepper's parents,
Juda and Schifra, had both come to Vienna from their native Poland

so that Erwin's father could study accounting at the university. The family lived in a nice apartment, at No. 11 Georgsiglgasse, near the Danube Canal in the Leopoldstadt area that had become known as Mazzesinsel—Matzo Island—because of its concentrated Jewish population.

FRITZI AND ELIZABETH Zinger also lived with their parents in an apartment, at No. 7 Rauscherstrasse, near the Danube and the lovely green parks not far from the canal. "I was always busy playing ball on the porch of our apartment, and of course the ball would always fall down to the street below," remembered Elizabeth, who was born in 1933 and known in the family as Lisl. "My mother would come to the rescue by looking down and asking whoever was walking by to please deposit the ball in a basket and bring it back up to the apartment. So that was even more fun than being outside." Her older sister Fritzi would roll her eyes at Lisl's childish antics, but the two girls were extremely close. Their mother regularly dressed them in matching outfits, accentuating the tight bond that held the Zinger girls together.

TEN BLOCKS AWAY, Kurt Roth lived with his parents, Hermann and Bertha, at No. 32 Treustrasse, tucked away near the Danube Canal in Vienna's working-class Twentieth District that, like the Second and Ninth districts, included a significant Jewish population. Kurt's parents, neither of whom were particularly religious, sent him to an afternoon Jewish school so that he could acquire at least a rudimentary knowledge of his faith and culture. But Kurt was more inclined to play hooky whenever he could get away with it, sneaking off with a friend from the neighborhood who owned an impressive collection of tin soldiers "with which we could conduct sweeping war maneuvers on the apartment floor."

. . . .

ALL THE WAY across town, Paul Beller lived with his parents at No. 48 Stumpergasse, in the more commercial Sixth District, which had a much smaller Jewish population than other parts of the city. His father, Leo, and two uncles were partners in a thriving plywood business that supported all three families very comfortably. Paul's mother, Mina, was an excellent cook and baker. "She enjoyed going to the park and talking with the other ladies," recalled Paul, who was born in 1931. "She liked playing piano and she loved classical music—Beethoven, Brahms and Mozart. Up until the time that the Nazis marched in, our family was living a very nice and comfortable life."

THE BRAUNS, WENKARTS, Teppers, Bellers, and others were just a few of the thousands of Jewish families that, during the early decades of the twentieth century, had little if any reason to question their rightful place in the fabric of Viennese life and culture. During the 1920s and early 1930s, Jews formed a sizeable community that, by and large, considered itself an indelible part of the city.

Not unlike those in the rest of Europe, Jews in Vienna had endured mixed blessings for hundreds of years. The first mention of a synagogue in Vienna dates back to 1204. Yet even though Emperor Friedrich II offered his protection to Jews in 1238, local Catholic Church leaders officially banned all social dealings between Christians and Jews thirty years later. Albert V, the Vienna-born archduke of Austria, issued a proclamation in 1420 that called for the expulsion of all Jews from Vienna and lower Austria; the city's original synagogue, built in an open plaza that later came to be known as the Judenplatz, was destroyed. By the end of the sixteenth century, a small number of Jews had been allowed to settle once again in Vienna, though they would soon be restricted to a ghetto in the area that would later become Leopoldstadt, named for Emperor Leopold I, who in 1670 ordered a second expulsion of Jews from Vienna. Within only a few years, however, a handful of wealthy "court Jews" had been permitted to return as a reward for their role as military suppliers and financiers.

A more enduring turn of good fortune occurred in 1782, when Emperor Joseph II issued his Edict of Tolerance, wiping away a variety of discriminatory laws directed at Jews. In the wake of Austria's 1848 revolution, which threatened the ruling monarchy, Vienna's Jews gained additional rights, including official recognition of the Israelitische Kultusgemeinde—the organization representing the city's Jewish community. Austria's new constitution, drafted in 1867, further liberalized attitudes toward Jews, granting them the unrestricted right to live in freedom and practice their religion throughout the country. Vienna's Jewish population skyrocketed during this period—rising from a tiny community of 2,600 in 1857 to more than 40,000 by 1870. By the end of the nineteenth century, Vienna was home to nearly 150,000 Jews, which accounted for about 9 percent of the city's overall population of 1.7 million people.

Although a virulent wave of anti-Semitism washed over the city at the turn of the century, the outbreak of World War I triggered yet another influx of Jewish arrivals. Some 50,000 to 70,000 Jews sought refuge from the battle-and-pogrom-scarred eastern regions of the Austro-Hungarian Empire, principally in the Galicia region. Although many of these migrant Jews returned to their homes once the worst of the horrors along the Eastern Front had passed, Vienna's Jewish population continued to rise. The high-water mark came in the early 1920s, when roughly 200,000 Jews accounted for more than 10 percent of Vienna's total population. In many ways, Jewish culture during this period became synonymous with café culture, as Jewish journalists, writers, and intellectuals exerted a palpable influence over the social, political, and cultural life of the city.

Yet the safety and security of Jewish Vienna remained fragile.

Undercurrents of deep-seated anti-Semitism were gaining swift momentum in the aftermath of Germany's crushing defeat in World War I and the disappearance of the Austro-Hungarian Empire. Jews once again were singled out as scapegoats, cast as the chief culprits responsible for Germany's descent into ashes, the humiliating terms of the peace treaty with its wartime enemies, and the catastrophic economic conditions that brought Germany to its knees in the years following the war.

By the time that Adolf Hitler became Germany's chancellor in 1933, Vienna's Jewish population had drifted slightly downward to about 185,000, which still made it the third largest Jewish community in Europe, trailing behind only Warsaw and Budapest. More Jews lived in Vienna than in Berlin, the German capital, which counted 160,000 Jews during Hitler's first year in power. Over the next six years, half of Berlin's Jews left the city in response to the Nazis' incremental, but increasingly hostile, campaign to rid the Reich of its Jewish inhabitants. In Vienna, as the winter of 1938 was about to give way to spring, the happy childhoods of Robert Braun, Henny Wenkart, Helga Weisz, Kurt Herman, and thousands of other Jewish children dissolved almost at once into a nightmare.

CHAPTER 4

What people don't understand is that in the beginning you could get out. Everyone could get out. But nobody would let us in.

—HENNY WENKART

VIENNA
MARCH–APRIL 1938

The young girl sat upright in bed, struggling to hear the voices that crackled out from the large console radio that her parents kept in the living room of their apartment. Henny was not quite ten years old but, sadly, knew plenty about the rapidly deteriorating world around her. After listening for a few more moments, she recognized the strained voice on the radio as that of Kurt Schuschnigg, Austria's chancellor for the past four years. She also grasped at least the vague outlines of Schuschnigg's solemn address. The German

army was on its way to Vienna, and the beleaguered Austrian leader
had no intention of spilling any blood in a futile challenge to Adolf
Hitler's lightning-fast move to swallow up Austria into the Third
Reich. "And so, I take leave of the Austrian people with a word of
farewell uttered from the depths of my heart," Schuschnigg som-
berly informed his radio audience. "God protect Austria." It was
the evening of Friday, March 11, 1938, and once Schuschnigg had
concluded his speech, a radio announcer dispassionately informed
listeners that, as of the next day, Austria would no longer exist as
an independent nation. At that very moment, German troops were
amassed along the border, waiting for orders to enter the country.

The radio station began playing the opening strains of Beethoven's
First Symphony. Before the broadcast had ended, Austrian Nazi Party
members and supporters began streaming through Vienna's streets
with lusty shouts of "*Sieg Heil!*" while waving swastika banners and
cheering Hitler's unopposed annexation of the country. As Henny lay
in bed later that evening, she heard her mother and father talking in
whispers. She was unable to make out what they were saying.

A few days later, Hermann Wenkart took his daughter for a walk
in a nearby park. Already small metal plaques had been attached to
almost all of the long wooden benches, announcing that the benches
were reserved for Aryans. With a deep sigh in his voice, he began
telling Henny about the Anschluss and what it foretold for themselves, along with their relatives and friends. Henny looked up at her
father and said, "Well, I already know that." He smiled and then
told her something that came as a great surprise. He had awakened
at four o'clock that morning and made his way to the American consulate, where he took his place in a long line that had already formed
outside the building in the predawn darkness. Everyone there had
the same objective: getting their names on a rapidly expanding waiting list for visas to America. Henny was taken aback. Nobody she
knew was ever up at four in the morning, other than the men who
drove the horse-drawn milk wagons that delivered bottles of fresh

milk and cream before dawn each day. Hermann looked into his daughter's eyes and made a solemn promise: "I give you my word of honor that you will be all right."

Adolf Hitler returned to Vienna on the morning of Saturday, April 9, arriving by train from Berlin at the city's Westbahnhof station and stepping into his six-wheeled Mercedes limousine. The motorcade, with Hitler's car in the lead, drove down Mariahilfer- strasse, Vienna's main shopping avenue, only a few blocks from Paul Beller's apartment building. Three weeks earlier, *Völkischer Beo- bachter,* a leading Nazi Party newspaper, noted that the street was the most "Jew-infested" commercial thoroughfare in Vienna. On the day of Hitler's return, however, "Vienna is again a German city," exclaimed the newspaper. One day later, on April 10, 99.7 percent of Austrians voted yes in a plebiscite that formally approved Hitler's takeover of the country.

Within the first ten days of the Anschluss, the Viennese police reported nearly one hundred suicides throughout the city, virtually all of them Jews. By the end of April, the number of suicides had jumped to at least two thousand. Among the victims was Henny Wenkart's pediatrician, who took his life by jumping out a window. It took less than a year to wipe out Vienna's once-plentiful ranks of Jewish doctors, all of whom, in the name of Aryanization, were no longer permitted to practice medicine. A city that had once been home to two thousand Jewish doctors—including, most famously, Sigmund Freud—now had none. Freud himself had been given per- mission to leave for London in June 1938, traveling on the Orient Express with his wife and daughter.

Between March 1938 and March 1939, nearly half of the city's Jewish population had departed. The vast majority had hoped to immigrate to the United States, especially since so many of them had relatives already living there. But America's immigration laws created an insurmountable obstacle for most German and Austrian Jews seeking safe haven in the United States. First, fixed quotas

capped the number of immigrants from every foreign country, resulting in a long waiting list for tens, if not hundreds, of thousands
of Jews. Second, America would only admit refugees who were
able to guarantee that they would not require any sort of public
assistance once they arrived. Stymied by the United States' closed-
door policies, many of Vienna's Jews instead dispersed to other far-
flung corners of the earth—Shanghai, Havana, Buenos Aires, and
elsewhere. A few even managed to sneak into Palestine despite the
strenuous efforts of the British authorities to prevent more than a
trickle of Jews from legally entering the Holy Land and disrupting
the fragile Arab-Jewish balance that His Majesty's government was
vigorously attempting to maintain.

From the earliest moments of the Anschluss, newspapers and magazines throughout the United States and the rest of the world were
filled with detailed accounts of Hitler's takeover of Austria and what
it meant for the country's Jews. "Their fate is even worse than that
of the Jews in Germany, where the persecutions were spread over a
period of several years," the *New Republic* magazine informed its
readers in April 1938, only weeks after the Anschluss. "In Austria,
the full force of the sadistic Nazi attack has come overnight." Hitler's
Nuremberg laws, which had gradually stripped German Jews of their
civil rights over a period of five years, were instantly put into effect.
Hermann Göring, Hitler's field marshal, had wasted no time in issuing a blunt warning that Jews were no longer welcome anywhere in
Austria. Vienna, he announced, would become purely German again.
"The Jew must know we do not care to live with him. He must go,"
Göring told foreign journalists. Throughout Vienna, groups of Jewish
men, pious rabbis among them, were forced to scrub clean the few
anti-Anschluss symbols that had been painted on streets and side-
walks prior to Hitler's arrival. Newly emboldened members of the
Hitler Youth organization set out across the city, taunting and ter-
rorizing Jewish shopkeepers and whitewashing swastikas, skull and
crossbones, and *Jude* across their storefront windows.

Within days of the Anschluss, in an early morning raid that was carefully planned well in advance, the Gestapo shut down the Israelitische Kultesgemeinde—Vienna's official Jewish community office—and arrested the organization's president, two vice presidents, and executive director. Six weeks later—on May 3, 1938—Adolf Eichmann, a thirty-two-year-old SS lieutenant who had been dispatched to Vienna to plan and enforce the *Judenrein* policy, officially permitted the Kultusgemeinde to reopen and released some of the arrested leaders. But Eichmann had only one purpose in mind for Vienna's Jewish leaders: to help him carry out the removal of every Jew—man, woman, and child—in the city. By the summer of 1938, more than twenty thousand people had made their way to the Kultusgemeinde's headquarters at No. 2 Seitenstettengasse, where they often had to wait for hours to officially register for emigration papers. Long rows of wooden filing cabinets on the second floor of the building, located only a few blocks from the Gestapo's headquarters at the Hotel Metropole, spilled over with thousands of cardboard index cards that meticulously listed Jewish families desperate to leave Austria as soon as possible. Eichmann and other Nazi officials were determined to fulfill Hitler's dream of a *Juden*-free Germany and Austria. Only one question remained: Where would all those Jews go?

The visa section at the American consulate office in Vienna was overrun with applicants hoping to gain admission into the United States. Long lines of people would form early each morning, anxiously waiting for the consulate to open its doors at 9:00 A.M. The overworked staff would often remain at their desks until 10:00 P.M., seeing as many as six thousand people and conducting up to five hundred interviews each day. Given the limited number of spaces allotted to Germany and Austria, the consulate officers knew that most of the individuals and families who were pleading for visas would have to wait as long as five years before their turn would come up.

To help expedite the forced Jewish exodus, Eichmann had set up the Zentralstelle für Jüdische Auswanderung—the Central Bureau for Jewish Emigration—which established, in a highly bureaucratic and assembly-line manner, a brutally efficient process for ridding Austria of Jews. Eichmann also found—or rather, annexed—what he considered to be an ideal location for his Zentralstelle. The ornate palace that occupied a full city block at No. 22 Prinz Eugenstrasse had, until recently, been the home of Albert Rothschild, a member of the Vienna branch of the famous European Jewish banking family. Designed in the French neo-Renaissance style, the imposing nineteenth-century building—one of five palaces belonging to various Rothschilds who lived in Vienna—was set back from the street, with a courtyard and a U-shaped layout. The entrance hall led to an enormous marble staircase, and throughout the building were crystal chandeliers, gold leaf, and polished parquet floors.

On August 20, 1938, Josef Bürkel, who had been installed as the Nazi gauleiter in Vienna after the Anschluss, spelled out the new function of the Rothschild palace in a memo sent to all Nazi state and party offices throughout Austria. "Undesirable interruptions and delays have occurred in the emigration of Jews. In addition, the question of Jewish emigration has been dealt with inefficiently by certain offices," wrote Bürkel. "To assist and expedite arrangements for the emigration of Jews from Austria, a Central Office for Jewish Emigration has therefore been set up in Vienna, at Prinz Eugenstrasse 22."

Eichmann and other Nazi officials took enormous satisfaction in converting the Rothschild mansion into a one-stop facility for hastening the fulfillment of *Judenrein*. "This is like an automatic factory, let us say a flour mill connected to some bakery. You put in at the one end a Jew who still has capital and has . . . a factory or a shop or an account in a bank," Wilhelm Höttl, an SS officer who served under Eichmann, later recounted. "He passes through the entire building, from counter to counter, from office to office. He comes out the other end. He has no money, he has no rights, only a passport in which it is written: you must leave this country within two weeks. If you fail to do so, you will go to a concentration camp."

IN THE WAKE of the Anschluss, even the youngest Jews felt the sense of peril that had descended over the city. Elizabeth Zinger was five years old and had recently started kindergarten. Sitting quietly in her classroom one morning, the little girl raised her hand, trying to get her teacher's attention so that she could request permission to go to the bathroom. The teacher, however, continued to ignore her, even as it became obvious why she wished to be excused. Finally, Elizabeth could not wait any longer, and she wet herself. Her teacher shot her a scolding look and grabbed the frightened girl by the collar of her blouse, pulling her out of her chair and in front of the rest of the class. "You see. This is what the *Juden* do. They make in their pants," the teacher announced to the other students, after which she shoved the sobbing girl back into her seat. "After that horrendous experience, my mother didn't send me back to school," Elizabeth remembered, "which was just as well, because very shortly thereafter it was announced that I could not come back. Nor could my sister—and all because we had committed that terrible crime of being Jewish."

Jewish children all throughout Vienna quickly learned to live in fear of the Nazis and their sympathizers. Kurt Herman's path literally intersected with Hitler's celebrated arrival in Vienna. At the age of seven, he was walking with his mother across a bridge that spanned the Danube Canal, not far from their home in the city's Second District. Suddenly a long motorcade of black cars, each adorned with a small red swastika flag that flapped in the breeze, rumbled through the streets, passing directly in front of Kurt and his mother. Standing in the backseat of one of the cars was the German chancellor, who would repeatedly thrust out his right arm in a gesture that, even at his young age, Kurt recognized as the Nazis' salute. The young boy stood there, motionless. Everyone around them was cheering loudly and waving their arms in enthusiastic salutes. The young boy and his mother, worried about standing out in the crowd, timidly held out their arms as well.

A few weeks after the Anschluss, Robert Braun walked into his fourth-grade classroom at the Schubert Schule and took his usual seat at a desk in the middle of the room. All of the other boys began filing in as well and then waited for their teacher to quiet them down—not an easy task for a classroom filled with rambunctious ten-year-old boys. Robert noticed that a yellow line had been painted in front of the last row of seats in the room. After all of the boys had arrived, the teacher stood up in front of the class and began speaking in a somber tone. "The authorities have ordered that we rearrange the seating in the room," the teacher announced. He pointed to the yellow line on the floor and proceeded to call out the names of all of the Jewish boys in the class. From now on, he said, they were to sit in the row of seats behind the yellow line. In the weeks that followed, some of the boys in the class began showing up at school in outfits that Robert had come to recognize as the Hitler Youth uniform—dark-colored short pants, khaki-colored cotton shirts, knee-high white stockings, and red armbands emblazoned with black swastikas. He quickly learned to steer clear of those boys as best he could, although sometimes they would chase him, taunt him, or try to throw punches at him. One of them hurled a small rock. It left a scar across his scalp that would still be visible seventy-five years later.

On March 13, 1939—precisely one year after the Anschluss—the Vienna correspondent for the Jewish Telegraphic Agency filed a story that cited a depressing litany of statistics about the rapid disintegration of Vienna's once-vibrant Jewish community. During the previous twelve months, 7,856 businesses had been "Aryanized"—that is, Jewish owners had been forced to hand their business over to new Aryan owners for little, if any, compensation. Another 5,122

Jewish-owned businesses had simply gone bankrupt. More than 12,000 Jewish families had been summarily evicted from their apartments, and almost all of the city's Jews had been herded into the already congested Leopoldstadt district, essentially creating a Jewish ghetto. Thousands of Jewish men had been arrested and sent to concentration camps located in unfamiliar places with names such as Buchenwald and Dachau. While these places had not yet given way to the death camps of the Final Solution, there had already been reports of the ashen remains of some of the men—husbands, fathers, uncles, grandfathers—being returned to relatives in Vienna following their unexplained deaths while incarcerated.

CHAPTER 5

All Vienna's Synagogues Attacked; Fires and Bombs Wreck 18 of 21

Jews Are Beaten, Furniture and Goods Flung From Homes and Shops — 15,000 Are Jailed During Day—20 Are Suicides

Wireless to THE NEW YORK TIMES.

VIENNA, Nov. 10.—In a surge of revenge for the murder of a German diplomat in Paris by a young Polish Jew, all Vienna's twenty-one synagogues were attacked today and eighteen were wholly or partly destroyed by fires and bomb explosions.

Anti-Jewish activities under the direction of Storm Troopers and Nazi party members in uniform began early this morning. In the earlier reported to have attempted suicide; about twenty succeeded.

Scores of bombs were placed in synagogues, blowing out windows and in many cases damaging walls. Floors that had been soaked with kerosene readily caught fire.

Fire brigades were summoned to fight fires in eighteen synagogues, and the fire engines remained in their neighborhood all day. Two of the synagogues were not being used for religious purposes.

Our apartment was visited by the Brown Shirts, who were the bully boys of the Nazi Party. They looked in every room and in every closet for an adult. My father never came home from work that night.

—ERWIN TEPPER

VIENNA
NOVEMBER 1938

On the morning of Monday, November 7, 1938, seventeen-year-old Herschel Grynszpan carefully loaded a handful of bullets into the chamber of a revolver that he had purchased the day before and then walked from his uncle's apartment, where he had been staying, to the German embassy in Paris. Ten days earlier, Herschel's parents—along with thousands of other Polish Jews who had been living for years in Germany—had been arrested, their homes and property taken away from them, and packed into trains that left them stranded near the Polish border town of Zbaszyn. Grynszpan's father had managed to mail a postcard to his son, pleading with Herschel to do whatever he could to help the family. Upon arriving at the German embassy, Grynszpan asked to see an official, explaining that he had an important document to deliver. Moments later, he pulled out his revolver and unloaded the bullets into the abdomen of Ernst vom Rath, a twenty-nine-year-old low-level embassy officer. The mortally injured German was rushed to a nearby hospital while the Jewish teenager quickly surrendered himself to the French police. In his pocket was a postcard that he had written to his parents, lamenting what had happened to them and the other Jews trapped in Zbaszyn. "May God forgive me," he wrote. "The heart bleeds when I hear of your tragedy and that of the 12,000 Jews. I must protest so that the whole world hears my protest, and that I will do."

Nazi leaders in Berlin wasted no time in reacting to Grynszpan's desperate act. One day after the shooting, the authorities banned all Jewish children from attending public schools and suspended the publication of all Jewish newspapers throughout Germany and Austria. Within hours of vom Rath's death from his injuries on November 9, Joseph Goebbels, Hitler's propaganda minister, set in motion a violent retaliatory pogrom—he described them as "spontaneous demonstrations"—aimed against all Jews throughout the Reich. Shortly after midnight that evening, Reinhard Heydrich, the deputy head of the Gestapo and the SS, sent a top secret telegram to police officials throughout Nazi Germany that laid out the guidelines for the riots that had already broken out against the Jews. Heydrich made it clear that the police were not to interfere with rioters. He also ordered the immediate arrest and detention of "healthy male Jews who are not too old," who would later be transferred to concentration camps.

Throughout the night and into the predawn hours of the next day, more than seven thousand Jewish shops were burned and destroyed throughout Germany and Austria. Although physical violence against Jews had not been specifically sanctioned in Heydrich's telegram, nearly a hundred Jews were beaten to death. Synagogues were ransacked and burned, with only one left standing in Vienna. The Nazi-ordered pogrom quickly came to be known as Kristallnacht—the Night of Broken Glass—because of the sounds of shattered storefront and synagogue windows. "Anti-Jewish activities under the direction of Storm Troopers and Nazi party members in uniform began early this morning," reported the *New York Times* from Vienna on November 11. "In the earlier stages Jews were attacked and beaten. Many Jews awaiting admittance to the British consulate-general were arrested, and according to reliable reporters others who stood in line before the United States consulate were severely beaten and also arrested. . . . Many of those arrested were sent to prisons or concentration camps in buses. Mobs of raiders penetrated Jewish residences and shops, flinging furniture and merchandise from the windows and destroying wantonly." The official Nazi press praised party members for practicing restraint during the Kristallnacht riots even as Nazi officials accepted full responsibility for the violence. "It is true that the Propaganda Ministry accepts responsibility for today's events," said a ministry spokesman. "The police did not intervene in the spontaneous demonstrations against Jewish shops."

Goebbels called off the riots a day after they had erupted. "The justified and understandable anger of the German people over the cowardly murder of a German diplomat in Paris found extensive expression during last night," he declared. "Now a strict request is issued to the entire population to cease immediately all further demonstrations and actions against Jewry, no matter what kind. A final answer to the Jewish assassination in Paris will be given to Jewry by way of legislation and ordinance." Within days, Hermann Göring imposed a fine of one billion reichsmarks—equivalent to $400 million—on the collective Jewish population of Germany and Austria in retribution for vom Rath's murder in Paris.

In reporting the horrifying events of Kristallnacht, the *New York Times* also described the frightening new reality facing Jews living inside Germany and Austria. "All Jewish organizational, cultural and publishing activity has been suspended," the newspaper reported. "It is assumed that the Jews, who have now lost most of their possessions and livelihood, will either be thrown into the streets or put into ghettos and concentration camps, or impressed into labor brigades and put to work for the Third Reich, as the children of Israel were once before for the Pharaohs."

Over the course of three days, somewhere between thirty-five thousand and fifty thousand Jews—mostly adult men—were arrested throughout Germany and held as prisoners either in local jails or concentration camps. A news brief published by the Jewish Telegraphic Agency's correspondent in Berlin on November 14 stated that "virtually every Jewish doctor" had been arrested in the aftermath of Kristallnacht, "as well as practically all practicing Jewish attorneys." Although most of the arrested men would be released over the next three months, more than two thousand prisoners died, either from illness or from beatings.

Other men were lucky and narrowly avoided being arrested during Kristallnacht. Erwin Tepper's father was not at home when a marauding group of Brown Shirts forced their way into the family's apartment. Several months earlier, Juda Tepper had lost his salesman's job at a women's lingerie shop, a casualty of Aryanization. But the new owner of the shop had little sympathy for Nazis and, in anticipation of the Kristallnacht riots, bravely agreed to hide Tepper inside the shop. "My father spent that night and the following day and the following night hidden in the back of the store, where he used to work," Erwin recalled. "The owner hid my father until it was safe to go home."

Fritzi and Elizabeth Zinger's father was also hidden away during Kristallnacht—concealed behind a large armoire in the family apartment. "My mother grabbed my father and shoved him behind the closet," remembered Elizabeth. "She then told me and my sister, 'Don't say anything when the Nazis come looking for him.' Of course, we knew where he was, but we were smart enough not to say. When the storm troopers came, they looked around for father, and then said to mother, 'If he's not here when we come back, we're going to take you.' She had saved his life, and for some reason Kristallnacht was called to a close for that night. I guess they had captured enough Jews to send off to the concentration camps."

Emil Weisz's stall in the Fleischmarkt was among the thousands of Jewish businesses that were vandalized during Kristallnacht. Looters freely made off with his cash registers, scales, and butcher's knives. The shop itself was heavily damaged, and the entire inventory was stolen. Weisz knew that non-Jewish shopkeepers had eagerly helped themselves to things from his store, but he also realized he no longer had any recourse. Complaining to the police only resulted in a beating, along with stern orders that he clean up the mess that was left. Shortly after Kristallnacht, the shop itself was confiscated, although Weisz was still forced to pay taxes on a business that he no longer owned with money that he could no longer earn. One night, while his eight-year-old daughter, Helga, lay fast asleep, Weisz slipped out of the family apartment, intent on selling his wedding band in order to scrape together at least some of the money that he owed in taxes. He never returned that evening, and his family would not learn until several months later that he had been arrested and sent off to Dachau.

The steady, somewhat orderly exodus of Jews from Vienna that had begun with the Anschluss now gave way to a panic-fueled effort to find any possible way out as quickly as possible. "All of a sudden, you had people at home all day long. They didn't have their businesses any longer," said Paul Beller, whose father and uncles had lost their successful plywood business. "Suddenly it was a different kind of a life, with all of the stress and hearing conversations about trying to get visas and trying to find ways out. In most cases, if you didn't have somebody to sponsor you in the United States, you were not going to get a visa. And there were the grim thoughts that if you were not going to get one, were you going to be one of those who was not going to survive."

For many Jewish families, such thoughts were exacerbated by the depressing realization that they had few, if any, hopes of even qualifying for a visa to America—or anywhere else, for that matter. "My parents had been trying to get visas, but they had no connections," remembered Robert Braun. "They had no relatives close enough in the United States that they could call on for an affidavit, and it all looked quite hopeless. Of course, there were rumors going around that you could buy a visa to get to Cuba or to Shanghai or places like that. But my parents were not wealthy. We were strictly lower middle class, and my father by then had lost what little business he had. I don't think they had any hope of being able to leave."

Families without relatives in the United States also tried anything they could to find ways, despite overwhelming odds, of somehow getting to America. "My mother was so desperate that she went to the telephone company and picked out some telephone directories from the United States," said Kurt Herman. "She looked up our last name, copied down all the addresses, and got an interpreter to write letters in English to see if they would sponsor us. Of course, that didn't work. But that's how desperate she was."

The Nazis were now enforcing their policy of *Judenrein* even more aggressively. Men who had been arrested and sent off to concentration camps in the days and weeks following Kristallnacht would often be released only if they could obtain exit visas. They were typically given only a couple of weeks to leave the country, and faced being arrested and sent back to the concentration camps if they were unable to do so.

In the wake of Emil Weisz's arrest and imprisonment in Dachau, Helga and her mother, Rosa, had been forced out of their spacious apartment and were now living, with two other families, in a cramped three-room apartment in Leopoldstadt. Helga's aunt and uncle, along with their two children, occupied one room. Helga and her mother—Helga's sister had recently escaped to Palestine—lived in a second room. Yet another family was crammed together in a third room. Rosa Weisz spent her days in a frantic effort to find out what had happened to her husband and whether she might be able to obtain a visa that would allow the family to leave Vienna. For Helga, the viciousness of Kristallnacht continued on the day that she, along with her other Jewish classmates, were thrown out of their school. "You can't come to school because you're a dirty Jew," one of her classmates told her. As Helga—who had once fantasized about singing like Shirley Temple—stood crying in the hallway of the school, waiting for her mother to take her home, a sympathetic teacher came over to her, lifted up her chin, and said, "I'm very sorry this is happening to you. This is not right."

The day after the Kristallnacht riots, eleven-year-old Kurt Roth was also sent home from school, even though he attended a private Jewish school that, for the moment at least, was still permitted to operate. The school's principal, frightened by the likelihood that the school would be singled out for attack by Nazi thugs, instructed the students to go home without explaining why. But rather than dismiss all the students at once, the principal filtered them out a few at a time so that the neighboring streets would not suddenly be filled with Jewish children who would be easy targets for the anti-Semitic mobs still rampaging through the streets of Vienna. "I began walking home, but I didn't get home," said Roth. "There was a synagogue near our house on one of the main streets in our district. I walked by there, and I saw this huge crowd around the synagogue. I had no idea what was going on, and I kept pushing myself into the crowd to see what was happening." A few moments later, he found himself in front of the temple's smoldering ruins. "I left the crowd and walked home, but I still had no idea what was going on. It wasn't until I got home that I learned what was happening out there in the streets. I also found out later that one of my uncles had been arrested during that first night of Kristallnacht."

A few weeks later, a young couple showed up at the Roths' apartment, brandishing an official notice declaring that the apartment now belonged to them. The Roths moved into a small apartment on the same street, just a couple of blocks away. The front of the building had been occupied by a store, whose Jewish owner had already been evicted. The Gestapo had stored the owner's belongings in one of the apartment's rooms, locking the door leading into the room and pasting a paper seal across the door. Kurt's mother leaned a small dining table against the door to prevent anyone in the family from accidentally tearing the Gestapo's official seal. "I sat at that table during every meal," Kurt recalled years later, "filled with terror from thinking what would happen if I broke the seal."

CHAPTER 6

The members of Brith Sholom are extremely eager to bring fifty refugee children from Germany to the United States. They are ready to provide a home and education for them.
—Gil's letter to Assistant Secretary of State George Messersmith

PHILADELPHIA–WASHINGTON, D.C.
FEBRUARY 1939

Gil had spent the past several hours scrutinizing a thick stack of documents he had spread across the leather-top mahogany desk that dominated his office on the tenth floor of Albert Greenfield's Bankers Securities Building. Despite his aptitude for figures, Gil was confused by what seemed to be an inexplicable discrepancy in the jumble of numbers before him.

As he continued to dig through the papers detailing the government's immigration quotas and the actual numbers of visas that had been issued to fill them, Gil could not reconcile the number of would-be immigrants from Germany and Austria with those who ultimately had arrived here. Unless he was missing something, the number of visas that had been issued did not match up with the number of immigrants who arrived under the quota.

Assuming that Gil was deciphering the figures correctly, the number of visas appeared to exceed the final number of immigrants. Given how difficult it was to obtain a visa, he could not understand why any would have gone unused, particularly when tens of thousands—perhaps hundreds of thousands—of Jews living inside Nazi Germany and Austria were so desperate to leave. Something was not right.

After agreeing to take on the rescue project, Gil had immediately embarked on a crash course in America's heavily regulated immigration system. In an attempt to curtail the waves of immigrants flooding into the United States, Congress in 1924 had established the quota system that fixed the number of immigrants allowed in from every foreign country. By the end of World War I, America had ceased to be a nation that warmly invited immigrants from around the world. Throughout the 1920s and 1930s, a virulent xenophobia pervaded the United States, and the once-idealized sympathy for those millions of "huddled masses yearning to breathe free" had long since vanished into thin air. The noble words of Emma Lazarus's "The New Colossus" sonnet remained engraved on the bronze plaque affixed to the pedestal of the Statue of Liberty, but increasingly restrictive laws designed to keep most would-be immigrants at a distance all but silenced Lazarus's plea to send the world's "homeless, tempest-tost" into the embrace of that "mighty woman with a torch."

Once he had completed yet another review of the latest figures from Germany, Gil was now absolutely certain that the total number of visas issued exceeded the number of people who had actually entered the United States. Why would that be? he kept asking himself.

He simply could not understand why any of those visas—those golden tickets to freedom—would go unused.

Prior to Hitler's takeover of Austria, the United States had maintained separate annual immigration quotas for Germany (25,957) and Austria (1,413). Once Austria lost its status as an independent nation, the quotas for the two countries were combined into an overall annual quota of 27,370. Based on the formula under which visas were distributed among several American consulates in Germany and Austria, combining the quotas actually resulted in better odds for Austrian Jews to obtain visas for the United States.

Gil was surprised, meanwhile, to discover that the annual quota for Germany had never been filled throughout the 1930s. This was largely due to a combination of procedural roadblocks and an initial reluctance on the part of German Jews to fully grasp the severity of Nazi policies. In 1933, during Hitler's first year in power, only 1,445 German immigrants—slightly more than 5 percent of the quota—came to the United States. Three years later, as Hitler's policies began to weigh more heavily on Germany's Jewish population, the quota had still only been 27 percent filled, with 6,642 refugees entering the country. Even as late as 1938, at which point there was no longer any doubt about the gravity of the Jews' plight, the quota remained less than two-thirds filled. During Hitler's first six years as Germany's Nazi dictator, more than 106,000 quota spaces for would-be refugees from that country went unused.

The Anschluss, reinforced by the shocking violence of Kristallnacht, dramatically altered the algorithm of the combined German and Austrian quota. Suddenly Jews seeking visas inundated the American consulates in Germany and Austria. Unfortunately, those seeking safe haven in the United States were stymied both by America's immigration laws and the burdensome bureaucratic responses on the part of American government officials responsible for interpreting and carrying out those laws. "The Department of State was not set up for rapid action or for humanitarianism," Henry

Morgenthau, President Roosevelt's treasury secretary, wrote in his diary at the time. "The typical foreign service officer lived off paper. His instinct was always toward postponement, on the hallowed theory of all foreign offices that problems postponed long enough will solve themselves. Moreover, many State Department officials had small personal sympathy for the humble and the downtrodden. . . . The horrors of Dachau or Buchenwald were beyond their conception. They dealt with human lives at the same bureaucratic tempo and with the same lofty manner that they might deal with a not very urgent trade negotiation."

It hardly helped matters during this period that the State Department was filled with senior officials who were openly anti-Semitic or did little to conceal anti-Jewish attitudes. As early as 1934, James Wilkinson, a senior official in the State Department's visa division, warned that a more sympathetic view of the inflexible 1924 immigration law would create "a grave risk that Jews would flood the United States." In a memo to A. Dana Hodgdon, chief of the visa division, Wilkinson also wrote: "Experience has taught us that Jews are persistent in their endeavors to obtain immigration visas, that Jews have a strong tendency, no matter where they are, to allege that they are the subjects of either religious or political persecution [and] that Jews have constantly endeavored to find means of entering the United States despite the barriers set up by our immigration laws."

Sitting in his law office with the dizzying array of immigration figures and quota numbers spread out in front of him, Gil almost certainly had to question his own ability to overcome the monumental challenge of bringing Jewish children into the United States. He quickly realized that he would need to find someone at the State Department in Washington who could better explain the intricacies of the quota system and perhaps offer at least a sense of whether there might be even a remote chance of getting children out of Germany and into America. Gil himself did not know anyone at the State Department, but he knew someone else in Washington who might be able to help.

Leon Sacks was a few years younger than Gil, but the two men had come to know each other through various Philadelphia connections. Sacks was born and raised in Philadelphia's South Side—rough-and-tumble neighborhoods filled with Jewish and Italian immigrants that paralleled New York City's immigrant-dense Lower East Side—which stood in sharp contrast to the far more genteel surroundings of Gil's Philadelphia childhood. But Sacks and Gil had attended Penn both as undergraduates and as law students, and Sacks, like Gil, had quickly begun making a name for himself within the city's business and Jewish communities after starting out as a lawyer in 1926. Unlike Gil, Sacks was intent on a political career. Following a brief stint as a deputy attorney general for the state of Pennsylvania, Sacks won election to the U.S. House of Representatives as part of the Democratic landslide that accompanied Franklin Roosevelt's first reelection campaign in 1936.

Sacks quickly assured Gil that he would gladly help with Brith Sholom's noble, though vaguely defined, rescue project. To move matters along, he arranged for Gil and Louis Levine to meet with George Messersmith, a career Foreign Service officer who had been serving in Washington, D.C., as assistant secretary of state ever since he had returned in 1937 after several years of overseas postings. Although in his current position Messersmith had no formal role in refugee matters, his previous Foreign Service postings in Berlin and Vienna had heightened his awareness of the mounting urgency for Jews to get out as quickly as possible. Fortunately, for both Gil and everyone else at Brith Sholom, Messersmith did not share the brazenly anti-Semitic attitudes that were common among so many of his State Department colleagues. George Kennan, the veteran diplomat and historian, later described Messersmith as "a dry, drawling peppery man, his eyes always glinting with the readiness to accept combat." He was, Kennan added, "incorruptible in his fight for what he considered right and decent." Many of Messersmith's colleagues incorrectly assumed that he himself was

Jewish, which presumably explained his sympathetic views toward them. Instead, those views were shaped wholly by his personal contempt for Nazi ideology and policy.

Messersmith had served as consul general at the American embassy in Berlin from 1930 to 1934, where he witnessed firsthand Hitler's rise to power and, with his ascendancy, the increasing menace posed by the Nazi Party. By the time that Hitler became chancellor, Messersmith had been dispatching a series of cables to the State Department in Washington that spelled out the Nazis' escalating anti-Jewish policies. "The extreme brutality with which the anti-Semitic movement has been carried through will, I believe, never be appreciated by the outside world," Messersmith wrote in a lengthy confidential letter to Under Secretary of State William Phillips in September 1933. "While physical attacks may have stopped almost entirely . . . the measures against the Jews are being carried out daily in a more implacable and a more effective manner. . . . It is definitely the aim of the [German] government . . . to eliminate the Jews from German life." In an earlier nine-page memo to Secretary of State Cordell Hull—written only a few weeks after the Nazi Party scored big gains in German federal elections in March 1933—Messersmith described the impact of the Nazi threat to something as ordinary as the F. W. Woolworth department stores, which were popular throughout Germany: in the wake of the recent election, "uniformed members of the National-Socialist party throughout Germany made difficulties for department stores, one-price stores and chain stores. The uniformed men in many cities picketed stores, posted themselves in front of them with placards warning the public not to enter or buy and, in some cases, compelled the closing of the stores. The Woolworth stores in various cities were among those which were affected."

Messersmith also made it abundantly clear to his superiors in Washington what was behind the Nazis' new campaign. "The movement against these stores," he concluded, "is largely influenced by the fact that the large department stores are owned by Jews and this general interference with stores of this type is therefore one of the manifestations of the anti-Jewish sentiment so actively displayed in these days throughout the country." During his tenure in Berlin, Messersmith earned a well-deserved reputation for speaking frankly with high-ranking Nazi officials, and Hitler himself reportedly "frothed at the mouth" whenever Messersmith's name was mentioned.

After four years in Berlin, Messersmith was appointed U.S. minister to Austria, a role that he filled during the years that led up to the Anschluss. Once again, his diplomatic posting offered a front-row view of the dangers that the Nazis had brought with them from Germany. In a cable sent to Acting Secretary of State R. Walton Moore in November 1936, Messersmith mentioned that National Socialists in Austria had been organizing Nazi military units and "openly address[ing] each other with '*Heil Hitler*' and the Nazi salute."

Messersmith returned to Washington the following April, where he was placed in charge of a project to reorganize the entire State Department. Along with his official duties, however, Messersmith continued to keep a close eye on the situation in Nazi Germany. In particular, Messersmith maintained a steady personal correspondence with Raymond Geist, another veteran Foreign Service officer who was stationed at the American embassy in Berlin and who, for the most part, shared Messersmith's disgust with the miserable conditions of Jews trapped inside Germany. "The Jews in Germany are being condemned to death. Their sentence will be slowly carried out, but probably too fast for the world to save them," Geist wrote in a private letter to Messersmith in December 1938, less than a month after Kristallnacht. "This is a struggle to save the lives of innocent people and not only to save their lives, but spare them years [of] indescribable torture and privations."

Despite Messersmith's personal sympathies, he was also an unyielding defender of America's immigration laws. Only a few days after Kristallnacht, Messersmith warned Labor Secretary Frances Perkins that the State Department strongly opposed her "illegal" proposal to allow German Jews already in the United States on temporary visas to remain in the country rather than force them to return home.* In a "personal and confidential" memo written to Geist in early December, Messersmith sharply criticized Perkins for advocating "extraordinary measures" aimed against existing immigration policies. "All of us who are decent and human are appalled by what is happening in the world," wrote Messersmith, "but we cannot permit the problem to be accentuated at home or abroad by hysterical action."

Although Messersmith readily agreed to meet with Gil and Louis Levine, he made it clear during their discussion that he was in no position to offer official support or encouragement for the Brith Sholom attempt to rescue Jewish children. He also pointed out that America's immigration laws made it extremely difficult to bring children into the country, while adding that those laws were not likely to change anytime soon, if ever. As far as the State Department was concerned, Messersmith told Gil, the Nazis' growing appetite for control of Europe was not going to result in easing the quotas that applied to those trying to find asylum in America. Messersmith, perhaps with a hint of resignation in his voice, added that the number of people from Germany and Austria who had already applied for visas would fill the annual quota for those combined countries for at least the next five years.

Toward the end of the meeting, Gil finally raised the discrepancy that had been bothering him for the past several days. Messersmith offered several reasons that might explain why the quota and visa

---

* Despite Messersmith's strenuous objections, President Roosevelt announced on November 18, 1938, that visitors' visas for 12,000 to 15,000 German Jews would be extended for at least six months. "It could be a cruel and inhumane thing to compel them to leave here," Roosevelt said at a press conference. "I cannot, in any decent humanity, throw them out." Several weeks later, Roosevelt's immigration commissioner estimated that the actual number of Jewish refugees in this category was fewer than 5,000.

numbers did not match up. In some cases, Jews who had been waiting for visas to America wound up escaping instead to places like Shanghai or Cuba—two destinations that had proven relatively open to Jewish families desperate to leave Europe. (In Shanghai, Jewish refugees had already created a "Little Vienna" neighborhood, with streets that were lined with Viennese bakeries, cafés, and delicatessens.) In other cases, visas had been issued to Jews who could no longer afford to make the journey to the United States.

This was the result of one of the cruelest paradoxes of the Nazis' policy of *Judenrein*. The Nazis wanted Jews to leave and readily allowed Jews to leave. But it took money to go someplace, and Hitler's anti-Jewish laws and policies had stripped virtually all Jewish adults of their wealth and means of earning a living.

As he listened to Messersmith's coldly realistic assessment of America's immigration policies, Gil had a flickering thought about how he might be able to bring in some children. It was only a tiny glimmer of hope, but it was certainly worth mentioning. Might it be possible, he asked, to set aside some of the unused visas that would otherwise simply expire if they could not be used in time? Rather than letting these so-called dead visas vanish into thin air, Gil suggested that they be reserved for children from families who were already waiting for their own visas to the United States. As Gil and Louis Levine had already explained to Messersmith, Brith Sholom was willing to pay for boat tickets and all other expenses that would be required to transport a group of children out of Nazi Germany and into the United States. Equally important, Gil also promised that the plan would fully comply with all of the requirements of America's immigration laws. In particular, each child would have a financial sponsor who would guarantee that the child, once in America, would not become a "public charge"—someone dependent upon any type of public support.

Messersmith listened politely to Gil's proposal. It was an intriguing idea, he admitted—and certainly one that had never been suggested by anyone else. He was willing to run it by Geist and others at the American embassy in Berlin, where the visas would have to be issued. Beyond that, however, he could make no promises.

On Friday, February 3, shortly after their meeting in Washington, Gil typed out a two-page letter to Messersmith that described the general outline of the Brith Sholom plan to bring fifty Jewish children from Germany to the United States. Gil again assured Messersmith that there would be no attempt to circumvent the immigration laws or the existing German quota. "We will supply satisfactory affidavits and guarantees from individuals of good standing and character to fulfill the public charge requirements. Each child shall have his own affidavit," wrote Gil. He also reminded Messersmith that there were "ample private funds to provide transportation of the children from Germany to Philadelphia and for their support, maintenance and education." Gil's letter further explained his own role—and that of Eleanor's—in the unfolding rescue plan. "To accomplish our purposes as promptly as possible, Mrs. Kraus and I are prepared to go to Germany to arrange with the proper governmental authorities for the selection of eligible children, the filing of the affidavits, and the transportation of the children." He closed the letter with a request that Messersmith offer some word in reply "concerning the feasibility of our plan and news from Germany."

On the same day that Gil wrote his letter to Messersmith, the State Department official sent a two-page cable to Geist in Berlin. The cable began with a reminder that "all sorts of steps are being proposed to bring children into this country in various ways." Messersmith mentioned that several bills were expected to be introduced in Congress that would allow for children living in Nazi Germany—Jewish and otherwise—to be admitted into the United States above and beyond the quota limits. "My own view is that all these bills will probably die if they are introduced," Messersmith candidly told Geist. "Although I am generally sympathetic to the idea of the admission of children under 15 years of age in a certain number . . . I believe the administrative difficulties in carrying through such a mission are tremendous and perhaps insuperable." Besides, he added, debating any kind of immigration legislation "is going to raise discussion which we want to avoid." Messersmith, above all else, was a political pragmatist who was well aware that anti-immigrant members of Congress would seize on any excuse to restrict immigration even further.

Without mentioning Brith Sholom by name, Messersmith's cable referred to "a responsible group" that was hoping to bring in children "under the quota whose parents for some reason or other may not be able to emigrate." In order to determine whether the plan might work, "a man and a woman of this organization intend to go to Germany and talk over certain matters with you and to go into certain aspects of the problem." Gil and Eleanor were both Jewish, he explained to Geist, but "I told them that I did not see any reason why an American Jew or Jewess should not go to Germany on such legitimate business and I did not believe that they were running any special risk in so doing. As to whether a Jew or Jewess could find a proper hotel to stay in, I was uncertain and that I would write you." Messersmith ended his cable with a request that Geist reply with either a "voyage feasible" or "voyage not feasible" response.

Three days later, on February 6, Messersmith sent a letter to Gil saying that he thought Brith Sholom "thoroughly understands our immigration laws and practice" and that Gil's proposed plan "is, I believe, the only sound and feasible way to approach this problem." But, as he had emphasized during the meeting, Messersmith stressed that "there is nothing which this Government or this Department can do which involves sponsoring any such procedure."

Messersmith was willing, however, to take quieter steps aimed at giving at least an unofficial nod of approval to the rescue effort. Not long after his meeting with Gil, Messersmith sent a memo to A. M. Warren and Eliot Coulter, the senior State Department officials in charge of the visa division. "I believe that this group is a responsible one and they do seem to be a sensible one," Messersmith wrote. "They have made a very favorable impression on me and their one thought is to carry through this project, which involves the initial bringing in of some 50 children, completely within the framework of our present immigration laws and practice." He sent a similar message to Geist in a second cable to Berlin that described the Brith Sholom plan in more detail. "They have approached this whole problem in a much more sensible and understanding way than most people. I think you may give any representatives of this organization, whose names I would eventually send you, full cooperation within the framework of our existing immigrations laws and procedure."

Two weeks later, on Monday, February 20, Messersmith received a telegram from Geist. It simply said: "Voyage entirely feasible."

CHAPTER 7

ADMISSION OF
GERMAN REFUGEE CHILDREN

HEARINGS
BEFORE THE
COMMITTEE ON
IMMIGRATION AND NATURALIZATION
HOUSE OF REPRESENTATIVES
SEVENTY-SIXTH CONGRESS
FIRST SESSION

What is American citizenship worth if it allows American children to go hungry, unschooled and without proper medical attention while we import children from a foreign country? Let the sympathies of the American people be with American children first.
—SENATOR ROBERT REYNOLDS OF NORTH CAROLINA

WASHINGTON, D.C.
FEBRUARY–MARCH 1939

On the morning of Thursday, February 9, 1939, Senator Robert Wagner, a Democrat from New York, rose to his feet next to his polished mahogany desk in the chamber of the United States Senate. After being recognized, Wagner announced the introduction of a bill he had authored that, if enacted, would dwarf the plan that Gil had been discussing with George Messersmith at the State Department.

Wagner, who had been elected to the Senate in 1926 after spending several years as a New York state legislator and judge, knew first-hand what it meant to be an immigrant looking to America for safe haven. As a young boy, he and his parents had come to the United States from Prussia (which later became part of Germany) and settled in New York City's Yorkville neighborhood. After attending the city's public schools, Wagner enrolled in the College of the City of New York (which later became City College) and later earned a law degree from New York Law School. While serving in the New York State Senate, he led a committee that investigated the tragic Triangle Shirtwaist Factory fire, the 1911 disaster that claimed the lives of 146 garment workers, most of whom were young Jewish or Italian immigrant women. Throughout his political career Wagner remained a steadfast supporter of immigrant rights. By early 1939 he had been working on his children's rescue measure for weeks, aided by refugee relief groups and influential individuals. Wagner's bill—formally known as Senate Joint Resolution 64—would allow twenty thousand children from Germany to enter the United States over the next two years, above and beyond the existing German immigration quota. "Millions of innocent and defenseless men, women and children in Germany today, of every race and creed, are suffering from conditions which compel them to seek refuge in other lands," Wagner said as he introduced his bill. "Our hearts go out especially to the children of tender years, who are the most pitiful and helpless sufferers." Passage of his bill, he added, would provide them with much needed relief "from the prospect of a life without hope and without recourse, and [would] enable them to grow up in an environment where the human spirit may survive and prosper."

Five days later, Edith Rogers, a Republican congresswoman from Lowell, Massachusetts, proposed identical legislation in the House of Representatives. "In Germany you have the situation where families . . . are willing to have their children come to a place where they feel they are safe," said Rogers, who had been one of the first members of Congress to take up the cause of Jewish victims of Nazism.

"I have also had the hope that many of the children would go back to their parents later. I do not feel that Hitler will always be in power in Germany."

The Wagner-Rogers bill at least in part was inspired by the British government's decision in late 1938 to ease its immigration rules and allow thousands of Jewish children into England. Jewish leaders in Britain delivered an urgent personal appeal to Prime Minister Neville Chamberlain five days after Kristallnacht, which resulted in Parliament's swift approval of a bill that waived immigration requirements for children under the age of seventeen, who would be permitted to live, at least temporarily, with British foster families. The first group of nearly two hundred children left Berlin on December 1, 1938, and arrived in England the next day. Over the next nine months, some ten thousand children—most of them from Germany and Austria—were evacuated to safety in England, sent away on trains and crossing the English Channel in boats that, collectively, came to be known as the *Kindertransport*.

Within weeks of the introduction of the Wagner-Rogers bill, scores of newspapers around the country published high-minded editorials in favor of allowing the twenty thousand children into the country. "It is difficult to see how anyone with humanitarian impulses can oppose" the bill, declared Virginia's *Richmond Times-Dispatch*. "Those of us who have enjoyed a normal and happy childhood should try to place ourselves in the position of these unfortunate boys and girls in the Germany of today, where they are treated as outcasts, scoffed at in public, and in many cases thrown out of orphan asylums and left on the verge of starvation. How can we, who profess to believe in democracy and human rights, sit idly by and allow such atrocities to be committed without raising a finger?"

But many of these same editorials, while lauding the humanitarian impulse to help Jewish children, also lobbied in defense of America's existing immigration quotas. These editorials made it clear that a special gesture to aid the children should not be viewed as an endorsement of a broader effort to liberalize the nation's overall immigration laws. "It is impossible to offer sanctuary in this country to all refugees, however urgent their need," maintained the *Galveston News* in an editorial published on February 20. "It would dishonor our traditions of humanity and freedom, however, to refuse the small measure of help" offered by the legislation.

These sentiments were broadly echoed in public opinion polls, which reflected overwhelming opposition to any relaxing of the immigration laws, even in light of the events unfolding in Europe. A 1938 survey conducted by the Roper polling company found that fewer than 5 percent of Americans favored more liberal immigration quotas. The same survey revealed that more than 67 percent of Americans were willing to stop all further immigration into the United States. The United States still bore the scars of the Great Depression, and restricting immigration was seen as a way to protect jobs for Americans, who for years had been plagued with staggering unemployment rates. But challenging economic considerations were not the only factors at play in the immigration debate. The American public simply was not moved by the dire situation in Europe.

Even 20 percent of American Jews said they favored a strict immigration policy. Many feared that efforts to allow more than a small trickle of Jewish refugees into the country would only add further fuel to the rising flames of anti-Semitism in the United States. Jewish leaders worried that any effort to liberalize the immigration quotas would quickly be interpreted as un-American, resulting in even more negative attitudes toward the country's Jewish population. These fears were not unfounded. A series of public opinion polls conducted in the late 1930s found that 60 percent of Americans held a low opinion of Jews, regarding them as "greedy," "dishonest," and "pushy." More than 40 percent believed that Jews held too much power in the United States—a figure that would rise to 58 percent by 1945. A Roper poll conducted in 1939 revealed that only 39 percent of Americans felt that Jews should receive the same treatment as all other citizens, while 53 percent believed that "Jews are different and should be restricted." One out of every ten Americans felt that all Jews should be deported outright.

The anti-Semitic rants of national figures such as Father Charles Coughlin—the so-called radio priest of the 1930s—further inflamed public attitudes against Jews during this period. Throughout the Great Depression, Coughlin frequently railed against "international bankers"—a long-recognized code phrase for powerful Jewish interests in the United States and Europe. In a national radio broadcast ten days after Kristallnacht, Coughlin offered a twisted explanation of the Nazis' rise to power in Germany as a logical reaction to Soviet communism, which he and many others felt had been heavily influenced by Jewish leaders: "It is my opinion that Nazism . . . cannot be liquidated until the religious Jews in high places—in synagogues, in finance, in radio and in the press—attack the cause, attack forthright the errors and the spread of communism, together with their co-nationals who support it." In the same speech, Coughlin insisted that any potential danger to 600,000 Jews in Nazi Germany "whom no government official has yet sentenced to death" paled in comparison to millions of Christians "whose lives have been snuffed out, whose property has been confiscated and whose altars have been desecrated" since the 1917 Communist revolution in Russia.

Even more virulent anti-Semitic rants poured out of Fritz Kuhn, the German-born leader of the German American Bund, a pro-Hitler group that at the height of its popularity in the 1930s published four newspapers, operated twenty-two summer camps for children, organized a businessmen's league, and established nearly one hundred branches around the country. "All Jews are enemies of the United States," Kuhn declared in June 1938. "It wasn't the Jews who built up this country. They came later when there was something to grab." On the night of February 20, 1939, more than twenty thousand Bund supporters filled New York City's Madison Square Garden, where speaker after speaker riled up the crowd with taunts that included attacks on "Jewish leeches of class warfare" and snide references to President Roosevelt as "Franklin Rosenfeld."*

In defiance of these anti-Jewish sentiments, two congressmen from New York—Emanuel Celler and Samuel Dickstein—considered introducing a bill in the wake of Kristallnacht to allow unrestricted immigration for victims of religious or political persecution. Such a measure, which would have had no chance of success on Capitol Hill, also attracted widespread opposition from Jewish leaders and organizations, hardly the kind of attention that its sponsors had imagined. Rabbi Stephen Wise, the popular and charismatic leader of the American Jewish Congress, who had President Roosevelt's ear on such matters, dismissed the Celler-Dickstein proposal as being "so bad that it seems the work of an *agent provocateur*." Another national organization, the American Jewish Committee, warned that the legislation would create "bad feelings" by allowing Jewish refugees to take jobs away from Americans who were still looking for work during the lingering Depression. "As heartless as it may seem, future efforts should be directed toward sending Jewish refugees to other countries instead of bringing them here," declared the group. Celler and Dickstein quickly abandoned their proposal.

Within the Roosevelt administration, Labor Secretary Frances Perkins provided a lone sympathetic voice in support of allowing greater numbers of Jewish refugees into the United States. During a cabinet meeting held six weeks after FDR's 1933 inauguration, Perkins urged the new president to rescind a 1930 executive order by President Herbert Hoover that had required strict adherence to the public charge requirement in the immigration law. The change would have immediately made it much easier for thousands of Jews to come to America without requiring any changes to the quota

---

* Kuhn, who had become an American citizen in 1933, was convicted in 1939 of embezzling more than $14,000 from the German American Bund. He was later arrested during the war as a foreign enemy agent and his citizenship was revoked in 1943. After the war ended, Kuhn was deported to Germany, where he died in 1951.

system. But Secretary of State Cordell Hull, along with Under Secretary of State William Phillips, opposed such a move and convinced Roosevelt there was no connection between Hoover's earlier order and the low percentage of refugees who were being admitted from Germany. The public charge requirement would remain in the law. Perkins also lobbied for other revisions to the law, such as legal authority for the issuance of a financial bond in advance of an immigrant's arrival in the country, which would help to guarantee that the immigrant would not wind up on public assistance.

Perkins, of course, convinced Roosevelt in November 1938 to extend temporary visas for thousands of German-Jewish visitors already in the United States. Her actions, however, prompted a candid warning from C. Paul Fletcher, an official in the State Department's visa division, who told a colleague that the department would quickly incur the wrath of the American public if "ships begin to arrive in New York City laden with Jewish immigrants."

By early 1939, efforts to allow more Jewish children into the country had gained the support of a few influential national figures, notably Eleanor Roosevelt. The first lady had even provided, sotto voce, strategic advice to a coalition of refugee relief groups that had been trying to generate support for the children's rescue bill even before it was formally introduced by Senator Wagner and Congresswoman Rogers. "My husband says that you had better go to work at once and get two people from opposite parties in the House and Senate and have them jointly get agreement on the legislation you want for bringing in the children," Mrs. Roosevelt advised her friend Justine Polier, a New York judge and social welfare activist who also happened to be Rabbi Wise's daughter.

But the Wagner-Rogers bill almost certainly was doomed to fail from the moment it was introduced. Although the State Department never officially opposed the measure, neither did it offer any support. Instead, Secretary of State Hull sent a detailed letter to members of Congress that focused on how difficult it would be to carry out the children's rescue bill. Without saying so explicitly, Hull's message left little doubt that the State Department had no interest in seeing the legislation enacted.

Once public hearings began in the spring of 1939, a steady stream of individuals and organizations paraded before the House and Senate immigration committees to testify against the bill. Agnes Waters, representing a group of World War I widows, urged Congress not to let in "thousands of motherless, embittered, persecuted children of undesirable foreigners" who would grow up to become "potential leaders of a revolt" against the American government. "Why should we give preference . . . to these potential Communists?" railed Mrs. Waters. "Already we have too many of their kind in our country trying to overthrow our government." To be sure, the hearings also featured a variety of witnesses who offered impassioned testimony in favor of the Wagner-Rogers legislation. "I know it must be difficult to visualize the anguish those mothers [in Germany] must feel to make them willing and eager to give up their children and send them to a strange land, send them to strange people," actress Helen Hayes told members of Congress. "That is the most potent and the most moving evidence of the immediate need of those little children. I beg of you to let them in."

But the strong anti-immigration attitudes that already prevailed on Capitol Hill continued to align with the overall mood of the country—even when it came to saving children. While the Wagner-Rogers measure was being debated in Congress, Senator Robert Reynolds, a conservative North Carolina Democrat, introduced his own series of bills that, among other things, would reduce the immigration quotas for all countries by up to 90 percent. Other parts of his legislation would prohibit immigration altogether until America's unemployment levels dropped further, along with requiring the deportation of all foreign aliens found to be receiving any form of public assistance. Reynolds staked out a leading role in marshaling public and political opposition to the Wagner-Rogers bill. "Shall we first take care of our own children, our citizens, our country, or shall we bestow our charity on children imported from abroad," he asked in a national radio broadcast in March 1939. Reynolds summarily dismissed the claim, put forward by supporters of the Wagner-Rogers bill, that thousands of Americans were ready to open up their homes to Jewish children if the measure were to pass. "If that statement be true, then this is my answer, your answer, and America's answer," said Reynolds. "If homes are available for the adoption of alien children, Americanism demands that needy American children also be adopted into these American homes. My heart beats in sympathy for those unfortunate children across the seas. But my love and duty belongs firstly to our children here at home."

Throughout the spring, Washington was filled with talk, both public and private, about immigration and hardened attitudes toward allowing Jewish refugees into the country. During a Washington dinner party, someone asked Laura Delano Houghteling for her thoughts about the pending Wagner-Rogers bill. As the wife of U.S. Immigration Commissioner James Houghteling and also President Roosevelt's first cousin, she might have been a little more circumspect before offering her opinion. Instead, she casually remarked: "Twenty thousand charming children would all too soon grow up into twenty thousand ugly adults."

It is doubtful that FDR himself ever gave serious consideration to throwing his political weight behind the Wagner-Rogers bill. Although he was immensely popular among Jews in America, Roosevelt was also acutely aware of the cost he might have to pay by defying the broad public sentiments against increased foreign immigration. Roosevelt was a consummate politician with an ambitious agenda for the nation that, by 1939, included the challenge of preparing a reluctant American public for the seeming inevitability of a war in Europe. FDR and his closest advisers knew that highly visible efforts to help bring larger numbers of Jewish refugees into the United States would do little to help accomplish his broader agenda. Indeed such efforts would almost certainly result in a backlash among American isolationists and anti-immigration forces, which would make it even more difficult for the president to forge ahead with his priorities for the country. Saving Jewish lives—particularly those of innocent children—may well have appealed to FDR's humanitarian instincts. But it did not square up with his broader political agenda.

Eleanor Roosevelt tried on a few occasions to sway her husband in favor of the Wagner-Rogers bill. She also talked with Under Secretary of State Sumner Welles in an effort to win more support for the legislation. "He says that personally he is in favor of the bill and feels as I do about it," Mrs. Roosevelt wrote to Justine Polier, "but that it would not be advisable for the president to come out because if the president did and [the bill] was defeated, it would be very bad."

As the hearings on the Wagner-Rogers bill concluded in late spring, a New York congresswoman attempted one last time to find out where the president stood. "Caroline O'Day asked me last night at dinner if you would give her an expression of your views on the bill providing for 20,000 refugee children being allowed into America regardless of the quota status," wrote Edwin "Pa" Watson, Roosevelt's senior aide, in a memo typed on cream-colored White House stationery. In the upper right-hand corner of the June 2 memo, Roosevelt, in clear handwriting, noted his succinct response: "File no action FDR."

CHAPTER 8

Help Save America!

Don't Buy From JEWS!

Since the quota waiting list is so long, I am afraid the children whom we register now won't come in for at least another year.

—CECILIA RAZOVSKY

PHILADELPHIA
FEBRUARY–MARCH 1939

With a bang of his gavel, Louis Levine called to order the emergency meeting of Brith Sholom leaders that he had hastily convened on the evening of Monday, February 27. Acting in his capacity as the organization's grand master, Levine had summoned the officers from dozens of the group's Philadelphia area lodges to its national headquarters on Spruce Street, just a few blocks south of the city's historic Independence Hall. With Gil sitting off to the side of the meeting room, Levine formally announced the plan to bring a group of German refugees into the United States. As everyone listened attentively, Levine explained that once the children were safely out of Nazi Germany and in the United States, they would be put up for adoption, placed with foster parents, or sent to live with relatives. Additional children would be brought over once the first group had been settled in good homes.

The Brith Sholom leader solemnly added that the organization had the power to "make or break" the rescue plan. He then introduced Gil, though everyone in the room already knew him. By the end of the evening, the men from Brith Sholom promised to raise $150,000 in support of the plan.

Two days later, the Philadelphia *Evening Public Ledger* published a two-paragraph item announcing that a project "to bring refugee children from Germany to Philadelphia is under consideration" by the Jewish fraternal organization. A slightly longer article appeared in that week's Philadelphia *Jewish Times*. "Grand Master Levine was assured that the entire national membership is eager to cooperate," reported the newspaper.

Word was spreading about the rescue project. But not everyone liked what they heard. Brith Sholom was not the only organization—Jewish or otherwise—interested in bringing Jewish children into the United States. Others, in fact, had been trying for some time to set into action similar missions, but with little or no success to show for their efforts. "We had a telephone message from Philadelphia stating that Brith Sholom is collecting funds and is making arrangements to set up a home for fifty children who are due to arrive here very shortly," Blanche Goldman, the chairman of German-Jewish Children's Aid, wrote on February 28 to A. M. Warren, the State Department's visa official. "As you know, German-Jewish Children's Aid has been carrying on a project of bringing children to the United States within the quota on an individual basis, and that recently very few children have been arriving because of the delay in the issuance of quota visas to them." The Brith Sholom plan, she told Warren, "is naturally very embarrassing for our organization."

But Goldman's letter did not accurately reflect the Brith Sholom plan. She was under the impression, for example, that Brith Sholom had recently received a letter from Under Secretary of State Welles that supposedly authorized the group to bring in up to 250 children above and beyond the regular quota limits for Germany and Austria. Welles never sent such a letter, and Gil, for his part, was aware that all of the children would have to qualify under the existing German quota. In his response to Goldman a few days later, Warren made no mention of the supposed letter from Welles. Instead he wrote that he had just spoken the day before with Brith Sholom officials "who assured me categorically that they do not intend to bring any immigrant children into the United States outside of the quota restrictions."

These assurances did little to mollify Goldman's group, which had been trying, along with others, to bring Jewish children into the United States ever since Hitler came to power. In the fall of 1933, representatives from the American Jewish Committee, American Jewish Congress, and B'nai B'rith formed a committee to develop a plan for rescuing Jewish children living in Germany. They debated the matter for several months before the project was placed in the hands of German Jewish Children's Aid, which was led by Cecilia Razovsky, a social worker who strenuously advocated for admitting Jewish refugees. After a period of frustrating negotiations with various immigration officials, an initial group of ten Jewish children from Germany finally arrived in New York in November 1934. But news of their arrival was quickly followed by stinging criticism from a group that called itself the American Coalition of Patriotic, Civil and Fraternal Societies, which accused the government of cooperating in the "systematic importation of indigent alien children." German Jewish Children's Aid also found it difficult to find enough

Jewish families willing to take in children. As a result, only about one hundred children were admitted between November 1934 and April 1935, after which Razovsky's group stopped sending for more children. Although the group later resumed its rescue efforts, it was constantly frustrated by the rigid immigration rules and managed to bring in a total of fewer than four hundred children by the end of 1938. These children typically arrived one or two at a time rather than as part of larger groups. The Brith Sholom plan differed significantly because of its attempt to bring in a larger group of children all together.

Razovsky, meanwhile, had recently worked out an agreement with the Labor Department to bring in twenty children each month. But bureaucratic delays and other administrative obstacles made even that modest goal impossible. "We not only are not taking large groups, but we are even slowing up on those whom we have ordered . . . because of the long delays in the quota," Razovsky wrote in late December 1938 to the head of Atlanta's Hebrew Orphan Home, who had asked her about plans to bring in Jewish children from the Reich. "We get people coming in all day long who do nothing but scold us and regard us as personally responsible because the children cannot come in."

As conditions in Nazi Germany deteriorated, Razovsky and others grew more frustrated than ever with the rigid limits imposed by American immigration policies. Razovsky received a letter from the wife of Rabbi Wise, asking whether it might be possible to bring in the young daughter from a Jewish family she knew in Dusseldorf, Germany. "Since the quota waiting list is so long, I am afraid the children whom we register now won't come in for at least another year," replied Razovsky. A few weeks later, Mrs. Wise wrote again to Razovsky, this time as the chairman of the Child Adoption Committee of the Free Synagogue, the New York City synagogue led by her husband. Once again, Razovsky could offer nothing but discouragement. "I am afraid there will not be any children available for adoption in the near future in view of the terrible crowded condition of the quota at this time," she wrote. In the aftermath of Kristall-nacht, Razovsky's group became even more inundated with pleas for help. "Persons who received affidavits some time ago now want us to use our influence with Washington to get them out of Germany quickly," Razovsky wrote to a woman in Erie, Pennsylvania, who was concerned about the worsening situation in Germany. "Of course that is absolutely out of the question. There is nothing we can do to help these thousands of trapped unfortunates. They have no preference on the quota and their turns will come two years hence possibly."

Once it began circulating around Philadelphia that Gil had taken on the project, several of the city's Jewish leaders decided to try and talk him out of it. Some, convinced that he would almost certainly fail, were worried that the project would make it even harder for other rescue efforts to proceed. Others feared that it would generate additional backlash against Jewish groups throughout the United States. In early March, a group of men dropped by Gil's office only to find out that he was in Washington that day for a meeting at the State Department. They made an appointment to see him once he returned home. "A few days later, three of the most important and leading Philadelphia Jews called on Gil . . . and told him we must drop any idea or plan that we had at once," wrote Eleanor. "They told him that he could not possibly succeed."

Although Eleanor did not name her husband's visitors, she did identify one of the men who arrived the next day with a similar mes-sage: Kurt Peiser, the director of Philadelphia's Federation of Jewish Charities. Peiser, who was a few years older than Gil, had been born in Germany and brought to the United States with his family when he was twelve. He had worked for a variety of Jewish charitable groups in Milwaukee, Cincinnati, and Detroit before moving to Phil-adelphia. As Eleanor described the meeting, Peiser wasted no time in insisting that Gil "must scrap this idea at once. Nothing good could come of it [and] only danger and fiasco was in store for him." Peiser pleaded with Gil to abandon the rescue mission. "Surely, you would not want to subject your wife to this danger and embarrassment," he said. "If you continue with this plan, we will be obliged to take all necessary steps to prevent it."

Gil listened politely, but he had no intention of backing down. "He was perfectly willing to risk failure, discouragement or embarrassment," wrote Eleanor. "He knew the chances of failure were much better than those for success. But he didn't see why, if he were willing to go to Germany on this mission, he should be prevented from doing so."

While fears of an anti-Semitic backlash certainly had a role in this opposition, professional jealousy almost certainly also played a part. Why should Brith Sholom—a group that had never before been involved in refugee work—now get credit for saving children when other organizations—including some that had been trying for years to bring in refugees—had met with little success in their own efforts?

Throughout late February and early March, the pressure mounted. "This line of talk continued everywhere Gil went—at lunch and in his club," wrote Eleanor. "One would think we were trying to do something illegal or wicked, even degrading, and we grew more and more confused. It seemed like such a decent, desirable thing to be doing."

As Eleanor knew better than anyone, her husband was not a man easily swayed or discouraged. But even he began to wonder if he was doing the right thing. "I don't know what to do or where to go for advice," he told Eleanor one evening in March. "I don't know whether we should abandon this thing or not." Eleanor's spirits fell even as she continued to ask the couple's friends and acquaintances if they would be willing to sponsor the children and submit personal affidavits. "I began to feel as though I was doing all this for nothing," she wrote.

Gil realized that he needed a fresh perspective. He needed to talk with someone who could offer sound, impartial advice on whether or not to proceed. He reached for the telephone and called Rufus Jones. A retired philosophy professor at nearby Haverford College, Jones was one of the country's most prominent Quakers. Gil, of course, also knew that Jones had led the Quaker delegation that had gone to Germany in December in the unsuccessful effort to convince Nazi officials to ease some of the burdens on Jews trying to leave the Reich.

Jones, who grew up in a long-established Quaker family in Maine, was one of the founders, in 1917, of the American Friends Service Committee, the well-respected group originally formed to help civilian victims during World War I. All during the 1930s, the group had been doing whatever it could to help refugees escape from Nazi Germany. Several weeks before Kristallnacht, Clarence Pickett—another leading Quaker official immersed in rescue efforts—had traveled to Europe and met with Raymond Geist at the American embassy in Berlin. "We saw Mr. Geist, the American consul general, who certainly had one tale of woe," Pickett wrote in his private journal in September 1938. "The preceding Saturday 3,000 people had applied for visas to America. He was simply deluged with people who had heart-rending tales of woe . . . The large consular office was swarmed with people when we were there and that, [Geist] said, was a comparatively quiet day."

Jones, who had taught at Haverford for more than forty years, continued to live in a comfortable stone house on the campus since his retirement in 1934. He readily agreed to see Gil and Eleanor, inviting the couple to his home the following afternoon. They arrived at Haverford in the midst of a swirling snowstorm. Making their way carefully through the snow-covered campus, they found it difficult to find Jones's house. Finally, as they slowed in front of one of the buildings, they spotted a small, gray-haired, elderly man, bundled against the cold with his suit collar turned up. It was Jones, who had ventured outside to look for his guests.

Inside his cozy study, Jones poured cups of steaming tea while Gil explained the details of the Brith Sholom mission that he had been asked to carry out. He told the retired Quaker professor about the home in Collegeville that was large enough to house fifty children. He made sure to mention that Brith Sholom members had promised to raise enough money to care for the children once they arrived in this country. "We will need nothing from the public," said Gil. "But we have no pull with anybody. Just a plan that has not been accepted or turned down at the State Department." He also mentioned the strenuous efforts to block him from moving ahead with the project. Jones listened quietly as Gil described his predicament. Gil also had several questions for Jones about current conditions inside Germany. "Could we even go to Germany at this time?" he wondered. "Would we be in danger and be persecuted or attacked in any way physically? How were Americans being treated in Germany? How would American Jews be received there?" Gil was almost pleading with Jones for advice.

Jones seemed reluctant at first to answer Gil's questions, particularly the ones about whether or not Americans would be safe in Germany. After all, the situation there seemed to be changing with each passing day. He and his fellow Quakers had not been threatened during their own visit a few months earlier, but who knew whether or not the situation might have grown worse since then? After listening to Gil's detailed description of the proposed rescue project, however, Jones did not hesitate to offer encouragement. "Since you have the house and the money and the plan, I feel you should go," said Jones. "Indeed, you must go and find out if your plan will work." It was the surge of adrenaline Gil needed. "On our way back to Philadelphia, we decided that we wouldn't stop now," wrote Eleanor. "We would proceed as if we were going to Germany."

Although Gil did not know it, the State Department was also proceeding on that assumption. On March 2, Secretary of State Cordell Hull signed a confidential cable that was sent out at 6:00 P.M. to the American embassy in Berlin. "The Department desires you to obtain from each of the offices, Berlin, Hamburg, Stuttgart and Vienna, a statement giving the number of German-born children under fourteen years of age who have been refused . . . visas during the period from July 1, 1938, to February 28, 1939." The purpose of the cable, aimed at all of the American consulates in Nazi Germany, was to narrow down the exact number of children who might be potential candidates for the Brith Sholom rescue project. It took until March 23 for the embassy in Berlin to report back to Washington. "Visas have been withheld from some five hundred twenty-six children by reason of insufficient support," Raymond Geist wrote in his telegram to Hull. "Latter figure is of necessity [an] estimate only owing to lack of exact statistics."

One day later Messersmith received a one-page memo from Warren, in the visa division, along with a copy of Geist's cable from the previous day. The precise number of children mentioned in the cable "would appear to include a category of children in whom Congressman Leon Sacks [the Philadelphia Democrat who had first introduced Gil to Messersmith] is interested. If any of these children should receive assurances of support, they would appear to be otherwise admissible into the United States immediately because the cablegram indicates that their turns have already been reached on the waiting lists in Germany."

Although Eleanor had no way of knowing at the time that the State Department had now identified a precise group of eligible children, she certainly knew that she would have to work faster in order to complete the necessary paperwork. "Every day I did as much as time allowed, worked very hard and paid very little attention to anything else." She had discovered there was a lot more to the process than simply filling out the forms that made up each individual affidavit. Letters from employers were required to confirm the salary of a prospective sponsor. Several of the affidavits were coming from friends who, like Gil, were self-employed. All of them were required to furnish a copy of the previous year's tax return. Bank statements, life insurance policies, a complete listing of stocks and bonds, real estate property deeds—the list went on and on. "No one who had offered to make out an affidavit had realized how personal and complete a financial statement I required," she wrote. "There is one thing in this country no one wants to do, and that is reveal his income tax return."

Eleanor went to a local printer's shop, where she ordered hundreds of blank affidavit forms. As she immersed herself in the work, she discovered that it took nearly two weeks to complete a single affidavit, given the additional time required to request and receive the various supporting documents that were part of the affidavit process. She became a very familiar face in the Philadelphia printing shop, where she would make the photostat copies that were required by the government. After a few weeks of this painstaking work, Eleanor had started nearly twenty-five affidavits, though none had yet been fully completed. She was discouraged by her lack of progress and felt that she would need to move much faster. She also became alarmed when she reached thirty-six affidavits, only to realize that she had run out of names. But Gil reassured her that additional people had offered to sponsor the children. Every night he came home with a new list for her to work on.

Gil, however, still had problems of his own. "The telephone calls and visits continued," wrote Eleanor. "Every place he went, more people tried to discourage him. We kept our mouths shut when we could, said as little as possible and did not reveal our immediate plans." By this time, toward the end of March, word had also spread around Philadelphia that Gil and Eleanor had gone to see Rufus Jones, which led to rumors that the Quakers had become involved in the Brith Sholom project. One of the Philadelphia Jewish leaders called on Gil yet again, this time with a demand that he and Eleanor present themselves for questioning before the Federation of Jewish Charities. "Gil did not agree to this," wrote Eleanor, "nor would he agree at any time to permit me to be questioned by anybody. Our minds were made up, and we knew just what we were going to do. Right now, no one was going to stop us."

Until that point, Eleanor had been seeking affidavits mostly from Gil's closest friends and others who were directly involved with Brith Sholom and who, as a result, would be more inclined to sign on as sponsors. Still faced with a shortage, however, she and Gil realized they would have to broaden their efforts by approaching others who were not aware of the project. Eleanor invited a few couples over for dinner, during which she and Gil talked about what they were doing and what they hoped to accomplish. Several of their friends gladly offered to provide affidavits without hesitation. Sometimes Gil would call a friend or a business associate from his office, and then later that evening pass on the information to Eleanor, who would follow up with the financial questions and forms. As she filled in the blanks on the affidavit forms, Eleanor often found herself staring at the "astronomical" incomes or stock portfolios that friends and others had. "I never realized that anybody had this much money," she wrote.

As the weeks went by, Eleanor settled into a routine. She knew that the success of the rescue plan, at least in large part, depended on her ability to prepare affidavits that would withstand the intense scrutiny of American immigration officials. She knew there was no room for error or oversight. "My heels were running down, but the papers were piling up," she recalled. "It took six weeks, but I had accumulated fifty-four affidavits, four extra just in case anything went wrong. It wasn't really easy, and it wasn't really pleasant. But it was accomplished!"

CHAPTER 9

*I do not think you should go to Germany. In fact, I urge you most
strongly not to go.*

—GEORGE MESSERSMITH'S STATE DEPARTMENT AIDE

WASHINGTON, D.C.–PHILADELPHIA
MARCH 1939

On a cool, early spring morning toward the end of March, Gil
and Eleanor boarded a train to Washington for another round
of meetings with government officials. Their first stop was at the Department of Labor's imposing headquarters on Constitution Avenue,
only a few blocks from the White House. Dressed in his custom-
ary three-piece suit and wingtip shoes, leather briefcase in hand,
Gil blended right in with the solemn-faced, business-attired deputy
assistant secretaries, lawyers, and other government employees who

filled the marble-floored hallways and populated the cubbyhole offices throughout the building. The Labor Department was in charge
of enforcing all of the regulations that applied to child immigrants
coming into the United States, and Gil wanted to be absolutely sure
that nothing in the rescue plan would conflict with any of the rules.
Because each child would be coming into the country under the
sponsorship of a financially viable individual—Eleanor's affidavits
would make sure of that—Gil was fairly confident. But he wasn't
leaving a single detail to chance. They spent about an hour with an
official, thoroughly outlining every aspect of the Brith Sholom plan.
They left with the assurances Gil had been seeking: there would be
no objections from that corner of the federal government.

The sun was shining, and the couple decided they would walk
to their next appointment—another meeting with George Messersmith at the State Department. They strolled along Fifteenth Street,
turning left on Pennsylvania Avenue and stopping for a moment for a
quick gaze through the black wrought iron gates that stood in front
of the White House. Messersmith worked right next door, in the
ornate Victorian-style State, War, and Navy Building on the corner
of Seventeenth and Pennsylvania. Warmly ushering the Krauses into
his office, Messersmith was "most cordial and friendly as could be,"
wrote Eleanor. However, he remained "completely non-committal,"
explaining once again that the American government could not officially endorse a private rescue effort. Gil told Messersmith that he and
Eleanor would be ready to leave for Germany in about two weeks—in
fact, they were picking up their passports at the State Department
that afternoon. Messersmith said he would write again to Raymond
Geist in Berlin once Gil and Eleanor knew exactly when they would
be leaving. As he stood up to say good-bye, the diplomat reached out
to shake Gil's hand. "I wish you every success," he said. His encour-
aging words contrasted with his earlier warning that the government
could play no official role in supporting Gil's plan—a contrast fully in
keeping with the dichotomy between Messersmith's public demeanor

and private character. He was a man bound by—and fully committed to—the laws and policies of the American government. But he also knew exactly what was at stake for the children and families Gil was trying to help. His firm handshake and warm farewell further confirmed to Gil that he and Eleanor were on the right path.

In the spring of 1939, there were no legal restrictions on Americans wishing to travel, either for personal or business reasons, to Nazi Germany. Six years after Hitler's rise to power, the United States and Germany continued to maintain official—albeit increasingly strained—diplomatic relations. A few months earlier, President Roosevelt had summoned Hugh Wilson, the American ambassador to Germany, back to Washington as a gesture of diplomatic protest against the violence during Kristallnacht. Wilson had yet to resume his post, and it now seemed unlikely that he would be returning to Germany as ambassador anytime soon.* Even so, the American embassy in Berlin (with Raymond Geist now effectively in charge) continued to function, along with a handful of American consulates scattered across Germany and Austria. Messersmith and others in Washington, however, were convinced that war in Europe was imminent, even if the United States managed to formally remain on the sidelines of the escalating hostilities.

After obtaining their passports, Gil and Eleanor chatted for a few minutes with Messersmith's assistant, who had accompanied them to the passport office. As the couple was getting ready to leave, the assistant lowered his voice and said that he felt compelled to tell them something "off the record." He turned to Eleanor and asked if she and her husband had children. She replied that they had two young children at home in Philadelphia.

She was not prepared for what came next. "I do not think you should go to Germany. In fact, I urge you most strongly not to go,"

---

* Hugh Wilson never returned to Germany, and the United States did not send another ambassador there until 1955.

the State Department official told her. She and Gil listened intently as he explained about the chaotic conditions that currently existed in Germany. He warned them that war in Europe could break out at any time, and if it did, Americans might find it difficult to get out. Hearing this, Eleanor felt the same jolt of fear that she had experienced when Gil first mentioned the plan in January. For the moment, Americans traveling in Germany were "reasonably safe," added Messersmith's assistant. "However, I cannot advise any woman, including any American woman, to enter Germany at this time. The consequences may be too dangerous and too serious."

He acknowledged that the State Department could not refuse to provide Eleanor with a passport nor could it legally forbid her from going to Germany. "I have no official right to even be telling you all these things. But I advise you, in fact I plead with you, not to go," he urged her.

The assistant's words came as a bombshell. It was one thing for Jewish community leaders and others to try and talk Gil out of moving ahead with the rescue plan. But a warning from a State Department official about the dangers of traveling to Nazi Germany was an entirely different matter. "We picked up our passports and left the State Department," wrote Eleanor. "We were late, and we dashed into a taxi and drove as quickly as possible to the station for our train back to Philadelphia."

Once aboard the late-afternoon train, the couple headed straight to the club car and ordered a round of drinks. Eleanor was still shaken. She took a sip from her drink, looked at her husband, and said, "Now what?" Gil stared down into his glass, took a long swallow, and then looked back up at his wife. "One thing is for sure," he said. "You cannot go."

Gil and Eleanor ordered another round of drinks and continued to fret. Gil had been counting on Eleanor to assist with the work that would have to get done in Europe. There was no way that he would be able to take care of everything by himself. Gil also confessed to a more personal reason for not wanting to travel to Europe alone. "I couldn't live over there by myself without anybody to talk to, to work with, to go out with," Gil told his wife. She nodded in agreement, knowing full well that her husband could not be expected to execute the plan on his own. But how could they ask somebody to step into her place, particularly on such short notice and under such potentially dangerous circumstances?

As the train pulled into Philadelphia's Thirtieth Street Station, a thought suddenly occurred to Eleanor. She turned to Gil and exclaimed: "Bob Schless!" It took a few moments for Eleanor's excited suggestion to sink in. Gil looked at his wife and said, "That's a brilliant idea!"

Gil and Eleanor had known Doctor Robert Schless for years. He was their children's pediatrician and was also one of Philadelphia's most respected doctors. Coincidentally he also happened to speak fluent German. Schless's father, Samuel, had emigrated from Odessa in the 1880s while his mother, Julia, was a native of Austria. The Schlesses were Jewish, but like the Krauses, they were hardly religious. Bob Schless, who was born in Wilmington, Delaware, but grew up in Philadelphia, greatly admired the Quakers and for much of his life had adhered closely to Quaker teachings and principles.

He was a few years older than Gil, and both men had graduated from Philadelphia's Central High School. From there Schless enrolled at Jefferson Medical College, which in those years allowed students to enter medical school directly after high school. After obtaining his medical degree in 1916, Schless eagerly accepted an invitation from the British Army to serve in the Royal Army Medical Corps, where he was assigned to a military base outside of London. He later enlisted in the U.S. Navy, where he became one of the nation's first flight surgeons. In the years after World War I, Schless made a name for himself in pediatric medicine and, in 1925, was appointed to the post of assistant pediatrician at Philadelphia General Hospital. He later became chief of pediatrics at the city's highly regarded

Jewish Hospital. Along the way, he had gotten married, though by the spring of 1939 Schless was a widower with three sons at home.

Riding in the taxi back to Cypress Street, Gil and Eleanor grew more excited about the prospect of Bob accompanying Gil to Germany. "Imagine having a pediatrician on a trip like this," said Eleanor. "Assuming you will get the children, think how wonderful it will be to have a pediatrician to travel with, to examine the children and take care of all their ills." Of course, one big question still remained: Would Bob Schless even consider the idea?

It did not take very long to find out. The following afternoon, Gil and Eleanor seated themselves in the small waiting room outside Schless's office in the Medical Arts Building on Walnut Street, three blocks away from Gil's law office. A tall, slender man with thinning brown hair who favored gold wire-rimmed glasses and perfectly knotted bow ties, Schless arrived a few minutes ahead of his first patient and cheerfully invited the Krauses into his office. They wasted no time on pleasantries and breathlessly launched into the reason for their visit.

Bob did not hesitate for a moment. He assured Gil and Eleanor that he had no reservations about going to Germany. They suggested that he take at least a few days before giving them his decision. But he saw no reason to wait. "I've already decided," he told them. "I want to go if I can get somebody to take over my practice." He promised to let them know within a day or so. Bob telephoned Gil later that evening to say he had found another doctor to handle his patients during his absence. He had already arranged for his mother to look after his three boys. Gil said he planned to leave for Germany in two weeks. Bob assured him that he would be ready to go.

Over the next two weeks, Gil and Eleanor frantically prepared for Gil's departure. Gil made sure that his immediate business responsibilities at his law office had been attended to. He also traveled once more to Washington, this time with Bob Schless, to confirm the plans with Messersmith and to obtain Bob's passport for the trip overseas.

On March 29, Messersmith sent a cable to Geist in Berlin that served as a formal "word of introduction" to Gilbert Kraus and Doctor Robert Schless. "They are sailing, I believe, on April 7 and will go to see you in the matter of bringing over a number of children to this country," wrote Messersmith. "Both of these men are very first class people and I am sure that you can depend on their reliability. . . . You know, of course, that we are not in any way sponsoring this matter and could not do so. We do believe, however, that these people are reliable, that they want to work entirely within the framework of our immigration laws, and that they are worthy of your sympathetic consideration."

Eleanor, for her part, worked at a furious pace in order to finalize all of the affidavits. By the first of April, the job was complete. Every piece of paper was neatly organized. Every photostat was in its proper place. Every notary seal appeared exactly where it was required. As she looked at the stack of documents piled neatly on her dining room table, Eleanor took a few moments to revel in her accomplishment. And yet she also felt conflicted now that her part in the rescue plan had come to an end. Ever since she and Gil had returned from Washington, she had felt "a combination of being very disappointed and very relieved about not going to Germany. I would have been scared to death the whole time, and now there was great relief that I did not have to go. Disappointment too—I had to admit to a feeling of disappointment."

Eleanor also felt more than a little sorry for herself—she suddenly had nothing to do. It was time for a little bit of consolation, she decided. "What does a woman do when she is at her lowest point?" she wrote. "She buys a hat!" Spring was in the air, and Eleanor decided that a new wardrobe was in order. She set out for the millinery department at Bonwit Teller department store on Walnut Street, keeping an eye out for a hat she had recently spotted in one of the window displays. There it was—a "red tweed tricorn with a green bird that looked like a parakeet and a wonderful yellow veil."

Eleanor gasped when she turned the hat over and stared at the price tag. "I had never paid anything like this for a hat in my whole lifetime. Not even my wedding hat approached this staggering figure." She gently placed the hat back on its perch, only to quickly pick it up and try it on again. "It was the most entrancing, enchanting thing I have ever had on my head."

Eleanor knew she had to buy that hat. Besides, she rationalized to herself, it was much cheaper than a trip to Europe. "I bought the hat, and out I went with my consolation prize. I shopped the rest of the day for clothes and found a simple, lovely beige topcoat to go with the hat. Weary, but most gratified, I went home with my packages."

PART TWO

THE RESCUE

CHAPTER 10

There is no possibility of Gil succeeding in the rescue effort. Instead, by going to Germany he would only confirm the impossibility and return a failure.

—Jacob Billikopf

PHILADELPHIA–VIENNA
APRIL 1939

The dinner service began with a sterling silver dish filled with intensely flavored *caviar de Beluga*. It was followed by a small bowl of spicy *gombo de volaille Creole*, a French version of traditional gumbo Creole. Gil was a man who enjoyed gourmet dining, and the sumptuous surroundings of the Grand Salon—the first-class dining room aboard the RMS *Queen Mary*—provided the ideal atmosphere for the classic French cuisine that he and Bob Schless tucked into on their third night at sea.

After the gumbo had been cleared away by the liveried waiters who moved effortlessly from table to table, out came the two main courses for that evening's dinner: *delice de sole Veronique* and *poussin en cocotte paysanne*—delicate fillets of sole sautéed with green grapes and heavy cream and a hearty chicken casserole prepared with bacon, white pearl onions, and red wine. Side dishes of *haricots verts nouveaux* and *pommes Garfield* accompanied the main courses along with carefully matched pairings of fine French wines. The meal ended sweetly with crystal bowls of *coupe aux fraises* and rolling carts that featured artfully arranged trays adorned with frosted cakes and fancy pastries. Gil sipped his coffee as the waiters swept away the last of the dishes, looked across the table at Bob, and, for at least another moment, tried to push all thoughts of Nazi Germany out of his mind.

Three days earlier, on the evening of Friday, April 7, Eleanor—sporting her new tricorn hat—made her way down one of the interior hallways that traversed the main deck of the stately *Queen Mary*. She peered into the small windows of the ship's boutique shops, which offered for sale everything from men's silk neckties to dazzling diamond necklaces. The ship also boasted two indoor swimming pools, beauty salons, libraries, five bars, a music studio, and a lecture hall. State-of-the-art telephone equipment made it possible for passengers to place ship-to-shore calls anywhere in the world. There were outdoor paddle tennis courts, even a dog kennel. The ship truly was a "magnificent, floating palace," Eleanor thought to herself. A few minutes earlier, she had walked out of Gil's snug but handsomely decorated first-class stateroom so that he could finish a conversation with Louis Levine and a few other men from Brith Sholom who had squeezed into the room to discuss last-minute arrangements. Eleanor enjoyed her stroll around the ship, which had filled with passengers and guests like herself who had come aboard to say their farewells before the ship's evening departure.

Gil soon joined Eleanor on the main deck. She lingered in her

husband's arms, kissing him good-bye and fighting off an unmistak-
able chill. She did not want to leave, but the time had come for all
of the visitors to make their way down the gangplank and back onto
the dock. Standing alone on the pier, Eleanor continued to gaze at
the ship as it heaved away from its berth and made its way down the
Hudson River, toward the harbor. Thinking of her husband and Bob
Schless—"these two handsome men who were sailing away"—she
removed a handkerchief from her purse. "I shed a few tears very quietly. I prayed for their safe return and then went home by myself."

Back in Philadelphia, Eleanor received a late-night phone call from
Jacob Billikopf, a prominent figure in Philadelphia's Jewish and business circles. Billikopf for many years had been the executive director
of the Jewish Federation of Charities but had stepped down in early
1937 so that he could focus all his attention on efforts to get Jews
out of Germany. He spent nearly the next two years as the executive
director of the National Coordinating Committee for Aid to Refugees and Emigrants from Germany and continued to be involved in
rescue efforts even after leaving that post toward the end of 1938.
Gil knew Billikopf quite well through mutual business connections;
Billikopf was involved in labor-management matters, some of which
overlapped with Gil's legal work for Albert Greenfield's company.

Eleanor told Billikopf that Gil was "out of town" and could not
be reached anytime soon. Billikopf said he had heard of Gil's plan
to go to Germany as part of an effort to bring a group of children
into the United States. Saying that he was calling as "a very close
and dear friend" and not in any official capacity, Billikopf told Eleanor that he wanted Gil to be aware of the dangerous conditions in
Germany and the grave risks in proceeding with the rescue effort.
Eleanor continued to hold her tongue.

But Billikopf had another message that he wanted Eleanor to
pass along to Gil. He said there was "no possibility" of bringing
groups of children into the United States, and that Gil, in attempting
to do so, would only confirm this impossibility and would "return

a failure." Finally, he reminded Eleanor that Gil had an excellent reputation in Philadelphia and that he "should not do anything that would discredit or hurt him in any way."

Before ending the call, Eleanor promised only that she would pass along Billikopf's message when she next saw her husband. She hung up without ever letting on that Gil had already left for Germany.

Over the next several days, Eleanor made an effort to resume her normal routine. She visited her sisters. She spent more time with her children. But her thoughts were always with Gil, and she tried as best she could to convince herself—with varying degrees of success—that he would be all right.

Five days after leaving New York, Gil sent Eleanor a cable letting her know that the *Queen Mary* had landed safely in Southampton, England. From there, the adventure began. After crossing the English Channel by ferry, Gil and Bob boarded a train to Amsterdam. Gil went straight to the American Express office, where he set up banking arrangements for his upcoming travels. He also rented a safe-deposit box where he could store important personal papers, minimizing the risk of having them in his possession while inside Nazi Germany. From Amsterdam, Gil wired another telegram to Eleanor letting her know that the two men would be leaving for Berlin.

Upon arriving in the Nazi capital, they checked into the Hotel Adlon, one of the city's most elegant hotels, which had long been a favorite destination for international celebrities, politicians, and royalty. Kaiser Wilhelm II attended the hotel's opening in 1907, and over the years the hotel's guests included Enrico Caruso, Marlene Dietrich, Tsar Nicholas II, and Charlie Chaplin. After Hitler took power, the Adlon continued to serve as one of Berlin's prime social centers. Its popular bar, located just off the plush lobby, happened to be one of the city's notorious watering holes for Gestapo agents. The hotel was a short walk from the American embassy, which was housed in the former Blücher Palace, which stood at the edge of the city's grand Pariser Platz. Under the Nazis, the broad boulevard that led into the plaza had been lined with soaring columns draped with huge red banners that featured the thick black lines of the Nazi *Hakenkreuz*—the swastika—centered in white circles.

Just as George Messersmith had promised, Raymond Geist greeted Gil warmly when he and Bob presented themselves at the embassy. Gil took an immediate liking to Geist and also felt a sense of relief and reassurance upon meeting the embassy's senior diplomat. Geist was a man of imposing physical stature, with broad shoulders and a thick neck that was accentuated by his close-cropped hair. But he had an easygoing manner about him, along with a reputation for being unflappable. Despite his interest in Gil's rescue plan, Geist, like Messersmith, still offered no promises that the plan would actually work. He was aware of Gil's proposal to set aside unused visas for the children but made no guarantees that any such visas would become available.

From the time that Gil and Louis Levine had first discussed the rescue project, Gil always assumed that he would look for the children in Berlin. Even after six years of repression under the Nazis, Berlin's Jewish community, while diminished in size, still maintained an active organization that was now largely devoted to helping Jews leave Germany. One of Berlin's Jewish leaders, Julius Seligsohn, had been a well-known lawyer until the Nazis prohibited Jews from practicing law. By 1939, he was serving as the president of the Hilfsverein der Deutschen Juden—Aid Association of German Jews—which was Berlin's main Jewish social welfare agency. "Now that I cannot work anymore as an attorney, I am devoting myself entirely to the work on behalf of Jewish emigration," Seligsohn wrote that year to Cecilia Razovsky. "I hope I will have some success in spite of the enormous difficulties we must face."[*]

---

[*] Julius Seligsohn's wife and children obtained exit papers to the Netherlands in 1938. He chose to remain in Berlin in order to help other Jews who were still living in the city. He was eventually arrested by the Gestapo in 1940 and deported to the Sachsenhausen concentration camp, where he died in 1942.

In fact, Seligsohn and other Jewish leaders in Berlin, prodded by Nazi officials, had been remarkably effective in helping tens of thousands of Jews—both individuals and families—find their way out of Germany during the six years that Hitler had been in power. And while there were still plenty of Jews who remained in Berlin by the time Gil arrived in April, Geist knew there was a more pressing need elsewhere for the kind of rescue project that Gil hoped to pull off. He urged Gil to travel directly to Vienna, where conditions for Jews had been deteriorating at an alarming pace since the Anschluss. While he was in Berlin, Gil also met with Seligsohn and other Jewish leaders, all of whom quickly confirmed what Geist had said. Time was quickly running out for Jews in Vienna. That is where Gil should go and find the fifty children.

Eleanor was understandably confused when Gil sent a tersely worded telegram that said he and Bob were leaving Berlin and traveling immediately to Vienna. It divulged no further information. Her mind began to race but she reminded herself that Gil surely knew what he was doing. Or at least she hoped he did.

Gil had not been back to Vienna since his first visit there fifteen years earlier, as part of his idyllic European tour the summer before he and Eleanor were married. He still had vivid memories of the city's wide boulevards, bustling cafés, inspiring monuments, and stately palaces. He knew of its reputation for magnificent hotels and exquisite restaurants. Despite the serious nature of his visit, Gil nonetheless was excited to be back in a city that he had fallen in love with as a young man. After he and Bob checked into the sumptuous Hotel Bristol early in the morning following their overnight train ride from Berlin, Gil quickly unpacked his things and wandered back outside into the bracing air of an early spring morning.

He strolled down the shop-lined Kärntnerstrasse in search of a favorite restaurant where he had eaten breakfast several times during his earlier visit to the city. As he approached the restaurant, Gil smiled at the memory of the casual bantering friendship he had struck up with the owner. His smile melted away when he spotted a sign on the door that read EINTRITT JUDEN VERBOTEN—JEWS FORBIDDEN TO ENTER. Well, I suppose my old friend has become a Nazi follower. I'll go to another restaurant, Gil thought to himself. He quickly realized that every restaurant along Kärtnerstrasse featured the same sign. His mind raced back to the vague assurances from the State Department that, as an American citizen, he was reasonably protected while traveling inside Nazi Germany. On the other hand, Gil was a Jew, and he had no doubts that all of these JUDEN VERBOTEN signs were aimed as much at him as at any other Jew in Vienna. "You must walk past these signs and live in trembling and fear that somebody or something or some SS black-uniformed devil might come and do you harm," Gil recalled later. "When you go to Vienna, which is the home of music, culture, refinement, and gaiety, you are faced at every restaurant, hotel, moving-picture house, and public park with great big signs that read EINTRITT JUDEN VERBOTEN. Only then can you realize what the real situation is."

The next morning, Gil presented himself at the American consulate. Before the Anschluss, the United States maintained a full ministerial legation in Vienna, given Austria's status as an independent nation. Now that Austria had been folded into Nazi Germany, the American legation had been downgraded to a consulate, whose staff reported to the U.S. embassy in Berlin. Gil introduced himself to Leland Morris, the U.S. consul general, and others in the office, all of whom seemed generally, though somewhat warily, supportive of the Brith Sholom plan. But the underlying message was the same one that Gil had received from Messersmith in Washington and from Geist in Berlin: no one from the United States government could guarantee that any visas would be available to the children whom Gil hoped to bring back with him.

By the time Gil arrived in Vienna, the American consulate for more than a year had been besieged by Jews, most of whom had little, if any, chance of immigrating to the United States. Because of the quota limits, the sheer volume of people hoping to escape to America made it impossible for more than a fraction to make the journey. The number of families registering for visas had exploded in the days and weeks following the Anschluss. "The visa section is in a state of siege," John Wiley, Morris's predecessor as consul general, informed his State Department superiors less than two weeks after Austria was annexed by Germany. In a series of dispatches to Washington, Wiley reported that more than twenty-five thousand people came to the consulate during the last ten days of March 1938 to apply for visas; the small, overworked consulate staff conducted about eight hundred personal interviews during that period. Under normal circumstances, the consulate staff would receive three hundred visitors each month while issuing only about thirty visas. Wiley and the other consulate officials knew precisely why people like Hermann Wenkart were lining up in the predawn hours in order to register for a visa. "We hear constantly of an ever-increasing list of arrests, suicides and tragedies, house searches, plundering and confiscation," Wiley informed Messersmith in a cable that he sent a week after the Anschluss. "The tragedy here is greater than in Berlin. There it was gradual; here it came from one day to the next."

Yet even in the face of such dire circumstances, consulate officers in Vienna were trained to meticulously follow both the letter and the spirit of America's immigration laws, which offered little recourse to those most in need of it. George Messersmith himself had spelled out the circumspect duties of American diplomats abroad in a detailed memo he had written a few years earlier while he was still serving as U.S. minister to Austria: "The object is not, as some interpret it, to maintain the United States as an asylum or refuge for dissatisfied and oppressed in other parts of the world irrespective of their capacity to become good and self-supporting citizens of our country." Nor was the objective "to keep out certain classes of persons on account of their race, religion or political ideas." Rather, wrote Messersmith, "it is the duty of every Foreign Service Officer to administer the law fairly, reasonably and sympathetically, keeping in mind all of the many factors involved in immigration practice so that our procedure in this matter in these difficult times or at posts where the pressure may be the greatest, does not become a concern of the Congress, of the Departments concerned or of the general public."

Gil was well versed in the legal and political restrictions confronting the consulate officials in Vienna. He also knew that visas alone provided no guarantee that entire families might be able to leave Vienna. In many cases, Jewish families seeking to come to the United States had no one there to sponsor them. As for children, one of the vice consuls assured Gil there were plenty of them—at least several hundred—who belonged to families that had already registered for visas to the United States and were now waiting for their numbers to come up. These were the children who would be considered for Gil's plan.

For the first time since he had taken on the project, Gil felt the weight of selecting fifty children from among the hundreds whose parents had become desperate enough to send their children away—not knowing if they would ever see them again. He was grateful for Bob Schless's help, but Gil also knew that the responsibility for choosing the children would largely fall to him. Suddenly the burden seemed almost too much to carry. He wished Eleanor were with him.

On a gray morning in mid-April, Gil slipped out of his room at the Hotel Bristol and walked along the Kärtnerstrasse, which soon spilled into Stephansplatz, the large open square that marked the geographical center of Vienna. Gil stared up at the soaring towers of Saint Stephen's Cathedral with its distinctive roof covered with tens of thousands of colored tiles. A few blocks farther along brought Gil to the Fleischmarkt, where butchers, fishmongers, greengrocers, cheese sellers, and others offered their goods and wares to Vienna's housewives. Gil walked for a few more blocks until he reached No.

2 Seitenstettengasse. He entered the shabby three-story building that housed the offices of the Israelitische Kultusgemeinde. It was time to go to work.

Nothing transpired inside the offices of the Kultusgemeinde without the Gestapo's permission. By the time Gil showed up on that dreary April morning, the skeletal staff at the Kultusgemeinde knew about his rescue plan and had been alerting families to the possibility of a children's transport to America. They arranged for Gil to use a spare office in the building. They also offered the assistance of a young woman, Hedy Neufeld, who instantly dazzled Gil and Bob with her intelligence and fluent English, along with her charming manner and infectious smile. She was only in her early twenties, with vibrant red hair, deep-set brown eyes, and a pretty face dotted with freckles. Hedy, whose father was Jewish and mother was Catholic, had spent the past few years studying medicine and earning high marks at the prestigious University of Vienna. Because she was half-Jewish, however, she would not be allowed to work as a doctor, she had recently learned. Her younger sister, Lily, was already working at the Kultusgemeinde and likely had a hand in arranging for Hedy to assist Gil with his work.

Gil arrived at the Kultusgemeinde with an initial list of twenty-five children that he had been given at the American consulate. With help from Hedy and her colleagues, Gil cross-checked each of the children with the *Fragenbogen*—questionnaires—and other documents that Jewish families had submitted to the Jewish community office. It was painstaking work but necessary in order to formulate a final list of fifty children best suited for the possible trip back to the United States. By the end of the day, Gil discovered that, among the twenty-five names on his list, four of the families had already left Vienna. A few other children were under the age of four—too young, in Gil's opinion, to be considered. He thought of his own two children, comfortable and safe in the family's spacious house on

Cypress Street. Here in Vienna, Jewish fathers and mothers could now only dream of safety for their children.

Walking back to the hotel that evening, Gil felt exhausted yet satisfied in knowing that the real work had finally begun. He barely paid any attention to the EINTRITT JUDEN VERBOTEN signs and ubiquitous photos of Adolf Hitler that appeared in almost every window along the way.

CHAPTER 11

There is so much work to do here and very little time. I need you to come and help.

—GIL KRAUS

PHILADELPHIA–PARIS–LINZ
APRIL 17–28, 1939

Eleanor was not at home when Gil first tried to telephone her from Vienna. She had gone out to do some shopping and had not returned until late in the afternoon. The family maid had taken the call and told Eleanor that Gil would try again later that evening. It was Monday, April 17, and Gil had been away for ten days. So far she had received only the few cables he had sent about his arrival in England, his brief stopover in Amsterdam, and the last-minute decision to look for the children in Vienna rather than Berlin. "I was terrified," said Eleanor, when she heard that Gil had called. "I was sure something was wrong. I was sure he was in trouble. Perhaps he had been arrested. There must have been an emergency. Perhaps the whole plan had failed and he was returning home."

The second call came through at 6:30 P.M. It was past midnight in Vienna but Gil did not sound tired, especially when the couple's children, Steven and Ellen, grabbed the phone and began talking excitedly with their father. A few moments later, Gil asked the children to hand the phone back to their mother. He hurriedly assured Eleanor that he was fine, and that he had so much to tell her but could not possibly discuss everything during the trans-Atlantic telephone call. Gil quickly walked her through the chain of events that had brought him to Vienna. Eleanor hung on to every word as Gil's voice crackled through the long-distance telephone wire. She felt immense relief that he had not fallen into danger, that her fears about him being arrested—or worse—had not come to pass. But she had to catch her breath after hearing what came next.

"There is so much work to do here and very little time," said Gil. "I need you to come and help." She clutched the black receiver tightly in her grip and felt a jolt of nervous excitement. Her mind went blank for a second, and she almost missed Gil's mention of a ship that would be sailing from New York to Europe in a few days' time. Gil told her to call Louis Levine, who would help with all of the arrangements. Eleanor, fumbling for words, wondered out loud if it would even be possible to book passage on such short notice. Gil's ready response did little to soothe his wife's mounting fears. With war rumblings growing steadily louder in Europe, fewer Americans were crossing the Atlantic. He was quite confident that she would be able to reserve a stateroom aboard the SS *Washington*, which was the next ship leaving for the Continent.

Eleanor felt light-headed. All she could think of was the warning from George Messersmith's assistant a few weeks earlier. Gil, of course, had heard those same words but now tried to assure his wife that she would be safe in Vienna. Or at least safe enough.

The next few days were a blur of activity that left Eleanor and everyone around her in a state of continuous commotion. "I told the children I was going to Europe to join their father," she wrote. "I told them that he needed me and that I had to go, that he had a lot of work to do and that I had to help him." Decades later, her son, Steven, recalled that he was generally aware at the time that his parents were trying to rescue the children from Nazi Germany. Beyond that, however, he and his nine-year-old sister, Ellen, knew next to nothing about the specific risks that their parents were facing once they decided to travel to Europe. "I had no idea what the situation in Germany was like," said Steven, who was thirteen at the time, "except that it was dangerous, particularly for Jewish people."

The morning after the phone call with Gil, Eleanor made a list of all the things that had to get done before she boarded the SS *Washington* three days later. She had to notify the State Department about her travel plans and obtain travel visas for the countries—England, France, and Germany—that would make up her itinerary. Before Gil had left, he had signed over a power of attorney that gave her responsibility for the couple's financial matters. Eleanor now had to decide what to do, with both of them out of the country. It was not the sort of decision that she had ever been called on to make. She turned to her sister Esther, known in the family as Essie and with whom Eleanor was particularly close. Essie, conveniently enough, had been helping out recently in Gil's law office, which made it even easier for her to keep an eye on not only business but also personal matters while both Gil and Eleanor were away. As an added precaution, Eleanor, at her sister's urging, signed a will before leaving the country.

Just as Gil had predicted, Eleanor had no problem booking passage aboard the SS *Washington*, which was part of the United States

Lines' fleet of trans-Atlantic vessels. She decided to indulge herself by reserving a stateroom with a private bath, "an extravagance which I had not considered until Louie Levine had told me to do so." Next, Eleanor thought of all the things she needed to buy for the long journey ahead, which included "stockings, a new girdle and a pair of bedroom slippers."

Finally there was the matter of looking after Steven and Ellen. Essie promised that she would come by the house every day to look in on the children. Gil and Eleanor had household help—a husband-and-wife couple who took care of the cooking and cleaning, and who drove the children to school, among other chores. But Eleanor now arranged for another couple to move into the house specifically to watch over the children. Mary Gavin had been a nursemaid for years and had helped to take care of the children when they were younger. She had since married and was living in West Philadelphia. She and her husband agreed to stay with the children on Cypress Street. "This was the first time both Gil and I would be away from the children at the same time," wrote Eleanor. "I wasn't the least bit happy about leaving them."

On her last night at home, Eleanor stayed up with her sister, Sarah, until four in the morning, talking and making detailed notes about everything that needed looking after in her absence. After squeezing in a few hours of sleep, Eleanor faced the final task of packing for the trip. It suddenly occurred to her that she had no idea how long she would be gone. Six weeks? Two months? Perhaps even longer? "I began to arrange my clothes, gather suitcases and try to plan my wardrobe," she wrote. "I telephoned my sister Fannie and asked if she would come and do the packing for me for time was running out." There were plenty of last-minute errands to run—another pile of papers to sign at Gil's office, checks to be written to cover household expenses and salaries. Eleanor made sure that everything was completed before Steven and Ellen came home from school later that afternoon "so I could have several quiet hours with them."

After dinner at home with the children, Eleanor, accompanied by a couple of close friends, boarded an early evening train at Philadelphia's Thirtieth Street Station. Everyone was quiet in the taxi that drove them from New York City's Pennsylvania Station to the docks along Manhattan's West Side, where the ship awaited its passengers for the late-night departure. Louis Levine, Sarah, and her nephew Richard, all of whom lived in New York, were waiting at the pier, and everyone boarded the ocean liner and squeezed into Eleanor's compact stateroom for a bon voyage party. "We spent a very gay two hours, with my friends and relatives plying me with champagne and good wishes," wrote Eleanor. "I needed all the bolstering I could get."

It almost certainly escaped everyone's attention that this same day, April 20, had been celebrated in every city, town, village, and hamlet throughout Nazi Germany. It was Adolf Hitler's fiftieth birthday. "Never before had Chancellor Hitler been acclaimed with such demonstrations," reported the *New York Times*, "as when he motored through the beflagged streets of downtown Berlin en route to the reviewing stand or when he took innumerable curtain calls from the balcony of the chancellery." Some forty thousand storm troopers and SS guards lined up along the five-mile parade route, holding back the huge crowds, estimated at two million, hoping for a glimpse of Hitler as he passed by in his motorcade that proceeded up the broad Unter den Linden boulevard and past the soaring arches of the Brandenburg Gate. Earlier that morning, a steady stream of foreign diplomats had appeared at Hitler's office to sign a birthday register in his honor. Among those who offered their obligatory birthday wishes was Raymond Geist, acting in his capacity as the American chargé d'affaires in Berlin.

Eleanor's ocean crossing was not nearly as glamorous as the one that Gil had enjoyed aboard the *Queen Mary* two weeks earlier. The *Washington* was comfortable enough but fell far short of luxurious, which did not escape Eleanor's attention. The ship's main lounge inexplicably featured four enormous moose heads, straight out of a hunting lodge in the Adirondacks. "Nothing seemed sillier than crossing the Atlantic with these moose heads staring at you," she wrote. She spent most of her time reading, either in her stateroom or on deck. Most of the passengers were English tourists or business-men returning home, Eleanor noticed. "The trip on the whole was very dull, and I met no one of great interest," she said. She managed to strike up a friendship with one English woman, "and there were two English gentlemen who took us to drinks and sat with us after dinner in the salon." Eleanor's friends and relatives back home, wor-ried about her traveling into Germany, advised her not to tell anyone aboard the ship her final destination in Europe. "Whenever I was asked where I was going and why, I just said that I was going to Europe to meet my husband, who was there on business. We were going to have a holiday and return together."

Eleanor had originally planned to remain aboard the *Washing-ton* until it reached its final port destination in Hamburg. Gil would meet her there, and the couple would take a train to Vienna by way of Berlin. But midway across the Atlantic Ocean, rumors began making their way around the ship of dock strikes and other disrup-tions in Europe. Two days before Eleanor left New York, a French ocean liner, the SS *Paris,* mysteriously caught fire while docked at the French port of Le Havre. No one knew the exact cause of the blaze, which had resulted in two deaths and the complete destruc-tion of the ship, which had been left smoldering in its berth. One of the stewards on the *Washington* repeatedly urged Eleanor to get off the ship before it reached Hamburg. Without providing any details, he hinted that the ship might be seriously delayed in arriving at the German port. The ship captain insisted to Eleanor that the *Wash-ington* would arrive right on schedule in Hamburg. But Eleanor, who by now was in a state of heightened anxiety, arranged for a ship-to-shore cable to Gil that said she would leave the ship in Le Havre. From there, she would take a train to Paris, where she would meet him. Among other things, it meant they would be able to enjoy a brief romantic interlude in Paris before immersing themselves in their work in Vienna.

Eleanor's stylish red hat was a big hit with her fellow passengers on the train that carried her from Le Havre to Paris. Several children were particularly fascinated by the decorative green bird. One young boy kept casting mischievous glances in the direction of the bird, shrieking "tweet, tweet!" as Eleanor passed by in the train's narrow corridor.

She caught sight of Gil within moments of disembarking at Paris's Gare Saint-Lazare. "He looked most debonair, continental in fact," she wrote. "In one hand he carried a cane, which was a new acquirement, and in the other hand was a beautiful bunch of violets for me. I threw myself into his arms." Not knowing exactly when Eleanor was going to arrive, Gil had come to Paris a day early. From the train station, they took a taxi to Gil's hotel, where Eleanor eagerly freshened up. Later they stopped at an outdoor café, lingering over lunch and basking in the warm sunshine of a beautiful spring day. Eleanor was dying to hear all about Gil's time so far in Vienna. But Gil hesitated, telling his wife that such a serious conversation could easily wait until they were on the train that evening. "I don't think we should spoil our one afternoon here by talking about Germany," he told her. "Let's just enjoy Paris."

A few days before the couple's rendezvous, a foreign correspondent for the *New York Times* had described the jittery atmosphere settling across Paris in what had already become known, somewhat jocularly, as "Hitler's Spring." Everyone in the French capital, the correspondent wrote, seemed to sense that war in Europe loomed. "France is not the only place where this uncertain 'we don't know what plans to make' atmosphere is getting on everybody's nerves in this Hitlerian spring of 1939," the newspaper reported. But it was Paris, in particular, with its heightened appreciation for fashion, civility, and social customs, where the looming specter of war had created a palpable sense of anxiety. "Every Paris apartment house has been provided with sand to extinguish bomb fires. Everyone is supposed to have a gas mask," said the *Times*. "It is not possible in such an atmosphere to make plans. It is not even possible to think clearly. It certainly is not possible to do business."

For one sunny spring afternoon, however, Eleanor and Gil acted like two carefree Americans determined to enjoy every moment of a lovely, albeit brief, Parisian holiday. They strolled around the city. They window-shopped up and down the city's fashionable boulevards. They had drinks at yet another charming sidewalk café. The time passed by quickly, and by late afternoon they were back at Gil's hotel to collect their luggage before rushing in a taxi to the Gare de l'Est. At six o'clock that evening, the couple boarded the Orient Express and settled into a plush first-class sleeper for the overnight trip to Vienna. Not long after the train whistled its way out of the station, Gil and Eleanor ate an early supper in the gleaming dining car and returned to their berth. Eleanor was in a buoyant mood, still reveling in the memories of the gay afternoon and the comforting luxury of the Orient Express. But Gil turned somber as the French countryside whirred by and the train made its way eastward toward Vienna. "You don't keep a sense of humor very long in Germany," he told his wife. "I need to prepare you so that you are not too shocked. It's not going to be fun."

As she listened to Gil's description of the stark conditions that awaited them in Vienna, Eleanor once again felt a sense of apprehension in the pit of her stomach. She interrupted him several times, demanding to know, "But is it safe? Is it safe for us?" As the train edged closer to the German border, those words echoed loudly as Gil described a city whose gaiety and sophisticated culture had been trampled by Hitler's jackbooted forces. He cautioned his wife that she would see storm troopers everywhere—in hotels, restaurants, shops, and on the streets. "It's a terrible sight," said Gil. "It is heartbreaking, frightening, sickening."

Gil, however, also tried to assure Eleanor that they would both be safe enough, but he quickly added that he no longer felt that their own safety mattered much. Ever since he had arrived in Vienna, he told her, he had come to realize how imperative it was to carry out the rescue mission. Back in Philadelphia, he had relied only on newspaper accounts to help him understand the situation that confronted thousands of Jewish families in Nazi Germany. Now that he was here, he had witnessed the true horror of Hitler's campaign. Hundreds, perhaps even thousands, of parents would do anything they could to send their children away. "You'll see why once you're in Vienna," said Gil. "You'll begin to understand much better than I can tell you." In that moment aboard the Orient Express, Eleanor was struck by the dramatic change that had come over her husband in such a short period of time. "He looked older and so far away, and I couldn't believe it had been only a few weeks since I had seen him," she wrote. "He was so entirely caught up in the whole thing. Nothing in the past seemed to matter, only the present. He was completely absorbed."

The two talked all through the night, and it wasn't until nearly daybreak that they decided to get at least a little bit of sleep. At some point, Eleanor heard what sounded like the harsh clang of a metal bolt slamming against the outside of their compartment door. Gil explained that the doors were locked in compliance with Nazi orders that no one depart the train while it passed through a small portion of Czechoslovakia. The German army had moved into Czechoslovakia just five weeks earlier to complete the takeover of that country that had begun the previous year. Hitler himself had traveled to Prague to announce, in a speech from Prague Castle, that the country was now a German protectorate. As soon as the train crossed into Austria, the compartment doors were unlocked.

Eleanor's chilling introduction to Nazi Germany occurred even before they arrived in Vienna. Not long after crossing the border that divided Czechoslovakia and Austria, the train pulled into Linz for a brief stop. It was a beautiful spring day, and Gil and Eleanor decided to stretch their legs and take a quick walk along the station platform. As she stepped off the train, Eleanor was confronted by the sobering sight of storm troopers lined up, two by two, alongside the train tracks. Moments later, she heard a loud, shrill voice blasting out of loudspeakers hoisted throughout the station. She immediately recognized it as the voice of Adolf Hitler.

Precisely at noon on that Friday, April 28, Hitler appeared before hundreds of members of the Reichstag, who had assembled in Berlin's opera house, and delivered a fiery two-hour speech that was broadcast throughout all of Nazi Germany. Hitler's speech came in response to a letter President Roosevelt had sent two weeks earlier, seeking Hitler's promise that he would not attack or invade other countries in Europe. In his Reichstag address, Hitler rejected FDR's request and vigorously defended his military actions. Raymond Geist sat with scores of other foreign diplomats who had been summoned to hear Hitler's speech. Joseph Goebbels ordered millions of Germans to listen to the Führer in their homes, shops, factories—and train stations.

The eerie timing of Hitler's speech added a sobering note to Eleanor's arrival into Nazi Germany. Hitler had been born in a small Austrian border town but moved to Linz as a young child. He had lived in the area until he left for Vienna as a young man with aspirations of becoming an artist. On a warm spring day, Eleanor found herself standing next to armed storm troopers, listening to the staccato bursts of a savage dictator's diatribe aimed at the American president. "This was Hitler's birthplace," she wrote, "and my introduction to Nazi Germany."

CHAPTER 12

If you leave, your life will be saved, and then I will have a better chance of saving my own life.

—Rosa Weisz

Vienna
Late April 1939

The Orient Express chugged slowly into Vienna's Westbahnhof on a bright sunny day in late April, and with a final blast of its whistle, came to a stop. Eleanor glanced out the window across the platform at what appeared to be a sea of brown-coated storm troopers. While Gil flagged down a porter to help with Eleanor's luggage, she carefully stepped off the train and instantly broke into a broad smile at the familiar sight of Bob Schless, who had come to the station to meet them.

He had brought along Hedy Neufeld, who warmly greeted Eleanor with a beautiful bouquet of spring flowers. "I liked her at once," wrote Eleanor. "She had wonderful red hair, a face full of freckles and beautiful brown eyes. She stood tall and erect. Her English was perfect. She was gay and animated, and she spoke quickly and with much humor."

In the taxi from the train station to the Hotel Bristol, Eleanor leaned forward in the backseat and stared out the window as the others pointed out the various sights of the city. Scattered among the beautiful parks, Gothic churches, and grand monuments were the grim reminders of a city that had fallen under Nazi rule. The taxi drove past the Hotel Metropole, which had been closed to the public not long before and turned over to the Gestapo. The secret police now used the building as its headquarters and as a detention center for Jews and others who were routinely brought in for interrogation and torture. Kurt Schuschnigg, who had been deposed as Austria's chancellor during the Anschluss, had been held in solitary confinement in this building.

Along the magnificent boulevard that made up part of the city's Ringstrasse—the ring road—the taxi passed the Imperial Hotel, where Hitler preferred to stay during his visits. A few blocks away stood the imposing Vienna Opera House, the magnificent neo-Renaissance structure that had provided the city with sublime music and culture since 1869. At the turn of the century, Gustav Mahler served for ten illustrious years as director of the opera. By 1939 the city's embrace of Nazi ideology consigned Mahler, who came from a Jewish family (though he later converted to Catholicism), to a ridiculed category of "degenerate" artists whose work was banned by the Nazis.

The seven-story Hotel Bristol stood directly across the street. One of the city's finest hotels since its opening in 1892, the Bristol more recently had served as a clandestine trysting spot for England's abdicated King Edward VIII and Wallis Simpson, the

American "woman I love." Eleanor was delighted with the beautiful accommodations that Gil had arranged—a spacious double bedroom with a private bath. Tall French doors opened onto a balcony that looked out over the double row of leafy linden trees that lined the Ringstrasse.

As she unpacked, Gil told her to keep her most important belongings readily at hand. "This room is searched every day," he warned his wife. "We suspect it is the chambermaid, since things are usually much neater when we return than when we left." Since coming to Vienna, Gil had made a habit of leaving his papers and other documents on the desk, in plain view: "We conceal nothing. We put nothing away. This makes it easier for all of us, since we know they are searching our papers." Eleanor was both shocked and confused by her husband's apparent indifference to this invasion of privacy. "It doesn't matter, since we are doing nothing in secret," he explained to her. "The Gestapo knows exactly what we're doing, where we go, where we spend our time." Eleanor thought back to Gil's assurances that they would be safe in Vienna. As she finished unpacking, the idea of someone randomly sifting through her things every day hardly made her feel very safe at all.

As dinnertime approached, Eleanor wondered if they might first stop at the hotel bar for a drink. Instead Gil brought out a bottle of Scotch and poured a glass for each of them. "We don't go to the bars," he told her. "There are too many Germans, even at the hotel."

That evening, they went to dinner with Bob Schless and Hedy Neufeld in the main dining room of the hotel. A painted sign— familiar by now to Gil but alarming to Eleanor—was posted on one of the heavy wood-paneled doors that led into the room—*JUDEN VERBOTEN*. A large oil painting of Hitler hung at the far end of the dining room. Only a few tables were occupied, and everyone seemed to be eating in complete silence. Eleanor felt as if everyone in the room was staring at the four of them as they were shown to their table. "The waiter came to take our order, and our food arrived.

The four of us talked very quietly. Soon, we too lapsed into silence."
Halfway through the meal, two storm troopers appeared at the door
where the "Jews Forbidden" sign was posted. Eleanor froze, but Gil
quickly leaned over and whispered to her to remain calm.

"This is routine, and it happens everywhere," Gil said under his
breath. "They will leave in a few minutes. Go ahead and eat your
dinner." Eleanor tried to concentrate on the food in front of her. But
her appetite was gone. She managed to swallow only a few spoon-
fuls of soup and then waited for the coffee to arrive. She felt too
unnerved to eat or drink anything else.

After dinner, Gil and Eleanor retreated back into their room.
They stayed up late, going through papers and reviewing the next
day's busy schedule at the Kultusgemeinde. Once they turned out
the lights, Gil fell asleep immediately. Eleanor lay awake, finding it
difficult to relax in this strange, menacing environment. She eventually drifted off, only to be awakened in the middle of the night by
a loud, rumbling noise that sounded unlike anything she had ever
heard before.

"I opened the French door and stood looking out over the balcony. Soldiers were marching by. It looked like there were thousands
of them," she wrote. "Then came the heavier sounds of machines
as they went by. Machines I had never seen before. Machines with
mounted guns, heavy tanks, one after the other." She wondered if
she should wake Gil, and then began to think that maybe war had
broken out that very night. Yet again, her mind raced back to the
words of George Messersmith's aide. If war broke out while she and
Gil were in Europe, there were no guarantees that they would be
protected, despite their status as American citizens. Gil, meanwhile,
slept soundly, even as the soldiers continued to noisily trudge down
the ring road directly in front of the Bristol, accompanied by the din
of military materiel. Eleanor did not fall back asleep until dawn.

She felt Gil gently nudging her awake at seven-thirty. She wondered if the predawn parade of soldiers and machinery had appeared

only in her dreams. But Gil explained that the soldiers regularly marched late at night and calmly suggested that Eleanor would get used to it, as he already had. After breakfast in the hotel dining room, Eleanor marveled at how quiet and peaceful things were this morning along the boulevard. The sun was shining, and a gentle, warm breeze stirred the air. There was no evidence at all of the previous night's rumblings.

Gil and Bob preferred to walk each morning from the hotel to the Kultusgemeinde, since it was only about a half-hour's brisk stroll. But Gil was eager to arrive a little earlier that morning so that Eleanor could meet everyone and get acclimated. Driving in the taxi with Gil and Bob, Eleanor thought that Vienna looked a little bit like Philadelphia, at least when it came to the crowds of people on the street making their way to work in the morning. Whenever the cab slowed down, however, she was jarringly reminded that she was somewhere entirely different. Every shop window featured the same formal likeness of Adolf Hitler. Nazi banners, with their thick black swastikas, hung from every streetlamp and telephone pole. Stopped at a crowded intersection, waiting for a white-capped traffic policeman to wave the cars through, she caught sight of Brown Shirts keeping steely-eyed watch on all four street corners. Eleanor wondered what they were looking for.

As they neared their destination, the streets became narrower. The buildings in this part of the city were older and shabbier. The shops were smaller and much less chic than the ones near the Bristol. Eleanor noticed a printer's shop, a bakery, a tobacco store. She wondered how many of these businesses had once been owned by Jews.

Before entering the Kultusgemeinde, Gil pointed to the adjoining building on Seitenstettengasse and mentioned to Eleanor that, behind its nondescript facade, was Vienna's only remaining synagogue. The mobs that had firebombed and destroyed every other synagogue during Kristallnacht nearly six months earlier had spared the Stadttempel—the City Synagogue—but only because of a historical quirk. Dating back to 1825, the synagogue on Seitenstettengasse had been built behind an exterior facade of houses and apartments in compliance with an edict by Emperor Joseph II that permitted only Catholic churches to be directly visible on public streets. While Brown Shirts and other thugs had been given carte blanche by the Vienna police to ransack the interior of the Stadttempel, they were prevented from burning the synagogue to the ground in order to spare the attached building block.

The offices of the Kultusgemeinde were reached through a drab entrance hall with well-worn stone floors and an open stairwell that led to a warren of offices on the second floor. Hedy was waiting at one of the desks. "The families and children are here," she told the three visiting Americans. "Lots of them have shown up."

She led them toward the back of the building and into a small office that had been set aside for their use when Gil first arrived a few weeks earlier. There were two desks in the room, one set aside for Gil and the other for Bob. Hedy took a seat next to Gil. Eleanor settled into a chair off to the side of Bob's desk. Gil began arranging a pile of papers that had been sent over from the American consulate— more lists of Jewish families that had been waiting for visas in the wake of the Anschluss. He glanced down at the neatly typed list of names. *Bermann, Bloch, Blumenstein, Braun, Bruckenstein.* Every family on the list in front of him had at least one child the parents were hoping to send to America. *Dressler, Duschner, Eisen, Feldmann, Freuthal.* The list of names went on for several pages. *Gluck, Goldner, Gottesdiener, Griensteidl, Halote.*

Gil stared at the papers without saying a word and then looked up at Hedy. "I am ready," he told her. She rose from her chair and walked out of the small office. A few moments later, she came back in, this time accompanied by a woman and her young daughter.

Much earlier that morning, Rosa Weisz had awakened her daughter Helga, prepared a quick breakfast, and made sure that Helga was scrubbed clean from head to toe. Their apartment on Krongasse was more than two and a half kilometers from the Kultusgemeinde. In better times, Rosa and Helga would have taken a tram around the ring road and then walked the few remaining blocks to Seitten-stettengasse. But Rosa told Helga they would walk all the way this morning. As a Jew, she did not want to risk being caught riding on the tram.

A few days earlier, Helga had pleaded with her mother to remain in Vienna. Helga's father was still imprisoned in Dachau, with no word as to when or if he might be released. "I don't want to go. I would rather die with you than go without you," Helga had cried to her mother. But Rosa was keenly aware of what most, if not all, Jewish parents had long since come to realize about the prospects they and their families faced as long as they remained inside Nazi Germany. She looked into her daughter's glistening eyes and, fighting back tears of her own, told her, "If you leave, your life will be saved, and then I will have a better chance of saving my own life."

At the Kultusgemeinde, Rosa and Helga quietly took their place in the long line of parents and children that had begun to form early that morning. "I'll never forget standing there in that line with my mother. There were all these other people who threw stones and tomatoes at us and called us all kinds of names," remembered Helga. "Once we finally got inside the building, we had to climb up this long stairwell. But the railing had come off, so you had to be careful, with the crowding and everything, that you wouldn't end up falling down."

As each set of parents and children came in for their interview, Gil, impeccably dressed as usual, sat stiff and upright at his little desk, always keeping the pile of papers arranged neatly in front of him: school records, health records, family questionnaires, fathers' occupations, relatives in America. Gil wanted to know as much as he possibly could about each child whose parents hoped to send him or her far across the ocean. During the interviews, Hedy Neufeld or Bob Schless asked most of the questions, since they both spoke German. But Gil, who spoke and understood a little bit of the language, sometimes asked a question or two. "He had a map of Europe with him and he asked me to point out where Paris was and where Berlin was," recalled Robert Braun.

Among the four children of Bernhard and Regina Linhard, only two—thirteen-year-old Franzi and six-year-old Peter—were the right ages to be considered for the Brith Sholom transport. Bernhard had once owned a thriving restaurant in Vienna but had lost the business after the Anschluss. Although he had relatives in New York, Bernhard had not been able to find any way to get his family safely out of Vienna. His spirit was crushed further in early April 1939 when four men forced their way into the family apartment at No. 24 Taborstrasse and ransacked the place for money and valuables. They made off with a few bags of cash—the family's final supply of savings—that Bernhard had hidden away after losing the restaurant. On April 20—the day of Hitler's birthday celebration and two days after Peter's sixth birthday—Bernhard wrapped the cord of a Venetian blind around his neck and hung himself. A few days later his wife, Regina, stood in the long line outside the Kultusgemeinde, determined to send her two youngest children away to safety.

Many of the parents did whatever they could to make sure their child would leave a positive impression on the visiting Americans. "My parents did not give me this feeling that I might not ever see them again because of the tragedies that were occurring in Europe," said Paul Beller. "Instead my mother painted a very different picture. She said to me, 'How would you like to visit some of your relatives in New York and have a little vacation in America?' She presented it without any grimness or fear, even though in her own mind I'm sure she was thinking totally differently. So when I was interviewed, I presented a very positive picture. I made it sound like I wasn't afraid of leaving on my own."

Other parents worried that their children might say something that would jeopardize their chances of being chosen. "I asked if I could take my littler sister with me," said Henny Wenkart. "My parents were horrified to hear me say that, because they were afraid that would scotch the whole thing. But whoever was talking to me said, 'No, we're not taking any babies.' 'Oh, but I can take complete care of her, and she's almost out of diapers,' I said. But the answer was still no. I was leaving my parents and my sister in danger for their lives, and I was saving my own skin. I knew that, and I was just deeply ashamed of that. At the same time, of course, I knew my parents wanted me to go. If they didn't want me to go, they wouldn't have taken me there in the first place. They were trying to save me."

Despite the increasingly desperate conditions facing Jewish families in Vienna, the wrenching decision about whether or not to send a child away was not something that every parent could agree on. "I remember a discussion at home about whether or not I should leave," said Kurt Admon. "My mother was very worried because, well, she was a Jewish mother and she had heard that children in America were sometimes kidnapped. This went back to the Lindbergh baby, which happened several years earlier. But she was still worried about that and wasn't sure that she could send her son there without her supervision. My father was more practical. He was very sure by this time there was no way to stay and no minute to spare. He convinced her."

Klara Rattner's mother had a different concern. "I was just getting over the measles, and my father told my mother, 'You should have her go and see if she could be one of the fifty,'" remembered Klara. "But my mother said, 'No, she's still ill with the measles, and I can't let her go.' And my father said, 'Yes you will because we may die here. But Klara is not going to die. She's going to go and lead a life in America."

Gil and Bob were determined to pick children who they felt would best be able to withstand, both physically and emotionally, the long journey to America and the separation from their parents. They paid no attention to the financial status of the families and interviewed children of lawyers, merchants, grocers, and salesmen.

Since none of the men were allowed to work by this time, the question of family financial backgrounds was hardly relevant in any case. After spending a few minutes with the parents, Gil turned directly to the boy or girl sitting at the desk in front of him. "Would you like to go to America?" he asked, speaking in English while Hedy translated. "Would you be willing to leave your mother and father for a while and go with us to America and wait for them there?" Eleanor said very little during the interviews. "We spent hours doing these interviews, without interruption," she wrote. "I shook hands, smiled, and listened most attentively. All of the children were charming. All of the children were appealing. And all of the children stood in equal need of being rescued."

As she sat there during those longer, excruciating interviews, Eleanor felt her heart breaking at the painful realization that so many children would be left behind. To make matters worse, Gil was still unable to promise the parents that he would be able to take *any* of the children to the United States. No one in either the American embassy in Berlin or the consulate in Vienna had yet to guarantee that he would be given any visas for the children's use. "There *might* be a transport of children to America," was the best that Gil could tell the parents. "We still do not yet know for sure."

Gil and Eleanor did not go to the Kultusgemeinde on Monday, May 1. All throughout Vienna, the streets were filled with noisy May Day parades, which began early in the morning and continued throughout the day. They remained in their hotel room, reviewing interview notes, checking names off the list of families hoping to be chosen, preparing the paperwork that would soon be submitted to the American consulate. By late afternoon, they decided to take a break and venture out into the city.

As they strolled through the streets during the May Day celebrations, Eleanor found herself fixated on the ubiquitous JUDEN VER-BOTEN signs, which Gil had come to ignore. "They did something terrible to me inside," she wrote. "Technically, we were exempt by virtue of being Americans. But everywhere we went, Hedy came, too. Perhaps she had special permission, since she was an accepted official representing the Jewish community. I didn't know."

Hedy Neufeld had no such permission to ignore the signs. That did not stop her from joining the Americans for dinner one evening at a Hungarian restaurant. "Won't Hedy get into trouble if she is found here in the restaurant?" Eleanor whispered to Gil. "Yes," he whispered back. "She defies all the rules, but she doesn't give a damn."

"Do you think we are being wise?" asked Eleanor. "Aren't we breaking the rules as well and asking for trouble?" Gil glanced around the room and then back at his wife. "I don't know," he told her. "And I don't care."

CHAPTER 13

We can delay and effectively stop . . . the number of immigrants into the United States.

—Breckinridge Long, assistant secretary of state

Vienna
May 1939

On a mild evening in early May, Gil and Eleanor took a short walk, passing by the familiar stores and cafés along Kärntnerstrasse. Eleanor had been looking forward to dinner at the Drei Husaren, tucked away at No. 4 Weihburggasse, which for the past few years had been regarded as one of Vienna's finest restaurants. Its name came from the original owners—three former Hussar, or cavalry, officers who had opened the restaurant in 1933. Until 1938, the building that housed the restaurant had been owned by the

Zwiebacks, a prominent Jewish family that also operated a fashionable department store on Kärtnerstrasse. All of the Zwiebacks' businesses had been confiscated after the Anschluss, and the trio of gastronomic Hussars had turned the restaurant over to Otto Horcher, a flamboyant restaurateur from Berlin who specialized in catering to the social and culinary appetites of senior Nazi officials. His restaurant in Berlin was a particular favorite of Göring, Hitler's devoted second-in-command. Not long after Göring helped to engineer the bloody Night of the Long Knives, during which scores of Hitler's opponents and perceived enemies were murdered in the summer of 1934, the Nazi henchman hosted a dinner at Horcher's restaurant to thank his loyal subordinates. A few years later, in 1937, Nazi officials Heinrich Himmler and Joachim von Ribbentrop wined and dined the Duke of Windsor at the restaurant. Astonishingly, Horcher himself never joined the Nazi Party, although he was a savvy businessman who understood the political and financial benefits of running dining establishments that were held in such high regard by the Nazi elite.

Much to the Krauses' surprise, the Drei Husaren was nearly empty that night. Undeterred by the deserted dining room, the tuxedoed maître d' politely escorted Gil and Eleanor to a small table in the center of the restaurant. When the waiter came by and offered menus to the couple, Eleanor asked if there were any vegetables that evening. During her time in Vienna, she had noticed an almost complete absence of fresh fruit and vegetables in many of the restaurants. The waiter quietly replied that the kitchen had none to offer that evening. A few minutes later, he returned to the table carrying a small bowl of white radishes and placed them in front of Eleanor. "These have just arrived from a nearby garden," he told her.

Over coffee at the end of the meal, Eleanor teasingly questioned Gil about all of the wonderful things he had always told her about Vienna. She knew that her husband had so many fond memories from his earlier visit and had often gleefully described the city's stylish women and sophisticated sense of romance and culture. "Where are the beautiful women?" Eleanor wondered out loud. "Where is all the gaiety and romance? I've looked in vain on the streets, in the hotels, and in the few public places we've gone to." Looking around the vacant restaurant, Gil was painfully aware that, all these years later, he had returned to a vanished world.

Later that evening, Gil and Eleanor received an unexpected visit at their hotel from Ogden Hammond Jr., a vice consul at the American consulate who had assumed his duties in Vienna only two months earlier. It fell to Hammond to evaluate the affidavits that Eleanor had brought with her from Philadelphia. Hammond, whom Eleanor found "very good-looking, bright, most entertaining and polished," was the son of a onetime U.S. ambassador to Spain; his mother had perished when a German U-boat had sunk the *Lusitania,* the British ocean liner attacked off the coast of Ireland during World War I.

To Hammond's obvious delight, Gil produced a bottle of brandy and poured drinks all around. "After his third or fourth brandy, Mr. Hammond really got going," wrote Eleanor. "He spoke very freely. He named names." Hammond reserved much of his invective for Adolf Eichmann, the SS officer who had been sent to Vienna the previous summer to rid the city—along with the rest of Austria—of its Jews. Although Eichmann had already moved on from Vienna by the time of Gil and Eleanor's arrival, he left in place a system of filtering out Jews that had proven to be highly successful. "Perhaps this is why the Gestapo is permitting you to go ahead with your project," said Hammond. "The idea is to get rid of the Jews as fast as possible. Germany has no interest as to what country they are going to as long as they get out."

As the bottle of brandy slowly emptied, Hammond stepped up his vitriolic attacks on the Nazis. "He called them by every rotten name he could think of," wrote Eleanor. As Hammond continued his alcohol-fueled diatribe, Eleanor's thoughts turned to Gil's earlier warning about the Gestapo monitoring their every move in Vienna.

She began to fear that this conversation would get back to the Nazi authorities. "This was the first time we had heard such scathing denunciation by anyone," she wrote. "This was the first time we were in the presence of what I considered to be very dangerous talk." Hammond did not leave Gil and Eleanor's hotel room until well past midnight. "I was glad to see him go. I went to bed praying that there were no microphones hidden in our bedroom." Although Gil, as usual, slept soundly that night, Eleanor tossed and turned, fully expecting a violent knock on the door. The knock never came. But all through breakfast the next morning, Eleanor nervously sipped at her coffee, certain that the Gestapo was coming for them at any moment. Gil, characteristically, did not seem concerned in the slightest.*

Later that day, Eleanor had an appointment at the consulate with Parker Hart, another young Foreign Service officer who had been assisting Hammond with the thousands of visa applications that had been pouring in. The moment she produced her neatly organized pile of affidavits, Eleanor knew she was in for a frustrating afternoon. It seemed, she later wrote, as if Hart was "looking for fly dirt in black pepper," determined to spot problems in the affidavits that she had collected in Philadelphia. He started with an affidavit from a close friend of Gil's father who had worked for years in a real estate office in Philadelphia. Eleanor knew the man well and also knew that he had a steady job and was willing to provide financial support for one of the children. But Hart brusquely dismissed the affidavit as insufficient. Eleanor demanded to know why. Here was a man who had borrowed ten thousand dollars from his life insurance company,

---

* Hammond was later accused by State Department officials of favoritism and carrying on an illicit relationship with a visa applicant in Vienna named Lilly Stein, whom Hammond met in Vienna in May 1939. He later claimed that she loaned him money and gave him a gold watch for safekeeping. Shortly thereafter Stein received a visa and immigrated to the United States. Hammond saw her again in New York in March 1940, though he later said he did so only to return both the money and the watch. Although Hammond denied any impropriety, the State Department in 1941 asked him to resign from the Foreign Service.

he replied. A man like that was not a sound financial risk. The last thing any man in the United States did was to borrow against his life insurance policy.

As Hart spoke, Eleanor felt her face flush with anger. She knew that the man who provided the affidavit had a daughter who had recently gotten married. She was fairly sure that the life insurance loan had probably been taken out either to help pay for the wedding or for a new house for his daughter. Gil likewise had borrowed money from his life insurance policy two years earlier to help pay off the mortgage on their beach house. Eleanor glared at Hart, who had instantly been transformed in her mind from a polite young man to an "arrogant pip squeak with a Boston accent." She never imagined for a moment that her affidavits, which she had labored over so carefully, would come under such scornful scrutiny.

Hart was not through with his critique, telling Eleanor that he had come to the conclusion that all of the affidavits were "technically deficient." Although they had all been stamped by a notary, the State Department had recently changed its rules and now required a certified public accountant's seal. Eleanor could hardly contain herself. "Really sir," she said, her voice shrill with anger. "Do you really believe I could not have found a CPA to approve these papers if I had known that you required such a signature? Surely, it would have been just as easy for me to get an accountant to sign these papers as it was for me to have them stamped by a notary public."

Eleanor felt completely dispirited as she gathered up her bundle of papers and stalked out of the American consulate that afternoon. Later that evening, as she told Gil about the meeting, she wondered if Hart might have been under orders to make things as difficult as possible. While a few officials like Messersmith in Washington and Geist in Berlin were genuinely devoted to doing what they could to help the victims of Nazi persecution, many others went out of their way to thwart Jewish refugees' efforts to come to America. "We can delay and effectively stop for a temporary period of indefinite length the number of immigrants into the United States," Assistant Secretary of State Breckinridge Long later wrote in a secret internal department memo. "We could do this by simply advising our consuls to put every obstacle in the way and to require additional evidence and to resort to various administrative devices, which would postpone and postpone and postpone the granting of the visas."

On the same day that Eleanor met with Hart, Gil had also encountered a potential setback, in the form of a telephone call from Theodore Hohenthal, one of the American vice consuls in Vienna. Hohenthal informed Gil that not only were no visas expected to become available, but also that no one in the Vienna consulate even knew about the plan to set aside unused visas for the children. "I had never seen Gil so blue and downcast as he was that evening," wrote Eleanor. "He kept saying everything looked terrible and that everything was too mixed up to even straighten out."

Gil and Eleanor returned to the consulate early the next morning for a meeting with Hohenthal. Gil's main objective was to straighten out Parker Hart's problems with Eleanor's affidavits. But Hohenthal was not prepared to discuss the affidavits. Instead he turned the discussion back to the rescue plan itself and reminded Gil that nothing would happen until he could find out more about the possibility of using any of the "dead" visas. Otherwise he said the consulate would not have any new visas until July. Gil's rising frustration was exacerbated by the fact that Consul General Leland Morris, who might have been able to sort out these problems, had been away from the office for almost a week.

Over the next few days, Gil and Eleanor continued their work at the Kultusgemeinde without telling anyone about the potential roadblocks raised at the consulate. They had by now interviewed more than 150 families and were close to narrowing down their selection of the fifty children. Each evening, however, they left the building on Seitenstettengasse weighed down by the knowledge that every child left behind might well never have another opportunity to escape.

On May 4, Raymond Geist cabled a two-page letter to George Messersmith in Washington. "You will remember Mr. Gilbert Kraus, who came to see me with regard to a project of taking fifty children to the United States," the letter began. Geist then mentioned that he had informed the Gestapo about the plan so that there would be no mystery surrounding Gil's presence in Vienna.

The letter detailed the bureaucratic complexities that stood in the way of setting aside the fifty visas that Gil would need for the children. "I pointed out that he had arrived in this country to carry out his project at an unfortunate time from a technical point of view with respect to the handling of the [immigration] quota," Geist wrote. He told Messersmith that the German quota had "technically been exhausted" at the end of April, leaving no new visas available for either May or June. But Geist also seemed intent on finding a bureaucratic loophole that might still allow Gil to obtain the necessary visas. He advised Messersmith that the precise formula for distributing visas under the German quota had worked out in such a way that several dozen "leftover visas" might be assigned to American consulate offices scattered throughout Nazi Germany. "In view of the pains he had taken to come over here to arrange for the emigration of 50 children," wrote Geist, referring to Gil, "I was prepared to reserve 50 [visas] for the use of these children during the month of May."

Two days after Geist sent his letter to Washington, Leland Morris, who had returned to Vienna, notified Geist by cable that he had informed Gil that the consulate already had a large backlog of pending visa applications, "thus making it impossible to consider the children before July." Morris had also urged Gil to return to Berlin to see if the visas might be obtained there rather than in Vienna. "I have informed him that I know nothing of the situation at your office," Morris wrote to Geist on May 6, "but have suggested the above procedure as offering the only possible solution for the children to obtain visas before July. I have told him, of course, that I am not sure that your office can do any better for them than we can."

Gil and Eleanor hurriedly made travel plans for Berlin. Realizing that time was running out, Gil booked a compartment on the train that left Vienna at nine o'clock that same night. "We had a terrible train trip to Berlin," wrote Eleanor. "We were in the last compartment in the last car. We played 'crack the whip' all the way there. It was impossible for us to sleep."

CHAPTER 14

I peered at the people on the street. I had never seen so many self-satisfied faces in my life. Here was the "superior" race.

—ELEANOR KRAUS

BERLIN
MAY 7–8, 1939

The overnight train from Vienna pulled into Berlin's Anhalter Bahnhof early on the morning of Sunday, May 7. The cavernous train station, which had once been the largest in all of Europe and featured a separate entrance and reception area for visiting royalty, counted six different platforms from which trains departed or arrived every few minutes to and from Prague, Vienna, Rome, and Athens. In their haste to get to Berlin, Gil and Eleanor failed to realize that the American embassy would be closed on a Sunday, which meant they had a full twenty-four hours ahead of them before they would be able to see Raymond Geist.

Gil was no stranger to the city, but this was Eleanor's first time in the German capital. As the morning mist gave way to bright sunshine, the couple decided to spend the day on a sightseeing excursion around the city. Once they had checked into their hotel, Gil suggested that they begin their tour of the city with a brisk walk around the Pariser Platz, the city's grandest square, which was named in 1814 in celebration of Napoleon's defeat and the conquest of Paris by the Prussian and Austrian armies. The square had been laid out in the shadow of the Brandenburg Gate and also marked the western end of the tree-lined Unter den Linden avenue, the main route for torch-lit Nazi parades and pageants ever since Hitler had come to power. While Eleanor marveled at the magnificence of the Brandenburg Gate and other buildings surrounding the sprawling plaza, Gil pointed out the American embassy, which stood only steps away from the Gate's rectangular-shaped pillars. The State Department had purchased the nineteenth-century Blücher Palace in 1930 for use as both the ambassador's residence and as a centralized location for the American diplomatic and consular offices that were then scattered across the city. The building, however, was never used as a residence, and a fire in 1931 had gutted it, rendering it temporarily inoperable as an embassy. When U.S. Ambassador William Dodd arrived in Berlin in 1933, he objected to the embassy's location on the Pariser Platz, citing the plaza's frequent use as a site for Nazi rallies and marches. But the State Department stuck to its plans, and the embassy staff moved into the Blücher Palace in early 1939, two years after Dodd left his post and only a few months before Gil and Eleanor's visit.

As a woman who loved the finer things in life, Eleanor normally would have been dazzled by the jewelry stores and silver shops that lined Unter den Linden. A few blocks away, on Leipzigerstrasse, she likewise would have been entranced by a string of boutique stores that sold gorgeous bronzes, beautiful silks, hand-tooled leather goods, Dresden china, and other exquisite merchandise. But as they continued their walk around the city, she ignored the store windows and stared instead at the faces of the people she passed on the street. "I've never seen so many self-satisfied faces in my life," Eleanor remarked to Gil. After passing a young, blond, blue-eyed woman who was pushing a baby stroller, Eleanor wondered to herself what the young mother might be thinking. "I stared at her as hard as I could," she wrote later. "She looked arrogant, smug, superior—as if listening to secret voices." Gil and Eleanor stopped for lunch at a large restaurant that overflowed with families who were out enjoying a beautiful spring Sunday afternoon. But something was amiss. "I noticed the silence, the peculiar silence, at each and every table," said Eleanor. "There was no laughter, no smiling, no conversation, no affection. We stayed about an hour, eating our lunch in this strange, silent restaurant."

Later that afternoon, Gil and Eleanor climbed aboard a tourist bus that took them around the city, with an English-speaking guide who pointed out sights along the way. They stopped in front of one particular building, which the guide proudly declared one of Berlin's newest and tallest skyscrapers. "It is true in America that the Empire State Building is much taller," he told the passengers. "But they do not use the top floors, for it is impractical." Eleanor stared blankly at the building in front of her. She thought it was about as impressive as the Walt Whitman Hotel in Camden, New Jersey, which topped out at a mere eight stories.

As the day wore on, the enjoyment of sightseeing gave way to a gnawing anxiety about what the next day would bring. Back at their hotel, Gil confided that he was worried that Geist would have little, if any, time to see them. "We'd better go out and do something to get our minds off this or we'll go nuts sitting here all evening," he told his wife. They decided to take in an after-dinner show at the Metropol Theater, which was known for its splashy Ziegfeld-style revues and light operettas. With its crystal chandeliers and plush red velvet stalls, the theater impressed Eleanor, who was always ready for an entertaining night on the town. But she stiffened after discovering that at least half of the audience was filled with German officers and their wives—the men imposing in their black-and-gray uniforms and high-peaked hats, the woman elaborately dressed and heavily jeweled. Sensing his wife's discomfort, Gil urged her to ignore the patrons and focus on what was happening onstage. The two managed to enjoy themselves despite their surroundings.

Gil had suggested that Eleanor look her best for their meeting with Geist, and so she had packed a couple of her finest outfits. Gil, for his part, had brought along his "poker suit"—a dark gray woolen suit that always seemed to bring him luck when he wore it on poker nights with his buddies in Philadelphia. On Monday morning, as they left the hotel for their meeting, Eleanor carefully adjusted her handsome red hat with the green parakeet.

At the embassy, a smiling Geist warmly greeted Gil and Eleanor promptly at 10:00 A.M. and ushered them into his office. Geist complimented Eleanor on her hat and, explaining that he had been away from home for such a long time, innocently wondered how much a woman would have to pay for such a hat. Eleanor laughed a little nervously, and then offered a reply with some tactful diplomacy of her own. "I'd be ashamed to tell you, particularly with my husband present," she said.

After exchanging a few more pleasantries, Gil reminded Geist why they had come to Berlin. Geist listened patiently as Gil explained that, while the fifty children had now been chosen, it seemed unlikely that the consulate in Vienna would be able to provide any visas for them. Geist assured Gil he would do what he could to help. "If there are visas available, I will agree that they should be allotted to you," he said. While Geist could not promise that any unused visas would materialize, he encouraged Gil and Eleanor to proceed as if the children would be able to make the trip to America.

There was still the matter of Eleanor's affidavits. Geist introduced Gil and Eleanor to Cyrus Follmer, an embassy official who often reviewed affidavits prepared on behalf of Jewish refugees seeking to immigrate to the United States. While Gil met separately with other embassy aides about the logistics for traveling with the children from Vienna to Berlin, Eleanor took a seat at Follmer's desk and showed him several of her affidavits. He studied them for a few minutes and then looked back up at Eleanor. "These are terrific in every possible way," he said. "They are as complete as can be."

A huge smile broke out across Eleanor's face, and she let out a sigh of relief. Follmer produced a large rubber stamp from inside his desk and, with a declarative *thwack*, stamped his approval on every one of the documents.

By this time Gil had completed the arrangements for the children's travel. Each child would have to be examined at the Berlin embassy by a doctor on Monday, May 22. This meant that Gil, Eleanor, and Bob would have to leave Vienna with the children on an overnight train the previous evening. "We left the embassy in a state of happy excitement," wrote Eleanor. Of course, there was still the uncertainty about the visas themselves. But Gil was optimistic.

Eleanor returned to their hotel while Gil took a taxi to the Hilfsverein, the Jewish center he and Bob had visited before heading to Vienna. Berlin's Jewish leaders, like their counterparts in Vienna, were now solely concerned with helping Jews exit Nazi Germany as quickly as possible. Six years earlier, Berlin's Jewish population stood at 160,000, accounting for nearly a third of all German Jews. About 50,000 Jews in Berlin left within weeks of Hitler becoming chancellor in early 1933, though at least some of them returned within a year or so, unconvinced that Hitler was serious about his policy of *Judenrein*. Still, by the time of Gil and Eleanor's visit in May 1939, Berlin's Jewish population was only half of what it had been. The JUDEN VERBOTEN signs that appeared everywhere in Vienna were also a familiar sight in Berlin. The signs had temporarily disappeared during the

1936 Olympic Games, part of the Nazis' propaganda deception. But the signs—along with more repressive restrictions on Berlin's Jews—returned with a vengeance once the Games concluded and the world's athletes and other visitors returned to their homelands.

The once-thriving Jewish life of Berlin, with its lively cafés, cultural societies, and vibrant intellectual life had disappeared by the time of Gil and Eleanor's visit. Almost all of Berlin's synagogues had been destroyed during Kristallnacht. More than a thousand Jewish businesses had been turned over to Aryan owners, while ten thousand Jews had been arrested and imprisoned in the Sachsenhausen concentration camp twenty miles north of the city. Only one Jewish newspaper, *Das Jüdische Narchrichtenblatt,* was allowed to publish, and it existed chiefly to transmit the Gestapo's orders to the city's dwindling number of Jewish residents.

Three months before Gil and Eleanor came to Berlin, the Gestapo had set up the Zentralstelle für Jüdische Auswanderung—the Central Bureau for Jewish Emigration—which mirrored the assembly-line operation that Adolf Eichmann had earlier set up in Vienna. At the Hilfsverein, Gil met once again with Julius Seligsohn, one of the city's remaining Jewish leaders. Seligsohn told Gil that arrangements would be made to house and feed the children during their short stay in Berlin.

Gil had two more stops to make before he and Eleanor would catch their train back to Vienna. He walked into the booking office for the United States Lines and reserved fifty-three passages on the SS *President Harding* ocean liner—fifty third-class tickets for the children and three first-class tickets for himself, his wife, and Bob Schless. The *Harding* was scheduled to sail from Hamburg on the night of May 23.

Finally, Gil walked into a telegraph office and sent a cable to Louis Levine in New York. The cable assured Levine that the rescue project was moving ahead. Early that evening Gil and Eleanor checked out of their hotel and took a taxi back to the Anhalter Bahnhof, arriving in plenty of time for their overnight train to Vienna.

CHAPTER 15

To take a child from its mother seemed to be the lowest thing a human being could do. Yet it was as if we had drawn up in a lifeboat in a most turbulent sea.

—ELEANOR KRAUS

VIENNA
MAY 9–12, 1939

On the day that Gil and Eleanor returned to Vienna, Hedy Neufeld sat in her little office at the Kultusgemeinde and typed out a one-page letter, written in German and with a space at the bottom for Gil's signature. After weeks of interviewing hundreds of families, the visiting Americans had completed the difficult task of choosing the children who would return with them to the United States. Certainly every child they met deserved to escape from their grim surroundings. But they could only take fifty. Hedy arranged for Gil's letter to be delivered to the parents of the children who had been chosen for the rescue project. "I am genuinely delighted to be able to inform you that your child will be taken to the United States of America as part of our mission," it began. The parents and their children were to gather the next morning at the Kultusgemeinde and bring several documents with them, including the children's birth certificates, proof of residence, and various other papers that would confirm the identity of each child and his parents. Gil knew he would have no margin for error when it came to dealing with either the Nazi authorities or the American officials. He made sure that his letter underscored the importance of these documents and everyone's attendance at the meeting: "I expect your prompt appearance tomorrow; otherwise the enrollment of your child will be questioned."

The meeting was set for 9:00 A.M. on the morning of Wednesday, May 10. Gil, Eleanor, and Bob were at the Kultusgemeinde an hour early, intent on being there to welcome the families as they arrived. But all of the parents and children were already there, standing patiently in a line that had begun to form shortly after dawn. "We passed them in the hall as we entered the offices," wrote Eleanor. "There was no hysteria, no disorder, no noise. The children were washed and dressed in their best. Their behavior was perfect." Gil and Hedy took their seats at one of the desks, as they had done during their earlier interviews. Eleanor and Bob sat next to each other at the other desk.

One at a time, each family was brought into the small office. "We all shook hands. Gil told them that their child had been selected to go to America," said Eleanor. "Each parent received this news with great delight." Gil then turned to each child who appeared before him. "Do you want to go to America with me?" he asked. Bob, speaking in German, then added, "Will you be a good, brave child and not be homesick if we take you there?" Next it was Eleanor's turn. "We will be very good to you," she told each child, with a reassuring smile on her face as she spoke in English and waited for Hedy to translate her soothing words into German. "You will wait in America for your parents to come." Before the children left the office, Hedy pointed to Gil and said to each of them, "You will call him Uncle Gil now." Turning toward Eleanor, she added, "And this is *Tante* Ellen."

The meetings lasted all morning. Before each one ended, Hedy asked the parents to sign a document that formally transferred temporary custody of their children over to Gil "and those persons who have joined together for this undertaking." The document also stated that Gil agreed to serve as a trustee for each child "until that child could be returned to one or both of his or her parents." No one dared to mention that neither Gil nor any of the parents knew when—*or if*—they might be reunited with their children. The document asserted that each child would be returned as soon as one or both parents have "legally and permanently immigrated to the United States of America and can convincingly prove that I/we are able to assume full custody of my/our child."

Eleanor found it difficult to keep her composure as she sat at her desk that morning, watching the heartbreaking parade of parents who did not hesitate to formally turn their children over to a group of strangers from another world. She saw in their faces a mixture of relief, sadness, hope, and fear. But Eleanor also noticed a difference between the demeanor of the men and that of their wives. These were men from all walks of life—doctors, lawyers, salesmen, merchants, and shop workers. Regardless of their stations in life—or rather, the positions they had occupied before they were stripped of their livelihoods—they now appeared utterly defeated as fathers, as husbands, as human beings. "They looked so lifeless, so hopeless, so forlorn," she wrote. "Only one thing seemed to be left to these men, and that was pride in their children." Many of the mothers, on the other hand, seemed so animated. "They smiled and chattered. Their cheeks were flushed and their eyes were dancing. They were still useful human beings. They were protecting their children."

It occurred to Eleanor that though she had arrived in Vienna only two weeks earlier, it felt as if she had been in the city for months. Over the course of those two weeks, she had come to share the crushing sorrow of the mothers and fathers who were forced to give away their children without knowing if they would ever see them again. "Every bit of me was sick at this terrible piece of man's inhumanity to man," she wrote. Eleanor was painfully conscious of her role in the tragic circumstances that led parents to willingly offer up their children. "To take a child from its mother seemed to be the lowest thing a human being could do. Yet it was as if we had drawn up in a lifeboat in a most turbulent sea," she wrote. "Each parent seemed to say, 'Here, yes, freely, gladly, take my child to a safer shore.' Fifty times this question was asked, 'Will you leave your mama and papa and come to America with us?' And each time the question was asked, I died a little more."

Later that afternoon, the children and parents gathered inside the desecrated sanctuary of the Stadttempel synagogue, which adjoined the offices of the Kultusgemeinde. This was Eleanor's first visit to the synagogue, which had been ransacked during Kristallnacht. "The altar had been broken, and shameful words were written on the walls," she wrote. "The pews had been removed, and there were some hard wooden benches on the floors." Several of the children sat on the benches while others either stood with their parents or sat on the floor of the vandalized synagogue. Six-year-old Friedrich Lifschutz and his parents, Morris and Bertha, arrived a few minutes late. Unable to find a seat on one of the benches where the other children were sitting, Friedrich climbed onto a chair in the front of the room, close to where Gil and some of the Kultusgemeinde officials were sitting. From that moment on, Gil would always jokingly refer to little Friedrich as "the president" of the group.

Gil carefully explained the plans for leaving Vienna, traveling to Berlin, and then boarding the ship in Hamburg. He described the home that Brith Sholom had built outside Philadelphia and assured the parents that it would provide a suitable temporary home for their children. Using the few words of German that he knew, Gil tried to reassure the parents that their children would be well cared for. As he spoke, Eleanor kept a steady gaze on the faces of the parents and the children. "The children were very quiet," she said. The parents listened intently. No one said a word.

On Thursday, May 11, Gil sent another cable to Louis Levine, asking him to transfer $5,000 to the United States Lines, to cover third-class passage for the children. He also sent a cable to the Labor Department in Washington, confirming that he had assumed legal responsibility for the children and that their affidavits had been approved. Bob Schless spent the day at the American consulate, making sure that officials there had all of the children's paperwork that would need to be forwarded to the embassy in Berlin before any visas could be issued.

On that same day, officials at the Kultusgemeinde dispatched a letter to Julius Seligsohn in Berlin, written in German and marked at the top with the words "*Kindertransport* from Vienna to USA." The letter outlined the travel arrangements that Gil had already worked out with Seligsohn, including the precise time—9:20 P.M.—when the train carrying the children would leave from Vienna, along with the time of its arrival—7:52 A.M.—the following morning in Berlin. "Upon arrival, the children will travel via bus to the quarters you will provide where they will be served breakfast," read the letter. "After a short stay, mainly for the purpose of getting cleaned up, the children will be brought to the American embassy to carry out the required formalities. How long the children will have to stay there isn't possible to determine at this time."

On Friday, May 12, Gil and Eleanor woke up early and ate a hurried breakfast at the Hotel Bristol before setting out on the short walk to the Rothschild Palace on Prinz Eugenstrasse. Richard Friedmann, a thirty-year-old Jewish man Gil had met earlier at the Kultusgemeinde, was waiting for them outside the building. He had grown up in Vienna and had once worked as a journalist. Since the Anschluss, Friedmann had devoted all of his time and effort to helping Jews leave the city. By the time of Gil and Eleanor's visit, he had already obtained passports and other exit documents for thousands of Jews. "He was delightful and charming," wrote Eleanor. "His English was very good. All of us liked him tremendously." Friedmann, perhaps better than any other Jew in Vienna, knew his way around the bureaucratic maze that Adolf Eichmann had set up inside the gilded Rothschild mansion.

Gil and Eleanor arrived in front of the building on Prinz Eugenstrasse at 8:45 A.M., as Friedmann had instructed. They had a 9:00 A.M. appointment with a Gestapo officer, and Friedmann wanted to take a few minutes to explain precisely what would happen inside. "I will take you to see the officer in charge," he told them. "He will question you. It is better if you do not speak or appear to understand German. I will translate all of his questions and all of your answers."

Eleanor was dazzled by the building's immense entry hall, with its marble floors, shimmering crystal chandeliers, and a grand staircase that led to rooms upstairs that had been converted into a warren of small offices. She also noticed that some of the walls were draped in swaths of cloth that looked like bedsheets. Friedmann explained that the cloth covered valuable paintings that had belonged to the Rothschild family but had now been confiscated by the Germans, who had yet to remove them from the premises.* As Gil and Eleanor followed Friedmann up the marble steps, Eleanor glanced nervously at the storm troopers standing rigidly at attention at every doorway.

Upstairs Friedmann led Gil and Eleanor down a long corridor before stopping and knocking softly on a large wooden door and waiting a few moments. When they were told to enter, Eleanor stepped into the office behind Friedmann, with Gil bringing up the

---

* The Nazis eventually seized hundreds of artworks from the Rothschilds, including scores of paintings that were personally chosen by Hitler to be displayed in a grand museum that he envisioned for Linz, his boyhood home in Austria.

rear. Gil did not think to close the door behind him, which prompted an angry tirade from one of the rifle-toting guards. Gil understood just enough German to recognize the gist of the guard's ire. "I suppose people like you have butlers in their houses who close the doors after them!" the guard shrieked at Gil before slamming the door shut and briskly striding away.

The three remained on their feet as they stood in front of the Gestapo officer, who did not get up from behind his desk. Friedmann took a step closer to the desk and waited for the officer to speak. After asking the identity of the visitors and being told they were Americans from Philadelphia, the officer shifted forward toward the edge of his chair, looking as if he was about to rise from his seat. Instead he eyed Gil and Eleanor coldly for several seconds before turning his attention back to Friedmann.

"Who are these two?" the officer demanded to know, speaking brusquely in German. As he spoke, the officer cast a dismissive glance at Gil and Eleanor.

"These are two Americans—Mr. and Mrs. Kraus from Philadelphia, in the United States," Friedmann calmly replied. Eleanor froze at the mention of their names. Gil fought the urge to clench his fist.

The officer tilted slightly toward the edge of his chair again, as if he were preparing to stand up and finally greet his visitors. Instead he remained seated and, looking back at Friedmann, asked, "Are they Jews?"

"Yes," Friedmann replied. "They are *American* Jews."

Gil glanced away. He felt the muscles in his neck and back tensing up. Eleanor's hand brushed against his ever so slightly, and he responded with a gentle and reassuring squeeze.

"Do they speak German?" the officer demanded to know.

"No, they do not," said Friedmann.

Gil and Eleanor likely did not realize that their meeting with the Gestapo officer was essentially a scripted one. The officer, of course, knew in advance why two Jews from Philadelphia were there to see him. Richard Friedmann, who had spent countless hours in this building playing his necessary part in a cruel charade that Adolf Eichmann had engineered, equally understood that the Gestapo officer was merely playing out his own role. Rules had to be followed. Questions had to be asked. Paperwork had to be signed. And so it was that the officer turned his flinty gaze once again from Gil and Eleanor back to Friedmann, now demanding that he ask the two American Jews their purpose for coming to see him.

Friedmann turned toward Gil and Eleanor. "Why have you come to Vienna?" he asked in English. Gil looked at the young man standing next to him, and then turned toward the Gestapo officer. He answered in English, with a determined edge to his voice.

"We have come to take fifty Jewish children with us to America," said Gil.

The officer stared closely at Gil and then looked down at a sheaf of papers that he had spread across his desk. He shuffled through the documents for a few moments, and then looked back up at his visitors. "There is no objection," he said in a monotone, continuing to speak in German. "This couple may take these children with them. The passports will be issued."

Friedmann motioned for Gil and Eleanor to follow him out of the office. Instinctively, Gil started to extend his arm in order to shake the officer's hand, then quickly withdrew it. He was in Nazi Germany, not a business meeting in Philadelphia. The three visitors silently made their way back down the marble staircase, passing yet another contingent of storm troopers that had formed at the foot of the stairs in the palace's grand foyer.

Eleanor, who could barely breathe during the meeting, wanted only to flee the building at this point. But there was still plenty of business to conduct inside the Rothschild Palace. The families had gathered in a large room on the main floor. They had been told to appear in anticipation of the decision to grant the passports, which would entail completing reams of paperwork that were required by

Eichmann's highly bureaucratic emigration process. Gil had to prove that he was authorized to take the children with him to America. In one office, he produced the documents that the parents had signed granting him guardianship of their children. In another office, he paid what amounted to a head tax for each departing child. Before leaving the building, Gil also had to provide proof that each child had a ticket for the ocean passage to America. Throughout this painstaking process, the parents and children stood still and silent as statues. There were no seats provided for them. Gil was seething inside, but he remained outwardly calm throughout the long day, determined to keep focused on the task at hand without letting his anger get the best of him. It took nearly two hours to complete all the paperwork.

Finally it was time for the parents to be questioned by the Nazi authorities, a process that would involve the approval of yet another set of documents. There was no need for the Krauses to stay at the palace, Friedmann assured them. He would remain with the families until every last bit of paperwork was completed. Gil and Eleanor made their way out of the building and walked, weary but triumphant, back to their hotel.

CHAPTER 16

It would be illegal for the American consul general at Vienna to grant non-preference visas under the German quota.

—R. C. ALEXANDER, U.S. STATE DEPARTMENT

BUDAPEST–VIENNA
MAY 13–17, 1939

Gil had been working nonstop, almost around the clock, from the moment he arrived in Vienna. "Gil was so overworked, so taut, so used up that we both agreed that we needed a couple of days of relaxation away from Germany," wrote Eleanor. Bob Schless, who had visited Budapest a few weeks earlier, urged them to spend a weekend in the Hungarian capital. Budapest was the "gayest, most dazzling city in the world—far more entertaining than Paris," he told them. That was all the encouragement they needed. Eleanor in particular was eager for a respite from Vienna's storm troopers and Nazi banners, however brief.

As they would be gone for the entire weekend, Gil thought it would be prudent to check out of the Hotel Bristol in order to save some money. After telephoning the front desk several times, however, the bill never arrived. Gil had booked an evening train to Budapest and was running out of patience with the hotel staff, which by late afternoon still had not presented him with a bill. Finally he paid a visit to the front desk and, in no uncertain terms, demanded that the clerk hand over the bill. The clerk apologized for the delay, explaining that it had been a very busy afternoon and that the bill would soon be ready. Gil had been in Vienna long enough to realize what was happening. "The clerk had been trying to get orders from somebody as to whether or not it was all right to let us go out of the country," wrote Eleanor. Clearly, the orders had not yet come through. Eleanor kept glancing at the large clock above the front desk. The seconds were ticking away, and she and Gil had no intention of missing their train to Budapest. "Is that clock fast?" Eleanor asked the somewhat sheepish desk clerk.

Bob came downstairs to say good-bye and could not resist having a little bit of fun. "I see there are two kinds of time in Austria," he told the clerk, as a sly smile crossed his face. "Fast and half-assed." Gil and Eleanor broke out in laughter. The clerk looked blankly at the three Americans; despite his command of English, he clearly did not catch the meaning of Bob's pun. Finally, the clerk received permission to produce the hotel bill. Gil and Eleanor arrived at the train station with only minutes to spare.

They awoke the next morning in their hotel in Budapest feeling refreshed. "We felt as if we had been let out of jail," said Eleanor. "Our room was beautiful and sunny. When the waiter brought our breakfast, he did not say 'Heil Hitler.'" As she dressed for the day, Eleanor thought appreciatively of her sister Fannie, who had helped select her wardrobe during the hasty preparations for Eleanor's journey to Europe. Uncharacteristically, Eleanor had originally thought to restrict herself to relatively plain outfits in light of the somber purpose of her journey. But Fannie convinced Eleanor that, her mission notwithstanding, she still had no good reason to dress down. Eleanor crossed the ocean with an assortment of evening dresses, along with a fox cape, strands of her favorite pearls, and a variety of other jewelry and accessories.

Walking through the city on a bright Saturday morning, Eleanor felt her spirits lifting as she and Gil drank in the colorful Hungarian sights and sounds. "It was wonderful to look into a shop window without seeing a picture of Hitler," she wrote. "No banners, no soldiers, no parades. Just busy people going about their own affairs." Hungary, of course, was hardly isolated from the menacing shadow that Hitler had cast across Europe in the late 1930s. By the time of Gil and Eleanor's visit to Budapest, the country's 450,000 Jews had already been subjected to a variety of anti-Semitic laws put into place the previous year. Similar to Germany's anti-Jewish Nuremberg Laws, the Hungarian edicts stripped away all rights of equal citizenship that had been granted to Jews in 1867. But it would be another year before Hungary would formally align with Nazi Germany. While Gil and Eleanor were hardly naïve about Jewish persecution in Hungary and the rise of Nazi sympathies throughout the country, on this particular sunny weekend, Budapest appeared to Eleanor like a world apart from Vienna.

They dawdled over a delicious lunch at Gundel, the famed Budapest restaurant that opened in 1910 and had long been one of the city's foremost gathering spots for artists, writers, politicians, and business leaders. Coincidentally the restaurant's owner, Karoly Gundel, had just set up a temporary branch of his celebrated establishment on the grounds of the World's Fair, which had opened less than two weeks earlier in New York. Following lunch, Gil and Eleanor spent the rest of the afternoon taking in the sights, strolling along the Danube, marveling at the majestic Parliament Building with its Gothic spires and soaring dome, and—for the moment at least—feeling like carefree tourists. That evening brought them to dinner at Kis Royale, yet another of Budapest's fanciest restaurants. "I had never seen so many beautiful women in any one place in my life," wrote Eleanor, grateful once again that she had packed appropriately for the trip. The restaurant was known for both its Hungarian paprika chicken and its lively Gypsy music, along with small statuettes of the Duke of Windsor that were placed atop each and every table. Attached to each figurine was a note reminding diners that the recently abdicated king of England had frequented the restaurant during his younger days as the Prince of Wales.

On Sunday morning, Gil and Eleanor took another leisurely walk before making their way to the opulent Saint Gellert Hotel. Perched at the foot of Gellert Hill on the Buda side of the Danube, the art noveau-style hotel boasted one of the most beautiful spas—complete with a series of exquisitely decorated Roman-style thermal baths—in all of Europe. The Gellert spa also featured one of Europe's unique novelties—a gigantic swimming pool that provided bathers with the illusion of frolicking in the ocean. "The water splashed about in enormous waves," wrote Eleanor, who found the sight amazing. "There was some sort of machine that kept churning, and it was like swimming in an open surf."

A reminder of the purpose for their trip to Europe hit them during the Monday-morning train ride back to Vienna. Although Gil knew that the German authorities did not allow anyone to bring foreign currency into Austria, he discovered that they still had a small number of American dollars with them, which had gone unspent during the weekend in Budapest. "As the train slowed down on the Hungarian side of the border," wrote Eleanor, "Gil threw the money out of the window at a group of small children who were playing by the railroad."

Back at the Hotel Bristol, Hedy Neufeld had left a message that required their immediate attention. One of the children who had been chosen for the trip to America—a sweet-faced, five-year-old boy named Heinrich Steinberger—had fallen ill and would need to be replaced. Gil and Bob realized they could not take the risk of traveling with a sick child, particularly since the children would be examined in Berlin for any health issues before they would be allowed to leave Germany.

Eleanor was crestfallen at the thought of having to leave the little boy behind. The notes from the interview at the Kultusgemeinde with Heinrich and his parents described him as a "nice boy, intelligent, healthy" and without any history of serious illnesses such as tuberculosis or trachoma. His father, Josef, had worked in an insurance company in Vienna, and his mother, Hilda, was a housewife. The family had a relative who lived in Detroit. But none of that mattered now. Eleanor could not bring herself to think what might happen to Heinrich in the future. Gil, while sharing his wife's concern for the boy, confirmed they had no choice but to remove him from the group.

Gil and Bob went back over the list of those who had not been chosen for the journey to America. All of these children deserved to be selected; all of their parents lived in mortal fear of what might happen if they were not. Gil settled on Alfred Berg, a tall fourteen-year-old who was older than any of the other children in the group. But he was a logical choice because his younger sister, Charlotte, had been selected, and the group included six other sets of siblings.

But even as Gil attended to the arrangements for completing the paperwork and obtaining a passport for Alfred, new complications arose on the visa front. A State Department official in Washington drafted an internal memorandum on May 16 that appeared, at least on the face of it, to render it impossible to obtain the visas from the American consulate in Vienna. The memo, written by R. C. Alexander from the visa division, stated that "it would be illegal for the American consul general at Vienna to grant non-preference visas under the German quota so long as he has eligible preference applicants waiting for visas at his office." (The children all fell into the nonpreference category, as opposed to those eligible for preference visas, including parents and other immediate relatives of current American citizens.) On the same day, Leland Morris, the consul general in Vienna, received a tersely worded confidential cable sent out under Secretary of State Hull's signature. "Referring fifty non-preference German quota numbers assigned to you from Berlin for German children, such numbers should not be used in issuing non-preference visas if you have eligible . . . preference applicants waiting," read the cable. The next day, the Vienna consulate confirmed that it would return all fifty visas to the embassy in Berlin.

The cables only confirmed what Gil had already learned in his frustrating conversations with Morris and other consulate officials in Vienna: if there was any hope of bringing the children to America, the visas would have to come directly from the American embassy in Berlin. Gil could only hope that Geist was sincere when he had promised to do his best on their behalf.

Although he had no way of knowing it at the time, the project was ruffling feathers back home in America as well. Cecilia Razovsky, the refugee advocate at German-Jewish Children's Aid, happened to hear about Gil's mission to Vienna from someone who had recently bumped into Louis Levine in Philadelphia. Fearing that Gil's ploy to obtain visas would jeopardize her group's own rescue efforts, Razovsky fired off a letter on May 15 to A. M. Warren, chief of the State Department's visa division. "This plan, as carried out by Brith Sholom, is raising many inquiries in the minds of our officers and constituents," Razovsky informed Warren. "We have many free homes waiting to receive the children whom we had selected for over a year and, because of the wait in the quota, our children have not been able to enter. To learn now that children are in the process of being admitted through some other means is, of course, very interesting to us." In his matter-of-fact reply, Warren told Razovsky only that Brith Sholom had "informally" approached

Eleanor Kraus sits for a formal portrait that was taken sometime during World War II. She is wearing a pin that reflects her wartime volunteer work with the U.S. Army.

(COURTESY OF THE KRAUS FAMILY)

Gil and Eleanor Kraus pose in front of their home on Cypress Street in Philadelphia.

(COURTESY OF THE KRAUS FAMILY)

Gil Kraus in an undated formal portrait taken by Blank & Stoller, a well-known New York City photography studio.

(COURTESY OF THE KRAUS FAMILY)

Gil with his children, Steven and Ellen, in a photo taken at the family's vacation home on the New Jersey shore.

(COURTESY OF THE KRAUS FAMILY)

Congressman Leon Sacks from Philadelphia helped set the rescue project in motion by introducing Gil to George Messersmith at the State Department. (AMERICAN JEWISH ARCHIVES)

Louis Levine, Brith Sholom's "Grand Master," persuaded Gil to plan and carry out the children's rescue mission. (BRITH SHOLOM)

Assistant Secretary of State George Messersmith (UNITED STATES HOLOCAUST MEMORIAL MUSEUM)

Raymond Geist's telegram, sent on February 20, 1939, informing
George Messersmith that Gil's proposed trip to Germany was
"entirely feasible." (NATIONAL ARCHIVES AND RECORDS ADMINISTRATION)

Raymond Geist, chargé
d'affaires at the American
embassy in Berlin, played a
pivotal role in helping
Gil obtain U.S. visas for
the fifty children.
(U.S. LIBRARY OF CONGRESS)

ברית שלום וועט אַריבערברײנגען אידישע קינדער־פּליכטלינגע פון נאַצי־דײטשלאַנד

אַפידעוויטס פאַר ערשטער גרופּע פון 50 קינדער שוין אונטערגעשריבען

פילאַדעלפיא. — דער היגער „ברית שלום" אָרדען אַרבייט איצט אויס אַ פּלאַן, אַז זיינע 60 לאָדזשעס אין שטאַט זאָלען אַהער אַריבערברענגען אַ באַדייטענדע צאָהל אידישע קינדער־פּליכטלינגע אין עלטער פון 3 ביז 12 יאָהר. לויט דעם פּלאַן וועלען די קינדער געהאַלטען ווערען אין דער ברית שלום'ס וויל האום, נעבען קאָלעדזשוויל, ביז מען וועט זיי אַדאָפּטירען.

לויט עס ווערט געמאָלדען, האָט דער ברית שלום שוין דערווייל איינגעקראָגען אין פּלעדזשעס אַלס גרינדונגס־פאָנד די סומע פון 150 טויזענט דאָלאַר. עס זיינען שוין אויך אונטערגעשריבען געוואָרען פינאַנציעלע אַפידייוויטס און אַנדערע נויטיגע לעגאַלע פּאַפּירען אַריבערצוברײנגען די ערשטע גרופּע פון 50 קינדער. נאָכדעם ווי די ערשטע גרופּע וועט קריגען פּאַסענדע היימען, וועלען אַהער געבראַכט ווערען נאָך קינדער־פּליכטלינגע.

The March 2, 1939, issue of the Yiddish-language *Daily Forward* included an article about the proposed rescue mission. The headline reads "Brith Sholom Will Bring Fugitive Jewish Children from Nazi Germany." (COURTESY OF ROBERT BRAUN)

Robert Braun sits between his sisters Martha and Johanna, while being pulled by their father, Max. (COURTESY OF ROBERT BRAUN)

Elizabeth and Fritzi Zinger were among several sets of siblings who were chosen for the group of fifty children brought to America by Gil and Eleanor Kraus. (COURTESY OF ELIZABETH DAVIS AND FRITZI NOZIK)

Robert Keller with his parents, Amalia and Viktor, and his older brother, Ernest.
(COURTESY OF STEVEN KELLER)

Henny Wenkart holds her younger sister in a family photo that includes her parents, Ruchele and Hermann. (COURTESY OF HENNY WENKART)

Robert Braun, the last boy on the left in the second row, in his first-grade class in Vienna. (COURTESY OF ROBERT BRAUN)

Kurt Roth in a photo taken a
few months before his departure
from Vienna.

(COURTESY OF KURT ADMON)

Kurt Herman with his father,
Heinrich, in a 1933 photo.

(COURTESY OF KURT HERMAN)

Friedrich Lifschutz with his
mother, Bertha, in an undated
photo from Vienna.

(COURTESY OF FRED LIFSCHUTZ)

Charlotte Berg and her older
brother, Alfred, in front of their
home in Vienna. Alfred was
chosen by the Krauses at the last
minute after one of the other
children became ill.

(COURTESY OF MARIANNE BERG)

Helga Weisz stands between her parents Emil and Rosa. The photo was taken shortly after Emil's release from a concentration camp in Dachau. (COURTESY OF THE MILBERG FAMILY)

Memo from FDR's assistant Edwin "Pa" Watson seeking the president's views on the Wagner-Rogers bill, which would have allowed 20,000 children from Nazi Germany into the United States. FDR's handwritten response: "File no action." (FDR LIBRARY/NATIONAL ARCHIVES AND RECORDS ADMINISTRATION)

Father Charles Coughlin, the popular "radio priest" of the 1930s, was known for his virulent anti-Semitic rhetoric. (U.S. LIBRARY OF CONGRESS)

Richard Friedmann, a former Vienna journalist, helped the Krauses obtain passports and other exit documents required by Nazi authorities. He was killed at Auschwitz in 1944. (YAD VASHEM)

Adolf Eichmann converted Vienna's ornate Rothschild Palace into the Central Bureau for Jewish Emigration. This is where Gil and Eleanor obtained passports for the fifty children.

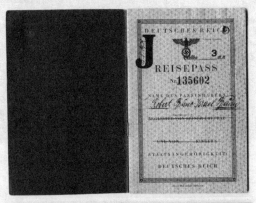

Heinrich Steinberger was taken off the list of fifty children after becoming ill shortly before their departure from Vienna. He died three years later at the Sobibor death camp. (CENTRAL ARCHIVES FOR THE HISTORY OF THE JEWISH PEOPLE/JERUSALEM)

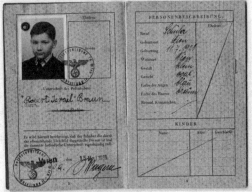

Robert Braun's passport, which was issued by Nazi authorities in Vienna on May 15, 1939. The Nazis required Jewish males with less than obvious Jewish names to use the middle name of Israel. The large "J" on the first page further identifies the passport holder as a *Jude*. (COURTESY OF ROBERT BRAUN)

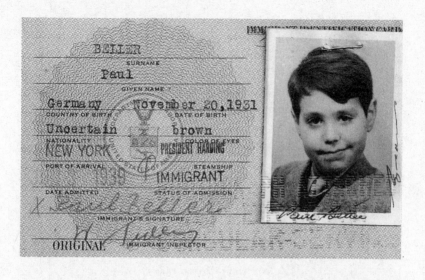

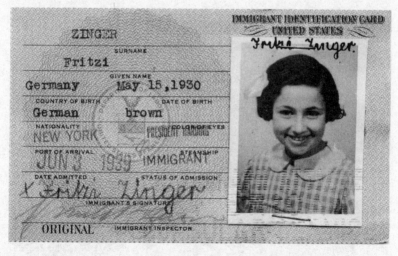

Each child received a U.S. immigration card at the American Embassy in Berlin.
(UNITED STATES HOLOCAUST MEMORIAL MUSEUM)

The parents in Vienna presented this porcelain sculpture to Eleanor as a Mother's Day gift for her "motherly love" in rescuing their children. (COURTESY OF ROBERT BRAUN)

Gil with two of the rescued children aboard the *S.S. Harding* shortly before leaving Southampton, England. (COURTESY OF ERWIN TEPPER)

Erwin Tepper, with his father, Juda, aboard the *S.S. Harding.* Juda, who had previously escaped to England, visited on the ship during its brief stopover in Southampton. (COURTESY OF ERWIN TEPPER)

The children, along with other passengers, participated in a lifeboat drill aboard the *S.S. Harding.* (COURTESY OF ROBERT BRAUN)

The lunch menu for the *S.S Harding* on the day before the ship arrived in the United States.

(COURTESY OF ROBERT BRAUN)

Marlit Bieler and Erika Tamar eating lunch on the day before the ship docked in New York City.

(COURTESY OF ROBERT BRAUN)

Several of the rescued children shortly after the *S.S. Harding* arrived in New York Harbor on June 3, 1939. (COURTESY OF ROBERT BRAUN)

The June 4, 1939, edition of the *New York Times* included an article about the arrival of the fifty children from Vienna.

The Vienna children salute the American flag at the Brith Sholom house in Collegeville, Pennsylvania. Gil and Eleanor's son, Steven, is standing in the top row between two saluting boys.
To the lower left of the flag, their daughter, Ellen, is in a white dress.

(COURTESY OF ROBERT BRAUN)

Two of the boys enjoy a friendly boxing match at the summer camp while the other children cheer them on.

(COURTESY OF ROBERT BRAUN)

Eleanor shows two of the rescued children a copy of the Declaration of Independence and a photograph of President Franklin D. Roosevelt inside the Brith Sholom house. (COURTESY OF ROBERT BRAUN)

Doctor Robert Schless and Hedy Neufeld in a 1939 photo taken in the United States a few months after they married in Vienna. (COURTESY OF THE SCHLESS FAMILY)

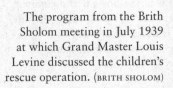

The program from the Brith Sholom meeting in July 1939 at which Grand Master Louis Levine discussed the children's rescue operation. (BRITH SHOLOM)

the State Department earlier in the year and that the department had neither approved nor sponsored the mission that Gil had proposed. Razovsky could hardly have been pleased with Warren's decidedly indifferent response.

Several days later, another leading Jewish refugee advocate sounded a similar alarm bell about the Brith Sholom effort. "It seems to me quite hazardous to permit this venture to go through," Jacob Kepecs, executive director of the Jewish Children's Bureau of Chicago, wrote to Clarence Pickett, the Quaker official who was now leading the recently formed Non-Sectarian Committee for German Refugee Children. "The Brith Sholom lodge to my knowledge has no experience whatsoever in the foster care of children. Its program, if permitted to go through, would constitute a hazard to the children involved and might discredit any other undertaking on behalf of children."

While Gil busily attended to the details of the upcoming journey back to America, Eleanor had a free afternoon to herself. She decided to get her hair done and walked to a hairdresser's salon located along the Kärtnerstrasse, near the hotel. During her time in Vienna, she had noticed that people rarely spoke to either Gil or herself when they were out together. But things were different whenever she ventured out by herself. That afternoon at the hair salon was no exception. The other women were eager to speak with her, particularly once they realized that she came from the United States. "Why does the United States want to make war against Germany?" asked one of the women, with others quick to nod in agreement. "Why does America threaten Germany all the time?" another woman asked. "We cannot understand why America wishes to start a war."

"My words of protest were wasted on them," Eleanor later wrote. "No matter what I said, I was not able to change their opinion." Although she made no reference to it in her account, it is unlikely that she would have happened to mention that she was Jewish.

Gil and Eleanor were invited to dinner that evening at the home of Emil Engel, who served as secretary of the Kultusgemeinde and who, with the approval of Adolf Eichmann, had been left in charge of the Jewish center when other community leaders had been arrested and imprisoned after the Gestapo raided the premises in the immediate aftermath of the Anschluss.

Up till that point, neither Gil nor Eleanor had been invited to anyone's home in Vienna. Eleanor braced herself for the visit with Engel and his wife. She knew that most Jews throughout the city had long since been forced out of their homes. The Engels lived in an apartment with several rooms that had already been converted into separate flats for families to share. The kitchen was bare, the table and chairs moved into another small room that served as the dining room. The Engels had also invited Bob Schless and Hedy Neufeld. Eleanor, while dismayed by the condition of the Engels' home, was delighted to see Richard Friedmann, who had guided them through their tense meeting with the Gestapo officer at the Rothschild Palace. Richard, it turned out, was the Engels' nephew.

Eleanor struck up an animated conversation with the young man. "I was surprised at how orderly and agreeable everything was at Prinz Eugenstrasse the day we got the passports," she told him. He responded with a hearty laugh, telling her that the Nazi officials had "put on one good show for you." Indeed Richard had gone in advance to inform the Gestapo officials that the two Americans would be arriving later to request passports for the children. Upon hearing about the visit, one of the officials barked out orders over the loudspeaker that the Krauses were to be treated with respect and courtesy, Richard said.

But what about the guard who had angrily shouted at Gil for not shutting the door behind him after they all had been brought before the Gestapo officer in charge? That hardly seemed like respect and courtesy, Eleanor pointed out. Richard laughed again. Apparently the guard had been in the bathroom when the orders had been given. He was the only one acting naturally that morning.

Engel's wife had prepared a delicious dinner of stewed chicken—no longer easy for a Jewish cook to come by—and the lively conversation around the bare kitchen table lasted well into the night. "We had a most enjoyable evening," wrote Eleanor. "These were all such delightful people. Gil and I were terribly impressed that people living under such circumstances could be so carefree and gay even for one evening." As the night wore on, Eleanor found herself thinking about her own dinner parties. Here in Vienna, the world had become such a foreboding place for people like Emil Engel and Richard Friedmann. The evening made her homesick for her children and the comfortable surroundings of her life in Philadelphia. Her heart broke for the cruelty that confronted every Jew who remained stuck in Vienna. She yearned more than ever to go home.

CHAPTER 17

Handwritten luggage tag:

THIRD CLASS

UNITED STATES LINES

PASSENGER'S NAME _Robert Braun_
STEAMER _Pres. Harding_
Sailing Date _May-24-1939_ Room No. _319/4_
From
PIER (No.) _____ City _Hamburg_
Booked to _N.Y.C._ Via _____
Full
Foreign Address _____

WANTED ON VOYAGE

STATEROOM

I have no interest in leaving Vienna until every other Jew has left. My hope is that I will be the last to go.

—RICHARD FRIEDMANN

VIENNA
MAY 18–20, 1939

Only a few days now remained before the departure from Vienna. Gil still had plenty of work ahead of him as he ironed out the endless details for transporting the group to Berlin and, from there, to the port in Hamburg.

"Gil and Hedy checked the children's baggage lists," wrote Eleanor. "They had to approve what apparel, trinkets, and toys the children would be able to take." The Nazi authorities imposed harsh restrictions on the amount of money that emigrating Jews were allowed to take out of the country. Each child would be permitted to leave with the equivalent of about ten dollars. "My father thought that was an awful lot of money for a child," recalled Henny Wenkart. When it came time to pack for his daughter's impending exodus, Hermann Wenkart carefully counted out only the equivalent of $6.75; he could not imagine Henny needing any more than that.

Gil and Eleanor, meanwhile, were happy to learn that Hedy Neufeld and Marianne Weiss, another young woman from the Kultusgemeinde, had been given permission by the Gestapo to help look after the children all the way to Hamburg.

Nothing was left to chance as the departure date approached. "We spent hours making out baggage tags for each child," wrote Eleanor. "It seemed there was no way we would ever be finished with the red tape and all of the paperwork." Gil received a phone call from the United States Lines informing him that payment for the children's boat passage, which had been arranged back in New York by Louis Levine, fell short by twenty-five dollars. The cruise line had also offered a complimentary first-class ticket to go along with the fifty third-class tickets that had been purchased for the children. Gil decided to give the free ticket to Bob Schless while paying for his and Eleanor's own passage.

As Gil and Eleanor checked off the remaining items on their to-do list, they also faced the emotional ordeal of hearing from parents whose children would not be making the trip to America. "We were deluged by letters, visits to our hotel and telephone calls from parents whose children had not been selected," wrote Eleanor. "We had always been most careful to refrain from arousing hopes for emigration among all these families. We could not blame these parents for persistence in trying their luck. They naturally enough did not believe we were restricted as to what we could do." Even as the parents begged Gil and Eleanor to take their children, she was struck by how politely they did so. It was wrenching to explain that they simply could not take more children with them.

Amid the packing and preparations for leaving Vienna, Gil had been slipping off in the evenings, walking to the Kultusgemeinde after dinner and not returning to the Hotel Bristol until well after midnight. "Gil was quite mysterious about these trips, and I couldn't imagine what it was he was doing there at night," wrote Eleanor. Finally, on the eve of their departure from Vienna, Gil explained that he had been spending the evenings inside the Stadttempel—the ransacked synagogue adjoining the Kultusgemeinde—with men who were intent on smuggling Jews into British-controlled Palestine. "It was a wonderful thing to see these men with hope again, willing to risk everything, even their lives," Gil told his wife. Eleanor had a very different reaction. "I was glad I hadn't known about them, and I was very pleased to hear it was over," she said. "I was afraid Gil would get into trouble."

On one of their last evenings in Vienna, Gil and Eleanor, along with Bob and Hedy, accepted Richard Friedmann's invitation to supper at his home. He lived in a tiny one-room apartment in the basement of a four-story building that had been owned by his grandfather and confiscated from the family after the Anschluss. His guests arrived to find a veritable feast laid out in the cramped apartment, accompanied by wine, beer, nuts, and candies. "The whole setting was sweet and touching," said Eleanor. She cast a knowing glance in Hedy's direction, surmising that the young woman had somehow managed to lend a hand.

Friedmann talked late into the night about the difficult life he had been leading in Vienna since the Anschluss put an end to his work as a journalist and pushed him into helping thousands of other Jews get out of Vienna. "But what about you, Richard," Eleanor asked him that evening. "Where will you go?"

"I have no interest in leaving Vienna until every other Jew has left," the young man replied. "My hope is that I will be the last to go." Gil and Eleanor had grown very fond of him and all that evening tried to talk him into coming to America. Gil offered to sponsor him if Richard wished to emigrate.

But Friedmann politely rebuffed Gil's invitation. "I will not enter another land where there is any anti-Semitism," he told Gil and Eleanor. "Austria is my home. And if I am forced to leave it, I will only leave for a piece of soil that I can truly call my own. We were betrayed here in Austria. We thought the soil belonged to us. Next time, I will have to make sure that it really will belong to me. And since I can no longer be an Austrian, I only wish to go where I can claim a bit of Jewish soil." Palestine was the only place on earth he wished to live.[*]

On the morning of Saturday, May 20, Hedy Neufeld telephoned Gil and Eleanor at their hotel to let them know that the staff at the Kultusgemeinde had planned a farewell reception later that afternoon to which all of the children and parents had been invited.

Eleanor did not think she had enough emotional strength to carry her through yet another such gathering; it had been difficult enough to get through the meetings and interviews with the children and their parents. But Hedy had promised that the Americans would be there. One more day, Eleanor kept reminding herself. She only had to make it through one more day.

When they arrived at the Kultusgemeinde, a few of the children presented Eleanor with little flower bouquets. Some of the parents then stepped forward, offering words of grateful appreciation for taking their children to safety. The children quickly occupied themselves with games and songs, leaving the parents to stand around a long table, where they chatted awkwardly among themselves while keeping steady gazes on their children. Parents kept approaching Gil to shake his hand and thank him for what he had done. Eleanor noticed that Hedy and Bob sat together in a corner of the room, immersed in

---

* Richard Friedmann never made it to Palestine. From Vienna, he moved to Prague, where he continued to help Jews obtain passports and other emigration documents. In February 1942, he was deported to the Theresienstadt ghetto and, two years later, was sent to Auschwitz. He was killed there in June 1944 at the age of thirty-five.

a quiet conversation. Eleanor made an effort to keep a smile on her face until she could do so no longer. "This entire party filled me with absolute misery," she said. She finally excused herself from the room and walked into an adjoining office, where she burst into tears. "I was unable to control myself and was too ashamed to return. It seemed so peculiar to me that I should be the only one who broke down. My lack of bravery was certainly no match for the parents who were charming and gay and acted as if nothing untoward was happening."

Before the party ended, the parents presented Eleanor with a gift. It was a delicately carved porcelain sculpture, set atop a wooden oval base and standing about eight inches high. The porcelain depicted two female figures, kneeling and facing each other. One of the figures was leaning toward the other, caressing the woman's hand and gently kissing it. Along with the sculpture was a note card with a vintage ink-drawn sketch of Vienna. The message inside, from "the grateful children and parents," was printed, in English, in an elegant script:

> *In memory of a Mother-Day*
> *in hard times never to be forgotten,*
> *of the day on which you have taken upon*
> *yourself with motherly love*
> *the care for Jewish children.*

For the second time that day, Eleanor's eyes filled with tears. It had completely escaped her attention that Mother's Day had been celebrated in the United States the previous Sunday.

Gil and Eleanor had one more social engagement to attend that final Saturday in Vienna. They had been invited to tea at the home of Arthur Kuffler, whom Gil had first met shortly after he had arrived in the city. Kuffler had been one of Austria's leading textile industrialists, heading a company that manufactured and traded cotton.

Five years earlier, in February 1934, Kuffler had visited several cities in the United States as part of an Austrian trade mission that had been appointed by Austrian Chancellor Engelbert Dollfuss. Three months later, Dollfuss was assassinated during a failed coup attempt by Austrian Nazis. Coincidentally, Kuffler and the other trade delegates had sailed to America on the SS *President Harding*.

Kuffler's business career, of course, ended with the Anschluss, after which he joined an effort led by a Dutch businessman to help wealthy Jews emigrate from Austria. When Gil and Eleanor arrived at Kuffler's home late in the afternoon, they were surprised to discover that he and his family were still living in a large apartment filled with splendid French furniture, Oriental rugs, tapestries, paintings, and other valuable objets d'art. Kuffler explained that he had been temporarily permitted to remain in the apartment until it was turned over to a high-ranking Nazi official. Eleanor thought of her own home and how much pride she took in it. As she looked around Kuffler's apartment, Eleanor was filled with both sadness and rage at the indignities that her hosts were forced to endure.

Kuffler's wife, Edith, carried in a pot of tea along with a tray that she had carefully arranged with small sandwiches and a few pastries. She quietly caught Eleanor's attention and pointed to the jewelry that she was wearing. "It all comes from the five- and ten-cent store," she whispered. "They took all my jewelry, and now I am wearing glass."

Gil and Kuffler spent part of the evening in a conversation about the situation in Palestine. The British government only days earlier had issued its "White Paper," which reinforced the limits on the number of Jews allowed into Palestine. Gil expressed the deep admiration he had for the young Viennese men he had met who were intent on settling there, legally or not. Eleanor was curious to hear Kuffler's thoughts about Britain's policy toward Palestine, which had flip-flopped over the years, stretching back to the 1917 Balfour

Declaration, in which the British government announced its support for a Jewish homeland. "It's really very simple, Mrs. Kraus," he replied. "England sold the horse twice. First it sold Palestine to the Jews and then it sold it back to the Arabs."

Kuffler's wife, who apparently had another agenda that evening, steered the conversation back to the plight of Jews still living in Vienna. She turned to Eleanor and asked if it would be possible to obtain an affidavit for herself, her mother, and her brother. Although her husband said he intended to remain in Austria, she was determined to leave. "Did you see the sandwiches? Did you see the pastries?" she told Eleanor. "I made them with my own hands. I could go to work for a caterer in America and support myself. All I need are affidavits to get myself, my mother, and my brother there." It pained Eleanor to hear this proud and elegant woman beg. And while she replied vaguely that she would try to help, Eleanor knew there was little she could do.

At the end of the evening, Arthur Kuffler walked downstairs with Gil and Eleanor. Before saying good-bye, he asked them to ignore his wife's pleas for affidavits. He was confident that he could easily obtain affidavits for himself and his family, which included two grown daughters. But he did not think that his wife's mother or brother, given their ages, were likely candidates for immigration to America.*

Eleanor felt completely drained by the time she and Gil returned to their hotel that evening. As she got ready for bed, it dawned on her that their work in Vienna had come to an end. Every last bit of paperwork had been completed, reviewed, and then reviewed again. Everything was in order for the next day's journey out of the city.

---

* Kuffler, along with his wife and daughters, immigrated later that year to South America. It is not known what happened to Mrs. Kuffler's mother and brother.

CHAPTER 18

Jews are not permitted to give the Nazi salute. If the parents raise their arms to wave, they will be arrested.

—HEDY NEUFELD

VIENNA
MAY 21, 1939

The sun was shining, and Gil and Eleanor had nothing to do on their final day in Vienna other than pack their luggage and settle their accounts with the hotel. The train to Berlin would not leave until that evening, and it felt strange to be dawdling over breakfast instead of rushing off to a meeting or an appointment.

As she finished her coffee in the hotel dining room, Eleanor was suddenly gripped with fear: What would happen if they got to Berlin with the children only to learn that the American embassy did not have any visas for them? "My God, don't think about it!" Gil implored her. "We're sure to get some visas. I'm afraid we won't know exactly how many until we get there."

Eleanor was hardly comforted. "Suppose there are only seven or eighteen or whatever other number," she said. "What will we do then?" Gil threw up his hands, even as he tried to remain calm and patient. He told her that she and Bob would continue on to America with as many children as they could. He would return to Vienna with the rest of the children. But there was no point in even considering such a gloomy scenario, he implored his wife.

In the afternoon, the sky began to darken and rain threatened. Gil and Eleanor walked a few blocks from the Bristol to Vienna's Kunstlerhaus, one of the city's main art exhibition halls, which had been built in the 1860s by the Austrian Artists' Society. Located next to the Musikverein, the home of the Vienna Philharmonic, the Kunstlerhaus, which had been designed to resemble a villa from the Italian Renaissance, was one of the earliest buildings constructed along the Ringstrasse. Gil wanted to visit an art exhibition that had opened two weeks earlier and that had originally been conceived by Joseph Goebbels. The exhibition was called Entartete Kunst ("Degenerate Art") and consisted of hundreds of modernist artworks that had been banned by the Nazis as either un-German or influenced by "Jewish Bolshevist" ideology. The paintings and sculptures on display were among thousands of pieces of art that the Nazis had confiscated from museums and art collections throughout the Reich. The exhibition, which included works by prominent artists such as Marc Chagall, Paul Klee, Max Ernst, and Otto Dix, was aimed at singling out the "perverse Jewish spirit," which the Nazis viewed as the sinister force behind the art. Hitler himself lavishly praised the exhibition at its opening in Munich, after which it traveled to nearly a dozen cities throughout Germany and Austria.

"I was profoundly shocked and deeply sickened by this display of German depravity," wrote Eleanor. "The deliberate ugliness of obscenity mingled with the beautiful—the mediocre next to the fine, the ridiculous next to the sublime, all labeled 'Jewish degenerate art.'" Surprisingly only a half-dozen or so among the more than one hundred artists whose works were shown were actually Jewish. But that was of no consequence to the Nazis, who were intent on ridiculing all artistic expressions that ran counter to their obsessive notion of pure German culture.

Gil and Eleanor returned to the Bristol late in the afternoon in order to finish packing and settle their bill, this time without any delays. Joined in the lobby by Bob Schless, the three Americans piled into a taxi for the short ride to the train station. Although a light rain began falling, the streets remained congested with crowds that had been enjoying the late spring Sunday. As the cab neared the station, Eleanor's thoughts turned to her first day in the city, only a few weeks earlier. During that initial taxi ride from the station to the hotel, she could hardly have been prepared for the emotional and physical impact the city would have on her. Now, as she traveled in the opposite direction, she was eager, desperate even, to leave Vienna behind. She was tired of being afraid, but above all else she missed her children and the comfort and safety of her own home.

The overnight train to Berlin was not scheduled to leave until 9:20 P.M., but almost every parent and child was waiting at the station three hours earlier. "We got to the train station early and saw that it was filled with storm troopers," remembered Kurt Herman, who stood with his mother in the anxious silence. "I think my mother immediately thought that the Germans had changed their minds and that they were not going to let us go."

"It was the first time in my life that I ever rode in a car," recalled Robert Braun, who came to the station with his parents and his older sister Johanna, who had also been selected for the trip. "My parents engaged a taxi to bring us to the station because they didn't want to be seen walking the streets with suitcases. It wasn't safe." Helga

Weisz clutched her soft brown teddy bear tightly to her chest as her mother and father—Emil Weisz had been released from Dachau shortly before his daughter's departure from Vienna—escorted her onto the platform, where everyone gathered in the long, tense hour or so before the children were allowed to board the train. "It was a very rainy night," remembered Helga. "The train was there, along with all of the soldiers with their guns, wearing brown shirts, black shirts, brown boots, black boots. There were German shepherds and dobermans and rottweilers. I mostly remember the darkness." That morning Helga had asked her mother to pack some of her favorite roast chicken for the train ride to Berlin. "I don't know where they got the money for it, but they managed. She packed it into a little sort of lunch box, along with some candy and a piece of fruit."

At last the children were allowed onto the train. Helga's mother and father gave her one last kiss good-bye. "My mother said to me, 'Be a good girl and listen to your foster parents and make sure you get a good education. Before you know it, we'll be there, and we'll all be reunited, and I'll see you in America.'" Helga had no way of knowing that she would never see her mother again.

Hedy Neufeld, meanwhile, was becoming agitated as she paced up and down the platform, keeping a watchful eye over the children but also monitoring the parents as well. She warned them they could not wave to their children as the train departed. When Eleanor demanded to know why, Hedy quietly explained that Jews were not allowed to give the Nazi salute. The parents risked being arrested if they raised their arms to wave good-bye.

They stood along the platform, staring in silence at their children through the train's glass windowpanes. Before boarding themselves, Gil, Eleanor, and Bob slowly made their way down the line of parents, shaking hands, solemnly promising to look after their children, attempting to offer words of hope and consolation. Hedy and Marianne, the other young woman from the Kultusgemeinde, were already on board and doing their best to comfort several of the younger boys and girls who had begun to cry.

"I was also in tears by that time," remembered Henny Wenkart. "It seemed as if the train was never going to leave, and we were all inside looking out the window and waving to our parents. I could still see my father's hat. He was standing on his tiptoes in order to see me. But my mother was shorter, so I didn't even see her while we were waiting."

Officials at the Kultusgemeinde had managed to arrange for all of the children to sit together in one train car. "I remember the smell of the locomotive so vividly," said Robert Braun. "All fifty children were in one car, and we were told that the doors would be locked until we got off in Berlin. On the platform, before getting on the train, there was a great deal of crying and wailing. But my sister, Johanna, and I did not cry because our parents had maintained a very cheerful attitude. They just kept telling us about this wonderful life we would have in America."

Finally the train sounded a piercing whistle as it slowly edged its way out of the station. Eleanor, surrounded by several of the children, peered out the window as the platform gradually receded from view. "The parents stood in completely orderly and quiet fashion. Their eyes were fixed on the faces of their children," she wrote. "Their mouths were smiling. But their eyes were red and strained. No one waved. It was the most heartbreaking show of dignity and bravery I had ever witnessed."

Gil, Eleanor, and Bob had booked sleeping compartments for themselves for the trip to Berlin. After finding their compartments, they rejoined the children. They made an effort to keep the mood as light as possible. "On the whole we were all very cheerful at the start," wrote Eleanor. "We turned it into a picnic." Helga Weisz was eager to eat her mother's roast chicken, and most of the other children hungrily began tucking into the suppers their parents had packed. Once they had eaten, however, many of the younger children began to cry as the night grew dark and the train traveled farther away from Vienna. The hard wooden benches in the train car were useless when it came to sleeping. Hedy and Marianne tried to console the younger ones who were becoming increasingly upset about leaving their parents. "It was really most unfortunate that our traveling had to be done at night," wrote Eleanor. "We had been told, however, that we would not have the right to engage sleepers [for the children], and it was thought that the children would be subjected to jeering if they traveled during the daytime. We realized that nothing could have been more uncomfortable or worse than the conditions we had. But we were stuck with them."

By two in the morning, all of the children, miraculously, finally managed to fall asleep. Their adult guardians—Gil, Eleanor, Bob, Hedy, and Marianne—remained in the car with them for a while, reviewing the next day's arrangements. But everyone was exhausted, both physically and emotionally. Gil suggested that Eleanor and Hedy get some sleep. He, along with Bob and Marianne, would remain with the children through the night.

Eleanor, reluctantly, made her way back to the compartment. But she was unable to sleep. "I could not get the picture of the parents standing on the platform out of my mind," she wrote. "Their eyes haunted me. I prayed that God might comfort each parent who had returned home to watch an empty bed." Her thoughts kept returning to the agonizing possibility of having to bring the children back to Vienna if Raymond Geist did not come through with the visas. "Would this all turn into one big fiasco?" Eleanor wrote. "Would we have to bring them back the next day? I cursed the Germans for their ways. And then I cried and cried for the parents."

As the first gray streaks of dawn filtered through the window of her compartment, Eleanor groggily returned to the children's car. She was surprised to find that all was calm. The younger children were still sleeping, and some of the older ones were sitting quietly, studying the passing scenery through the small windows. Nearly an hour before the train arrived in Berlin, the adults scampered around the car, gathering together the children's belongings, lining up their suitcases, and making sure everything was in perfect order for their arrival. The train pulled into the Anhalter Bahnhof at 7:52 A.M. on the dot.

CHAPTER 19

Mr. Kraus was yelling at the SS officer, who was yelling back at him in German. I thought the officer was going to shoot him right there.

—ROBERT BRAUN

BERLIN
MAY 22–23, 1939

Heinrich Stahl, the president of Berlin's rapidly dwindling Jewish community, was waiting at the station to greet the travelers from Vienna. Once a prominent insurance executive in Germany, Stahl had been presiding over the city's imperiled Jewish population since Hitler took power in 1933. Joining him on the platform was Julius Seligsohn, the Jewish leader with whom Gil had met during his earlier visits to Berlin. Several other men and women from the Hilfsverein—Berlin's Jewish aid group—stood alongside the two

Jewish leaders, ready to help shepherd the tired and hungry children as everyone made their way off the train. The Anhalter Bahnof, as always, was filled with storm troopers, many of whom gazed sternly at the arriving passengers. Eleanor this time brushed dismissively past them as she stepped off the train and onto the platform.

Once the children had been gathered together and their luggage and other belongings accounted for, Hedy and Marianne, assisted by the attendants from the Hilfsverein, shepherded them into several vehicles for the short ride to the nearby community building where they would be staying. The building had been set up as a dormitory, and as Gil had arranged, a hot breakfast was waiting to be served. Gil drove separately with Stahl, who—presumably because of his position in the Jewish community—appeared to own one of the few remaining private automobiles still allowed to Jews. At the age of seventy-one, Stahl was a proud man who had lived his entire life in Berlin. But he had long since devoted himself to doing everything he could to urge Jews to leave Germany. "To those . . . who have not yet decided to emigrate, I say there is no future for the Jews in this country," he declared nearly ten months before Kristallnacht.*

Eleanor and Bob gathered their own luggage into a taxi, asking the driver to take them directly to their hotel. Gil had booked rooms at the splendid Hotel Adlon, only a stone's throw away from the American Embassy. As the taxi wended its way through the morning traffic, "I cleaned myself up as best I could, putting on some powder and lipstick and combing my hair," wrote Eleanor. She also donned her red hat, adjusting it carefully as the taxi approached Unter den Linden near the hotel.

A few moments later, the driver turned around and announced

---

* In the spring of 1940, Heinrich Stahl tried to leave Germany and move to Belgium, where his children lived, but the Gestapo did not allow him to emigrate. In June 1942, Stahl and his wife, along with fifty other officials from Berlin's Jewish Community, were deported to Theresienstadt, the ghetto-concentration camp established by the Nazis in what was then Czechoslovakia. He died there in November 1942.

to his passengers that he could not go any farther, even though the hotel was still several hundred yards ahead. The street was blocked off for a parade, he said, speaking in German. Eleanor, though she did not understand what the driver was saying, could see for herself that the street, which spilled into the Pariser Platz, was blockaded. Bob asked the driver the cause of all the commotion. He explained that Galeazzo Ciano, Italy's foreign minister—who also was Mussolini's son-in-law—had just arrived in Berlin. He was there to sign a new military alliance between Italy and Germany, an agreement that would come to be known as the Stahlpakt—the Pact of Steel. With a beaming smile, the taxi driver announced that this would be a day of great celebration all throughout the city.

Indeed, Ciano had arrived in Berlin the day before and had been treated by his German host and counterpart, Foreign Minister Joachim von Ribbentrop, to a lavish motorcade from the train station to the Adlon, where he was staying. "The route over which Count Ciano passed to the Hotel Adlon was a swirling mass of color," reported a *New York Times* correspondent on the scene. "Bands every hundred yards provided martial music as the automobile cortege proceeded along the festively decorated streets. Massed formations of military and party organizations drawn up along the route presented arms and the large crowd lustily cheered as Ciano and von Ribbentrop drove past."

The enormous crowds had gathered again the following morning to continue their celebration. Later in the day, Ciano and Ribbentrop, along with Hitler himself, would formally ratify the Stahlpakt in an elaborate ceremony at the German foreign ministry, which was located not very far from the hotel. Inside the stalled taxi, Bob Schless abandoned his gentle, easy-going demeanor, and—speaking in fluent German—barked out orders to the driver. "We are staying at the Adlon! We certainly cannot get out here with all of our baggage. You will have to pull up in front of the hotel!"

It was a tone of voice that Eleanor had come to recognize during her stay in Nazi Germany. "I had discovered by this time that a German will always take orders if they are shouted with an air of authority," she later wrote. Bob's strategy worked like a charm. The taxi driver carefully steered the car back out into the blockaded boulevard and, moments later, pulled up directly in front of the hotel. "After we stopped," said Eleanor, "the driver turned to us and said, 'Pardon me, sir. Pardon me, madam. I did not realize you were part of the Italian party.'" The two Americans quickly got out of the taxi without saying another word.

Two rows of uniformed German guards stood between the taxi and the entrance to the hotel. Eleanor glanced nervously at Bob. "Walk right into the hotel," he said. "Don't look back. Don't wait for me. Don't do anything else. Just keep walking." Eleanor looked straight ahead as she walked along the plush red carpet that led up a few steps and into the hotel lobby, which was filled with dozens of men in German and Italian military uniforms. A loud chorus of "*Sieg Heils!*" echoed throughout the lobby as she made her way to the front desk. Her legs were trembling as the clerk brought out the hotel registry. "I glanced over to my left," wrote Eleanor. "Count Ciano and von Ribbentrop were in conversation at the foot of the stairs. I looked around and noticed about fifty Italian officers in black uniforms. I must admit they were the handsomest collection of men I'd ever seen."

Bob joined her at the front desk and, in the officious tone that had worked magic with the taxi driver, instructed the clerk to send a bellboy for their luggage. Eleanor suddenly found it difficult to focus on the hotel registration form the clerk had asked her to complete. Her nerves were at a breaking point. "I was stumped when it came to the question of my husband's birthday," she said. "I could hardly remember my own."

After receiving their room keys, Eleanor and Bob threaded their way across the congested lobby, which was humming with the animated conversations of German and Italian military officers. The

two Americans stepped into the metal-cage elevator, eager to retreat to their hotel rooms. The elevator operator did not follow them
into the cage, however, but hovered just outside, an anxious look
on his face. A few moments later, two uniformed men—deep in
conversation—entered the cage without so much as a glance at Eleanor or Bob. They continued their conversation while the elevator
operator tugged the metal gate shut with a resounding *clang* and
swung the lever that set in motion the elevator's ascent. Eleanor had
directed her gaze at the floor when the two men had walked into
the elevator car. Now, as the car climbed upward, she looked up.
She instantly recognized the two officers—Ciano and von Ribbentrop. Within moments the operator brought the elevator to a stop,
pulled open the gate, and waited as the two foreign ministers exited
and walked across a hallway onto a hotel balcony, where they stood
waving to the crowds gathered on the streets below. It felt to Eleanor
like an eternity before the operator pulled the gate shut and set the
elevator back in motion.

Gil had a standoff of his own earlier that morning. Having settled the children into the dormitory, he found himself in a heated
shouting match with an SS officer who had been sent to keep an eye
on the group. "A few of the older boys, including myself, were peek-
ing around and saw Mr. Kraus sitting in some sort of anteroom next
to this big room where we were all staying," recalled Robert Braun.
Gil, who was yelling in English at the SS officer, apparently needed
the officer's signature on a document, and the officer appeared to be
in no immediate hurry to cooperate. Gil's tolerance for bureaucratic
paper shuffling had long since been exhausted. Robert and the other
boys who caught sight of the altercation had never seen anything
like it before. "Anytime we saw an SS officer on the street in Vienna,
we'd make sure to get out of the way and try to pretend to be invisi-
ble," said Robert. "But here Mr. Kraus was yelling at the SS officer,
who was yelling back at him in German. I was frightened because I
thought that the officer was going to shoot him right there." After a

few tense moments, the officer finally picked up the pen and signed the paper.

Once she had settled into her room at the Hotel Adlon, Eleanor picked up the telephone and ordered a large pot of coffee to be sent up to the room. A stiff drink might have done more to calm her nerves, but it was a little too early in the day for that; the coffee would have to suffice. After freshening up, Eleanor went back downstairs to meet Bob and walk with him to the American embassy. By this time, Ciano and von Ribbentrop had left the hotel for the signing ceremony, and the crowds that had gathered earlier in front of the Adlon had begun to disperse. The surrounding streets remained crowded, but Eleanor and Bob were able to reach the embassy without incident.

Many of the children were already there by the time they arrived. "They looked very tired," she said. "As soon as the children saw us, some of them became very tearful. We did our best to comfort them and cheer them up." The younger children were especially upset by the strange surroundings and were suffering from homesickness. "They all looked so weary, and most of the little ones kept crying. The more I tried to stop them, the more they seemed to cry." Eleanor was told that Gil had already taken the first group of children upstairs to be examined by embassy officials. She grew anxious while she waited for him to appear. Finally he came downstairs and sat next to her in the hallway.

"What about the visas? What about the visas?" she asked in a trembling voice. Gil leaned close and whispered, "There are fifty visas waiting for us. All our worries are over." Raymond Geist had lived up to his word: he had set aside all of the unused visas that they needed. None of the children would have to return to Vienna. Eleanor looked up at her husband and, for the first time in weeks, allowed herself the luxury of pure relief.

There were still bureaucratic procedures to complete. Each child needed to be interviewed and to undergo a physical examination.

Many of the interviews were conducted by Cyrus Follmer, one of the American vice consuls who had been handling the visa requests that had been flooding the embassy. One child at a time was ushered into Follmer's office and seated on a chair in front of his desk. The vice consul, aided by his German-speaking secretary, asked his questions in a gentle and patient manner. However, some of the children, exhausted and disoriented by the constant change in their surroundings, found the process distressing. The questions themselves were perfunctory—name, address, and other identifying information that, according to procedure, had to be asked directly of each child, no matter how young they were. When eight-year-old Charlotte Berg was brought in, she nervously settled herself into the chair across from Follmer, looking "like an Alice in Wonderland figure, sitting there with her long blond hair and her bright blue eyes," wrote Eleanor.

"Can you write?" Follmer asked the quiet little girl. He smiled at her and waited for his secretary to translate his question.

"*Ja,*" she replied timidly, in German.

"Write your name here," said Follmer as he handed her a pen and pointed to the place on the form where he wanted her to sign.

Charlotte took the pen but suddenly began to sob. Eleanor leaned in close and heard the girl mumble something but was unable to make out the words.

"What's the matter?" Follmer asked Charlotte. "Don't cry. Raise your head. We can't hear you." But the little girl, her chin down, continued to cry into her lap.

Finally, she lifted her head and managed to speak clearly enough that everyone in the office could hear. "*Muss ich Sara schreiben?*" she asked as the tears continued to stream down her face. At first, Eleanor did not understand what the girl was saying.

The name on her German passport was listed as Charlotte Sara Berg. But Sara was not her middle name. In an effort to easily identify Jews, one of Hitler's edicts required Jewish females to list Sara as a middle name if their first names were not recognizably Jewish. Males were required to use Israel as their middle name.

Once everyone understood what the young girl was asking—"Must I write Sara?"—Follmer buried his face in his hands for a few seconds. He then looked back up at the pretty little blond-haired, blue-eyed girl sitting across from him with tears streaming down her cheeks. She was still clutching the pen in her hand.

"*Schreibe Charlotte*," he told her, speaking as soothingly as he could. Write Charlotte. "You will always keep your name where you are going," he said. "You will never have to write Sara again."

CHAPTER 20

It was an awesome sight to see this large ship that was going to take us to America, with the American flag flying.

—KURT HERMAN

BERLIN–HAMBURG–SOUTHAMPTON
MAY 23–25, 1939

After the children completed the interviews, they returned to their dormitory, where they continued to be looked after by Hedy Neufeld and Marianne Weiss. Someone from the Hilfsverein had invited a Jewish musician to entertain the children. He arrived with a banjo and spent about an hour singing songs in Yiddish and Hebrew, which he tried to teach to the children. "It's the only place where I ever heard a Yiddish song because I had never before heard anyone even speak Yiddish," said Robert Braun. "In Vienna, we always spoke German, and my parents didn't have any acquaintances who spoke Yiddish. As we were listening to these songs in Berlin, I realized that Yiddish sounded a lot like German, but not quite."

Gil and Eleanor went back to their hotel to get some rest and then returned to check on the children early that evening, just as supper was being served. "There's room for you here at our table. Why don't you come and sit with us?" Henny Wenkart asked Eleanor. "Oh, that's so nice of you, dear," replied Eleanor. "But we already ate at our hotel." Eleanor's response did not sit well with the sharp-tongued Henny. "We are all traveling together, and you're staying in a hotel while we're staying here?" she chided Eleanor. "I guess I hadn't become aware yet that I was now a refugee," she recalled years later. "I was not the lawyer's daughter from Vienna anymore."

Early the next morning, Bob Schless took a couple of the children to a dentist after they complained about toothaches. He and Gil were determined to avoid having to leave anyone behind because of health concerns. Fortunately, the toothaches proved to be minor.

Gil and Eleanor made their way back to the American embassy, where a few remaining children still had to be interviewed. By midmorning, the last of the paperwork had been completed. They walked back to the Adlon across the Pariser Platz with the fifty visas in Gil's briefcase. No amount of gold or diamonds could have been as valuable. Bob was waiting for them at the hotel. They quickly collected their luggage and took a taxi to the train station, where the children were already assembled. The train to Hamburg left the station right on time—a few minutes before noon. Eleanor, recalling the emotional departure from Vienna, was relieved to be leaving Berlin without another wrenching set of farewells.

"The weather was beautiful—sunny and mild," she wrote. "The children had a very good night's sleep. More than a dozen men and women had attended to them and had arranged our departure in a most orderly fashion." The children had been provided with lunches to eat during the three-hour train ride to Hamburg. Gil and Eleanor walked through the train throughout the journey, changing seats often so that they could sit with different groups of children along the way.

"The attitudes of the children were interesting to us," wrote Eleanor. "For Gil, they had lost all feeling of awe. He had become the father of them all. The little ones climbed on him and showered him with affection. The older ones clung to him and talked to him, sometimes even putting an arm about his shoulders." As for Bob Schless, some had begun calling him Uncle Bob while others continued to address him formally as Herr Doktor. "They were witty with him, but always conscious of his revered title," said Eleanor. "A doctor was a man to be respected, and they never forgot that."

And Eleanor herself? "I had become the fairy godmother. If I touched one child, the others were noticeably jealous. I had to be very careful not to show special attention or affection. I was not a replacement for their own mothers."

A pair of buses operated by the United States Lines ship company was waiting at the Hamburg train station to bring the children and adults directly to the company's offices. To Eleanor's chagrin, the German employees who worked for the United States Lines in Hamburg were a surly bunch. They acted put out to be helping Jewish children. "No one there was pleasant," said Eleanor. "The red tape was endless. We missed the friendliness and help we had gotten at the embassy. There was none of that attitude here. We were kept at the office for two hours until it was time to leave to make the steamer."

Finally, the buses brought the children and adults to the dock. Once all of the baggage had arrived from the Hamburg train station, there was yet another hurdle. Everything had to be inspected again, this time by the German customs authorities. "All of the children were lined up with their suitcases, and each one was opened for inspection," said Eleanor. "There was a complete search of every piece of luggage. Several boys and girls were selected and chosen for a search for money."

Few, if any, of the children had ever seen an ocean liner. As they waited to board, several kept staring, wide-eyed, up at the *Harding,* with its immense oil-belching smokestack and rows of lifeboats hanging off the side of the ship. "It was an awesome sight to see—this large ship that was going to take us to America, with the American flag flying," said Kurt Herman, who had never seen a boat larger than the small barges that would occasionally float down the Danube in Vienna. "This ship was something to be remembered."

As she waited on the dock with the children, Eleanor wanted nothing more than to board the ship. "I stared up at the gangplank," she wrote. "I thought to myself that any minute now we would be back on American soil."

Eleanor's joyful anticipation was marred only by the sorrow of saying good-bye to Hedy Neufeld. She had been allowed to travel this far with the children, but Hedy was not permitted to walk along the platform that led onto the ship; the Nazi authorities were not going to risk letting someone slip away that easily. Hedy and Marianne had no choice but to stand alone behind a wire fence and watch as the children boarded the ship with the Americans. "I felt so mean pulling away from them," said Eleanor. "We had all grown particularly close. It was a dreadful moment to see them both standing there, forlorn and dejected. It was sickening to leave her behind. I could see Hedy crying, and I could feel my own tears running down my face."

On board the *Harding,* the children were divided four to a cabin throughout the third-class deck. As the children made their way to their rooms, Eleanor caught the attention of a ship steward and handed him two of the children's suitcases, asking him to deliver them to their cabins. "I don't carry baggage for the steerage," the steward curtly replied. Livid, Eleanor told Gil about the steward's rudeness. Not wanting to make a scene, Gil quietly sought out the chief steward, diplomatically explaining the situation and agreeing to pay an additional sum of money—basically, an extra tip to all of the stewards—in exchange for their agreement to help, however grudgingly, with the children.

Not until everyone had settled into their cabins did Eleanor finally allow herself to relax. Throughout most of the ten-day voyage, Gil and Eleanor ate their meals with Bob in the ship's first-class dining room while the children ate in a separate area. On the first night, however, Eleanor remained with the children while they ate dinner. As she looked around the room, she attempted a head count to make sure that all fifty were on hand. Several children were flitting from table to table, and Eleanor found it difficult to keep an accurate count. "I just prayed that we hadn't lost anybody," she said. A waiter came in with a tray of marinated herring, which caused great excitement among the children. "*Rollmops! Rollmops!*" several of them shouted in unison as they recognized the sight—and perhaps pungent scent—of the pickled fish. "Can we have some? Oh please, can we have some?" Eleanor asked the waiter to bring trays of rollmops for all the children. As the dinner progressed, Eleanor pulled aside one of the busboys and asked if he happened to have any American cigarettes. "Sure, lady," he replied in a thick Brooklyn accent. He reached into his pocket and handed her a pack of Lucky Strikes. She lit one, took a long drag, and sighed contentedly. "I clung to the pack," she said later. "This was my first link with home. I was so grateful."

Rollmops and Lucky Strikes aside, Eleanor was far less impressed with the *Harding* itself, which she dismissed as "old, small and hideous." She and Gil had long since become accustomed to considerably higher standards of luxury and comfort when it came to travel. The *Harding* was hardly the *Queen Mary,* nor did it compare favorably even with the *Washington.* Despite their first-class fare, "our stateroom was most unsatisfactory," she said. "Our beds were so narrow that we were sure we would roll out if there should be a rough sea. The idea of spending ten days at sea this way seemed unendurable to us."

The ocean voyage also proved to be an ordeal for many of the children. Seasickness was a frequent problem. For some, the fears of their upcoming journey across the sea began even before the journey itself. "I was frightened even about walking across the plank onto the boat because there was the ocean below that plank, and I didn't know how to swim," recalled Helga Weisz. "I also couldn't understand anything that was being said to me, and I kept looking at the other kids who were looking back at me. A few of the older children knew English so they felt at home. But that wasn't the case for the rest of us." Gil and Bob wasted no time in dividing the children into smaller groups and conducting daily English lessons while at sea. "I paid a lot of attention because my parents had told me back home, 'Be sure you listen to anything in English so that you learn it faster.' At the time, the only English words I knew were *yes, thank you,* and *toilet,*" said Helga.

The ocean voyage also held a few unexpected delights for many of the children. Six-year-old Friedrich Lifschutz tried out chewing gum for the first time in his life. "I had no idea what it was," he remembered decades later. "But soon a lot of us were just chewing away on the boat. It was a real treat."

Two days after leaving Hamburg, the ship docked briefly at Southampton, England, where it took on more passengers and cargo goods before heading westward into the Atlantic. Some of the children had relatives in England who had been notified about the ship's port stop in Southampton and were allowed to come aboard for short visits. Erwin Tepper received an unexpected visit from his father, who had arrived in England from Vienna only a few weeks earlier. Juda Tepper was among a few thousand Jewish men from Germany and Austria who found refuge at Camp Kitchener—a former World War I army camp in Kent that had been turned over to a Jewish relief group in England. Although Erwin and the other lucky children were overjoyed to see their relatives, the stopover in Southampton was difficult for the rest. "These visits made all of the other children homesick, and many began to fuss and cry," said Eleanor. "We were glad to see the visitors go ashore."

Gil had a more pressing reason to get the relatives off the ship. Shortly after leaving Hamburg, he was horrified to discover a few pieces of jewelry hidden in a suitcase belonging to one of the younger children. The jewelry had gone undetected during the German customs search, and Gil only learned about it when the child handed the jewelry to a relative who had come aboard in Southampton. Gil flew into a rage, railing that the entire rescue mission might have been jeopardized had the jewelry been discovered by the Germans. In his anger, he even thought about sending the child back to Berlin. It took all of Eleanor's powers of persuasion to talk Gil out of taking such a drastic step, finally convincing him that it would be cruel to punish an innocent child for the parents' foolish action.

With England behind them, the children now spent long days at sea playing on the decks, writing letters to their parents, and concentrating on their daily English lessons. As part of their language exercises, the children learned to sing "My Bonnie Lies Over the Ocean," a decidedly odd choice for a group of refugee children from Vienna. In an effort to combine English lessons with a dose of American civics, the children also practiced singing "The Star-Spangled Banner" (which had been officially established as America's national anthem in 1931), only to be utterly baffled by the song's confusing lyrics and challenging melody. Despite the homesickness and other more minor maladies, the children turned out to be wonderful passengers. "It would be difficult for anyone to believe how good the children were," wrote Eleanor. "They were sweet tempered, and at all times they were obedient and courteous. I couldn't help but contrast the difference between what fifty American children would have been like against these Viennese children."

The group, however, was not without at least one young prankster. Eight-year-old Oswald LeWinter, whom Eleanor later remembered for his "twinkling brown eyes and wonderful smile," was also "our mischievous little boy" who always seemed to be doing something to attract a little extra attention. One morning, the young boy gathered up several keys that were used to lock some of the children's suitcases, merrily skipped over to the ship's railing, and dropped them into the ocean. "He said he did it to be funny, and I am sure that was his motive," said Eleanor. "Yet this caused great inconvenience, and the children were most resentful over having lost their keys."

Gil somehow managed to find other keys that opened the suitcases but in the process made an unexpected discovery. "Most of the children still had food packed in their suitcases, which had been provided by their mothers before they left Vienna," said Eleanor. "Since we were well on our way, having been out at sea four days, the food was beginning to smell." Gil and Eleanor promptly embarked on a thorough inspection of every suitcase. Soon enough, they were faced with a pile of spoiled food—everything from rotting pieces of fruit to pungent hunks of salami. The children's group included two brothers who came from a family that kept a strictly kosher home in Vienna. Their parents, fearing—correctly—that the boys would find no kosher food on the ship, had packed away some fish that had long since begun to go bad. "Somewhere out in the middle of the Atlantic Ocean, I remember seeing Mr. Kraus and a steward each carrying a small suitcase at arm's length, running up to the railing and dropping it into the ocean," recalled Robert Braun. "I thought that was hilarious because I had never seen Mr. Kraus run so fast."

Midway through the voyage, Bob Schless joined Gil and Eleanor one evening after dinner in the ship's first-class smoking salon. He was tense and unhappy that night, an unusual state for the mild-mannered and easygoing doctor. Eleanor asked him what was wrong. "I made a very great mistake in leaving Hedy behind," he confessed. "I am in love with her and want to marry her. I never should have left her in Austria."

Eleanor was never one to mince words. "Now you tell us!" she exclaimed. "Why didn't you think of it while you were there?"

Bob said that he had done just that many times during their stay in Vienna but did not want to act on his feelings until he was completely sure. "I know I have made a serious mistake," he confessed. In an effort to remedy the situation, he sent Hedy a ship-to-shore cable that included a proposal of marriage. "I was terribly pleased at the news, but I really could have kicked Bob for not having come to his senses while we were over there," wrote Eleanor. "I told Gil several times that I thought Hedy was falling in love with Bob. Gil said it was my imagination, and that she naturally was attached and devoted to all of us."

Early the next morning, Bob greeted Gil and Eleanor at breakfast with a broad grin on his face. Not only had Hedy received his cable, but she had already dispatched her response. She would gladly agree to get married. "It seemed like such a wonderful and magical ending," said Eleanor. "It was a happy, fairy-tale ending that we shared with Bob."

CHAPTER 21

The persons responsible for bringing the children into this country were strongly adverse to giving any information to newspaper men on board the ship.

—*The New York Times*

June 3, 1939
New York Harbor

A soft spring breeze and the promise of a warming sun greeted the passengers aboard the *President Harding* on the final morning of the trans-Atlantic passage that had begun ten days earlier in Hamburg. As the ship approached the wide mouth of New York harbor, the calm ocean felt as gentle as a smoothly flowing river. Ambrose Light—the floating station that marked the entry point to the harbor—was a soft pink in the early morning light. All seemed unusually quiet as the *Harding*'s noisy oil-burning engines began to decelerate. The ocean liner, its single stack no longer belching out plumes of black smoke, aimed for the piers that jutted out along the lower west side of Manhattan.

Despite the calm seas, Eleanor found herself maneuvering precariously at a sharp right angle down the narrow hallway outside her stateroom. Indeed, the boat was listing so hard to starboard that Eleanor had to grab hold of a wooden railing to keep from toppling over as she gingerly made her way to one of the upper decks. The ship's ballast had shifted during the night, resulting in the peculiar pitch at which the liner was now edging its way into the harbor.

On one of the lower decks, Bob Schless stood careful watch over several of the children who, despite the early hour, were already gazing eagerly out beyond the ship's railing toward the horizon. He pointed to a small object that was only barely recognizable in the morning mist but had already become a source of gleeful excitement among the children who were gathered around him. They knew they were on the verge of their first real glimpse of America. Some of the older children vaguely knew about the Statue of Liberty, either from their parents or from having seen pictures of it in newspapers or newsreels. "We all ran to the railing on one side of the ship to see the Statue of Liberty," recalled Helga Weisz. "I was crying because my parents had told me all about the Statue, and I just remember thinking, 'Well, I made it here.'"

As the soaring copper-green figure of a torch-bearing woman draped in flowing robes emerged more clearly into view, some of the younger children shrieked joyfully while waving little American flags. A few of the older children, while happy to have arrived, recognized the sobering significance of their first sighting of America. "Some of the older kids were certainly conscious of the fact that we had escaped Nazi Germany, where things weren't so good for Jews," said Kurt Herman. "And we knew that we were going on an adventure to a new country where we would have all these rights and freedoms. But we also understood, at least most of us did, that it was possible that we would not see our parents again."

After gliding past the Statue of Liberty, the children turned their wide-eyed attention to the incredibly tall buildings that loomed before them. The skyscrapers clustered toward the lower tip of Manhattan only seemed to grow taller and taller as the ship inched closer to its West Side berth. Eleanor delicately balanced her way to the ship's B Deck, where she joined Bob and the children for the *Harding*'s arrival into port. Gil, who had been up since before dawn, remained in his stateroom, reviewing arrangements for immigration and customs inspections. Louis Levine, the Brith Sholom leader, and Congressman Leon Sacks from Philadelphia had boarded the ship at Ambrose Light and had been working with Gil all morning to ensure a smooth transition onto shore. The three men did not emerge back up on the deck until just before the ship was tied up at the pier, which jutted out into the Hudson River at the foot of West Eighteenth Street in Manhattan.

Excited shouts and welcome-home greetings broke the morning silence as the ship's passengers made their way down the gangplank and into the embrace of awaiting family and friends. Eleanor stayed on deck with Bob and the children, bracing herself as she spotted newspaper reporters heading in their direction. "They made a beeline for the group of children I was standing with," wrote Eleanor. "Gil remained below with Louie and Congressman Sacks. I was cornered by the press." The reporters had been alerted that fifty German children were onboard the *Harding*. "We didn't want any publicity, yet I was afraid to say nothing at all about the children," said Eleanor. "I was as non-committal as I could be." As the reporters flung questions at her, Eleanor described the children's arrival as a "quiet, private project" that resulted from "friends of ours who had become interested in bringing some children into this country."

When Gil appeared on deck, he lost his temper, shouting that he did not want any publicity about the children's arrival. Gil remained acutely aware of the public's generally negative views toward opening up the country to Jewish refugees from Nazi Germany. He worried that news about the arrival of even a small group of Jewish children would not be greeted so warmly by others around the country.

Eleanor caught sight of a family friend waiting along the dock. The friend held up a small girl wearing a printed dress. Eleanor recognized the dress even before she could make out the girl's face. It was her daughter, Ellen. A boy kept bouncing up and down next to Ellen, and Eleanor flashed a smile at her son, Steven.

By this time, most of the ship's passengers had made their way off the ship. Gil and Eleanor had a considerable amount of luggage of their own to manage, along with all of the children's suitcases. "It was quite a procession off the ship, with all of our baggage and all our children," wrote Eleanor. "We tried to keep the children in line. We tried to keep them all together. We tried to unscramble their baggage, but everything did get mixed up." More than a dozen volunteers from Brith Sholom were waiting alongside the ship to help keep track of the children. Two school buses were parked nearby, ready to transport the children to the house outside of Philadelphia.

Some of the children's relatives—many of them had aunts, uncles, cousins, and others living in the United States—were also waiting on the dock. "They would find the child they had come to see and then the child would bring the relatives up to us and introduce them," said Eleanor. Paul Beller had an awkward moment with a pair of cousins who had come to see him. "They spoke to me in Yiddish because they figured I would understand since it was pretty close to German," recalled Paul, who managed to understand what his cousins were saying. "How do you like America?" one of them asked. "How am I supposed to know? I just got here," the boy impishly replied. "They probably didn't care for that answer too much."

At long last, it was Eleanor's turn to embrace her own children.

For the rest of the morning Eleanor clung to her daughter, holding her hand tightly. Her son, Steven, at thirteen, was more interested in roaming the grounds on his own.

Bob Schless, who had spent virtually every waking moment with the children during the voyage, came over to Eleanor and pointed to his own three boys and his mother, all of whom had traveled from Philadelphia to greet the ship. "Do you think it will be all right for me to go home with my children now?" he quietly asked Eleanor. She happily insisted that he should.

Gil remained hard at work. "He opened each child's suitcase very carefully as part of the customs inspection," said Eleanor. "He was so tired, so worn, and still working like a steam engine in order to get everything finished." It took more than two hours to inspect all of the suitcases.

By late morning, everyone had boarded buses for the three-hour drive to the Brith Sholom house in Collegeville, Pennsylvania. "What joy, what peace," said Eleanor. "I sat on a seat across from my sister, clutching my daughter all the way there."

As the familiar countryside rushed by, Eleanor's mind wandered over the events of the past six months, which seemed to pass in a blur. She thought back to the evening in January when Gil had first mentioned this fantastic idea to rescue Jewish children from Nazi Germany. She remembered the impassioned pleas from all of those who had been so intent on convincing Gil not to go ahead with his seemingly impossible plan. She could still hear the desperate voices of the parents in Vienna who begged them to take their children from them and bring them to safety in America. And now here they were—rumbling along a New Jersey highway with fifty children in their care.

Eleanor stared out the window again and then looked back down at Ellen. She squeezed the young girl's hand tightly in her own. She was home. She was back with her children. Everyone was safe.

PART THREE

NEW LIVES

CHAPTER 22

*For the first time in my life, tears of joy. God has granted you such
fortune, and granted us, the parents, to partake in it.*

—LETTER FROM HERMANN ROTH TO HIS SON KURT

COLLEGEVILLE, PENNSYLVANIA–HAVANA, CUBA
JUNE–AUGUST 1939

As the buses meandered through New Jersey and Pennsylvania,
Henny Wenkart's first taste of America took on the flavor of
inedible chocolate. "Someone had brought a Whitman's Sampler
to the dock, and the box made its way around the bus that I was
on," she remembered. One by one, each of the children bit into the
chocolates, which brought at least some of them to tears. "Viennese chocolate was so good," Wenkart remembered fondly. "And the
Whitman's chocolates were really awful!"

For Robert Braun, the bus ride to Collegeville provided a dramatic reminder of some of the stark differences between his upcoming life in the casual new world of America and the formal Old World that had been left behind in Vienna. Gil and Eleanor's son, Steven, had folded himself into a seat directly behind the bus driver, draping his legs over the chrome railing that separated the driver's seat from the rest of the bus. "That was so shocking to us," remembered Robert. "If I had done that in Austria, my parents would have clobbered me or the conductor would have thrown me off the tram. But here it seemed very relaxed."

Dozens of Brith Sholom members, their wives, and others were waiting on the lawn in front of the sprawling, one-story stone house to greet the children when the buses arrived later that afternoon. The house had been swept clean throughout, and every one of the twenty-five bedrooms had been outfitted with immaculate new furniture. The "ladies' auxiliary" of Brith Sholom had also excitedly prepared for the children's arrival. "The dining room was set for all of us," wrote Eleanor. "I had never seen so much food in all my life. Turkeys, pies, cakes—everything cooked and served by the women of Brith Sholom. No children the world over were ever more beautifully received or had a better welcome."

In spite of the effusive smiles and delicious feast that greeted the children, many of them remained understandably nervous as they took in the unusual sights and sounds of their strange new surroundings. The Brith Sholom house stood adjacent to the summer camp that the organization operated for children, which further confused the new arrivals from Vienna. "I had been very apprehensive from the time I got off the ship, particularly when someone told us that we were going to be taken to a camp," said Klara Rattner. "I didn't know what a camp was in the United States, but we had all heard about concentration camps back in Germany and Austria." The children's fears melted away as the afternoon wore on. There was clearly no reason to be frightened by a camp like this, one where delicious cakes and pies were freely served up to anyone who asked.

Gil excused himself from the hubbub of the dining room and closeted himself away with a group of men from Brith Sholom. With fifty children now in their care, he wanted to make sure that all of their needs would be met. Among the men was a dentist from nearby Norristown who readily volunteered his services. "He probably did more than any other one man for the children as all their teeth needed attention," wrote Eleanor. Several doctors also offered to help, guaranteeing that the children would receive ongoing care throughout the summer.

By early evening, the children had settled into their bedrooms. Most of the younger ones fell asleep immediately after the long and tiring day. A few of the older children stayed up a while longer, talking excitedly about everything they had seen, heard, tasted that day. Before long, however, a comforting silence had settled throughout the big stone house. Eleanor turned to Gil and asked, "Do you think I could please go home now? I'd like to be alone in my own house with my own two children."

It was very late when she arrived back home on Cypress Street. She was much too tired to even think about unpacking; it could wait until the morning. She looked in on her children, who had been taken home earlier by one of Eleanor's sisters. Minutes later, she was in her own bed and fast asleep, alone—Gil remained at the Brith Sholom house that first night. He did not want the children to wake up in a strange, new country without seeing at least one familiar face.

On Sunday, June 4, the *Philadelphia Inquirer* published a photograph that showed several of the children, their backs turned toward the camera, waving at the Statue of Liberty from aboard the *President Harding*. "An after-dinner discussion—started casually in the home of a Philadelphia lawyer last January—about the plight of the Jews in Vienna under the Nazi regime neared a happy conclusion yesterday with the arrival in New York of fifty Viennese refugee children," read a line from the accompanying article.

Other parts of the article were wholly inaccurate, which undoubtedly disturbed Gil, given his efforts to stifle any publicity about the rescue project. According to the newspaper, Gil and Eleanor "went abroad several months ago and got photographs of the children who need help. The pictures were sent to the backers of the [rescue] plan and the children were selected."

That same day, the *Inquirer* published another story, this one on the front page, about a disturbing development in the situation facing Jewish refugees from Nazi Germany. The Associated Press dispatch from Havana described a tense saga over the fate of 937 Jewish passengers who had sailed from Hamburg aboard the SS *St. Louis* ten days before the *President Harding* had left for New York. Although the Jewish passengers on the *St. Louis* had obtained visas to enter Cuba, by the time the ship arrived in Havana on May 27, government officials had changed their minds about honoring the visas. Despite a flurry of international negotiations, as well as desperate pleas from the passengers themselves, the Cuban government ordered the ship to leave on June 2.

American officials, including President Roosevelt, received a flood of urgent requests to allow the *St. Louis* into the United States. Cuba was not the final destination for the majority of the passengers; almost all were awaiting American visas. Roosevelt also received a telegram from some of those trapped aboard the ship. "Most urgently repeat plea for help for the passengers of the *St. Louis*," read the telegram, written in German. "Mr. President, help the 900 passengers, including over 400 women and children." The appeals fell on deaf ears. Even as the ship sailed within sight of the United States—at one point, passengers could see the lights of Miami from the deck of their doomed ship—American officials refused to relax the laws that stood between the passengers and freedom. A telegram from the State Department informed the passengers they must "await their turns on the waiting list and qualify for and obtain immigration visas before they may be admissible into the United States."

In the end, the Cuban government admitted only twenty-eight passengers from the ship—twenty-two of whom already had valid U.S. visas. One additional passenger was evacuated to a hospital in Havana after attempting to commit suicide while the boat was docked in the harbor.

Three days after the *President Harding* docked in New York Harbor, the *St. Louis* set sail for a return voyage to Germany. Jewish relief organizations, led by the Joint Distribution Committee, persuaded four other European countries to issue entry visas for the passengers. Among those, 288 were allowed into Great Britain and 224 were admitted into France. Belgium took in 214, the Netherlands 181. For many, sadly, the reprieve proved to be temporary. Of the 937 passengers who first set out for Cuba, 254 lost their lives in the Holocaust—victims of roundups and deportations that came in the wake of the Nazi occupation of Belgium, Holland, and France.

On Monday, June 5, Gil wrote a lengthy letter to Emil Engel, the Jewish community leader in Vienna who had been instrumental in helping with the rescue mission. "No doubt you received my telegram from the ship, which notified you of our arrival in America," said Gil, who wrote in English "since I am much better in expressing my earnest thanks and deep fondness for you in my own language, and I know you will understand each word." After reporting that the children "are all happy and well," Gil asked if Engel would notify the parents that their children were safe and that they had "behaved flawlessly" during the journey to America. "I would ask you to congratulate the parents for the selfless way in which they said farewell to their children." Immediately after receiving Gil's letter, Engel translated it into German and sent copies to all of the parents.

Two weeks later, Gil received a letter, in German, from the father of one of the boys from Vienna. Written just before he escaped to England's Camp Kitchener, Sigmund Zulawski expressed "my deep gratitude for the fatherly care" that Gil had provided to his only child, Hugo. "It is a great comfort and great reassurance during this difficult time to know that my boy is in good care. My wife and I will never forget this, and we pray hourly to God for your well-being."

Gil, meanwhile, made a point of writing another very important letter, now that the children had arrived in America. On June 8, five days after returning from Europe, Gil wrote once again to George Messersmith at the State Department. "It was my intention to come to Washington to personally thank you for your splendid coopera-tion and helpfulness in this project," Gil wrote in the one-page letter typed on letterhead from the law offices of Kraus & Weyl. "But because of the rush of things and now being the father of fifty ad-ditional children, I have been unable to move from my desk." Now that the rescue project had come to a successful close, "I frankly wish to say that if it were not for the cooperation, within legal limits, of the Department of State and the Foreign Service, our accomplish-ment could never have been possible." Gil closed the letter with an invitation for Messersmith to visit the children in Collegeville.

"I know that you must feel a personal sense of satisfaction in having carried through your mission so successfully," Messersmith told Gil in his reply. He added that he had already heard from Ray-mond Geist in Berlin "who tells me that he was very glad to be in a position to cooperate with you within the limits of our immigration laws and practice." Messersmith also mentioned that Congressman Sacks "called me on the telephone the other day to express appreci-ation" and to invite him to visit the children. He politely declined. "You will appreciate that it is difficult for me for the present to make any plans which take me out of Washington," he told Gil. The me-ticulous Messersmith sent copies of his correspondence with Gil to A. M. Warren, who headed the State Department's visa division. "You will wish to put this with the appropriate file," Messersmith noted in a cover memo. "I think Congressman Sacks and Mr. Kraus have carried through this project in a very commendable manner."

As the days grew warmer, the fifty children from Vienna became accustomed to the comfortable surroundings of the country house in Collegeville. The Brith Sholom ladies' auxiliary organized a clothing drive that in short order resulted in a steady stream of boxes brimming with dresses, trousers, shirts, swimming suits, and other apparel. "Within a week or so," wrote Eleanor, "these children owned more good clothes than any other children in the country."

They were also getting used to a variety of new foods, though some were decidedly more mysterious than others. Erwin Tepper was not the only child who was baffled one evening when, at the end of dinner, dessert arrived at the table. "It looked like some kind of jelly, which was bright red and with slices of banana inside of it," Erwin remembered. "I don't think I had eaten a banana more than two or three times in my life, so that was really a treat. But none of us knew what the red, wiggly stuff was, which we all very carefully scraped away. We thought it was some kind of preservative to protect the banana floating inside. Someone finally tasted the stuff and told us it was delicious." And so it was that Erwin and the rest of the children came to be introduced to the odd American dessert called Jell-O.

Henny Wenkart had a puzzling—even a little frightening— experience one night. She watched from afar as some of the counselors, staff members of the adjoining Brith Sholom summer camp, threw each other around inside the camp's recreation hall. "We had been told that America was a violent country," recalled Henny, which seemed to explain the counselors' rough-and-tumble antics. It wasn't until later that she discovered that they were simply dancing the jitterbug.

Gil, who drove from Philadelphia to Collegeville every day during the children's first week, quickly realized that no one was truly in charge. Although Brith Sholom officials had hired nurses, cooks, and others to care and provide for the children, no one had overall responsibility for running the house. On the following Sunday,

Eleanor's sister Sarah and her husband came for a visit. After Gil explained the somewhat chaotic situation, Sarah volunteered to take over. "She didn't even go home for a change of clothing," wrote Eleanor. "She stayed for two months and put the entire place in order. Her husband came every weekend. We never would have gotten through the summer without her help."

The children's English lessons, which had begun onboard the *Harding*, continued throughout the summer. On the weekends, the Sunday comics provided the children with a particularly enjoyable method for mastering their new language. "It was a great way to learn English," said Erwin Tepper. "You had all of the words inside the balloons, and you could look at the pictures, which also helped to figure out some of those words. To this day, the funnies are the first thing I read on Sundays before reading the rest of the paper."

Amid the lighthearted humor of Sunday comics and the mysteries of American baseball, at least some of the children continued to harbor dark fears that harkened back to their experiences in Vienna. Congressman Sacks visited the camp with his daughter, Myra, shortly after the children had arrived. She spotted one of the younger girls standing nearby on the sprawling lawn in front of the house. The young girl began walking toward Myra and her parents, then abruptly stopped at the edge of the lawn, a frightened look spreading across her face. Not long after the Anschluss, Jews were banned from Vienna's public parks. Instinctively, she was afraid to step on the grass, even though she knew there was no longer any danger in doing so.

In between their English lessons and sports activities, the children were required to write letters to their parents or other relatives in Vienna. "It is very hot here," one of the children, Robert Keller, wrote to his mother. "We are always busy. The food is wonderful. We are all healthy. I've already written to the grandparents. How are they? Every Sunday we go to the movies together with the American children. On the opposite side from us is the camp of Brith Sholom.

There are lots of Jewish children. Today we will have a bonfire. A thousand kisses, Robi."

The letters from Collegeville brought pure joy to the parents who remained trapped in Vienna. "Today is another beautiful day for me since I got mail from you," Rosa Zinger wrote to her daughters Fritzi and Elizabeth. "You do not know, my darlings, what it means to get a few sentences from you. You give your mother great pleasure. Did you get the pictures of Mama and Papa? Please write us as often as you can so that we may have many letters from you. Greetings and kisses from your loving Mother."

For some children, the letters only increased their homesickness by reminding them of the relatives and friends they had left behind. While the correspondence helped to keep them connected with their parents, it also underscored the uncertainty, at least in some cases, of whether the children and parents would see each other again. "Your letters are scribbled, but nevertheless we—I and Mama—could not restrain our tears of joy, picturing your young group being photographed with the Statue of Liberty," Hermann Roth wrote to his son Kurt less than two weeks after the children had arrived in the United States. "For the first time in my life, tears of joy. God has granted you such fortune, and granted us, the parents, to partake in it."

A week later, Hermann wrote again to his son, though this time with an added, and good-natured, parental admonition. "I must call to your attention again that in your letter, only the address on the envelope is legible. The letter itself is all scribbled, and you aren't even a doctor yet. You must write neatly."

The next letter, however, did not come from Vienna. Hermann Roth wrote it instead from a Nazi-operated work camp located outside of the city where he was now living. He had decided that it was too risky to remain in the city, where more and more Jewish men were being arrested and sent away to concentration camps. He felt that he was safer at the work camp, where the ability to perform hard physical labor seemed to provide an alternative to the risks of arrest. "I am well and have become more or less accustomed to the work, which is, of course, very strenuous. Maybe it's even good for me," Hermann wrote to his son on July 16. "How are you coming along with your English? I have my English books with me here but I study only on Sundays. On weekdays I am too tired."

Throughout the summer, Kurt's parents had been trying, without success, to obtain visas and exit documents for themselves and their younger child, Herbert. By the middle of August, Hermann had managed to book passage on a Holland Line ship that was scheduled to leave from Hamburg in late September and arrive in New York on October 3. But he had run into problems with his exit permits and now needed an extension on his passport. In an August 27 letter, he explained that affidavits from relatives in America also had to be renewed and that Kurt's mother had been going to the American consulate to try and resolve additional snags that were delaying their departure from Vienna. "The consulate [officer] was very nice," wrote Hermann, who was still living in the labor camp. "He played with Herberti, gave him candy and, at parting, said 'God be with you,' in reference to our situation, as you can understand." Once again, he reminded his son to "Write diligently, be obedient and well behaved. It is not always to be regretted. How is your English coming along?"

Five days later, on September 1, German tanks rumbled into Poland. Two days after that, Britain and France declared war on Germany. The formal outbreak of World War II put an end to the Nazis' policy of *Judenrein* in places like Vienna and Berlin. Instead of pressuring Jews to immigrate to other countries, a far deadlier formula for the Final Solution was about to take hold. Kurt Roth received no more letters from his father. On October 2, Hermann was deported to the Buchenwald concentration camp, where he was assigned to a forced labor detail. He died there twenty-two days later. He was forty years old.

CHAPTER 23

While the number fifty is but a small drop among the hundreds of thousands of lives yet to be saved, still in all each life is worth a world unto itself.

—GIL KRAUS

SUMMER 1939

ATLANTIC CITY–PHILADELPHIA–NEW YORK CITY

Shortly after 2:00 P.M. on the afternoon of Sunday, June 11, 1939, Leon Sacks stepped to the dais in the chandeliered Ritz Gardens ballroom inside the Ritz-Carlton Hotel in Atlantic City, New Jersey. The Philadelphia congressman looked out across the lectern at the hundreds of men and women gathered for the opening session of the thirty-fourth annual convention of the International Order of Brith Sholom.

"As I stand before this assemblage, proud of my being here, I know I am standing before a group of men and women, unselfish in their service to humanity and fearless in their endeavor to preserve American democracy," said Sacks. "Here meets an organization whose humanitarian endeavors stand today as a beacon light to all whose hearts beat for the oppressed." As a swell of applause rippled across the room, Sacks added, "May I take this opportunity of congratulating you for this noble work, especially in being the first to aid in bringing fifty living orphans to the shores of liberty and freedom."

Sacks, of course, had played an important supporting part in the rescue mission. He had used his influence as a member of Congress to introduce Gil six months earlier to George Messersmith at the State Department. Once the plan was set in motion, Sacks kept in touch with Messersmith and other officials as part of the effort to secure as much cooperation as could be expected from an otherwise recalcitrant State Department. In his speech, however, the Philadelphia congressman reserved his most glowing words of praise for Gil's role in the mission. "He has endeared himself to all of us and has become a most distinguished member of American Jewry," said Sacks. "Going to a land filled with hatred, he carried hope to our brethren in the throes of despair, stretched out his hand and by his ability and courage was able to rescue those innocent souls from the depths of hell such as you and I could not realize ever existed." Sacks then turned to Eleanor. He paid warm tribute to a woman "who left her own babies and went to this land of despair to salvage the lives of those whose only crime was that they were Jewish children." Sacks also singled out Bob Schless— who was not in attendance—for leaving behind his medical practice "to aid Brith Sholom in its noble cause" and who, in doing so, became a "true healer in the suffering of humanity."

Sacks was followed to the podium by Samuel Einhorn, a Philadelphia lawyer and Brith Sholom's vice grand master. Einhorn reminded the audience that Gil's father had led the campaign years earlier to save lives by building a sanitarium for tuberculosis patients. "It seems to me but fitting," said Einhorn, "that all these years later, Solomon Kraus's beloved son should sit down with others and think of saving lives, this time the lives of unfortunate children, this time the lives of those who all said could not be saved." Eight days earlier, Einhorn had been among the contingent of Brith Sholom officials that had met the *President Harding* when it docked in New York. "In my twenty-five years of communal work, I know of nothing in my life that has given to us greater happiness, happiness beyond measure, than meeting and greeting those children as they came off the boat," he said. "And the first individual that I saw, the first happy face that I saw—a face, however, that to me gave every evidence of having borne great grief, a face that showed every evidence of having been through great strain—was that of Gil Kraus."

Einhorn looked up from his notes and out across the ballroom. "These children are children like yours," he declared as ripples of applause began to spread around the room. "They were saved from that inferno in Germany by Gil Kraus." The applause grew louder as Einhorn motioned for Gil to come to the podium.

The applause died down as Gil, impeccably dressed as always, took his place at the lectern. "The credit for whatever achievements were accomplished is yours," he began. "My associates and myself were only the medium through which fifty souls were given the right to live and grow up into good American citizens." For the next thirty minutes, Gil delivered a speech that painted a grimly realistic portrait of the crumbling conditions facing Jews inside Nazi Germany. "If you could see, as I have with my own eyes, the sad plight of our people in Middle Europe, then would you realize the immediate need of palliative relief until something of a permanent nature could be accomplished," he said. "When fathers and mothers of small children are willing, and even plead for you to take their children from them out of the land of darkness into the light of liberty, you can well realize the dire necessity for relief. . . . While the number fifty is but a small drop among the hundreds of thousands of lives yet to be saved, still in all each life is worth a world unto itself, and each child shall be privileged to live and breathe in a land consecrated to freedom and liberty."

The crowd in the ballroom jumped to their feet, the room echoing with the sounds of loud, sustained applause as Gil concluded: "May I convey to you the warm and sincere thanks of fifty little children who, with one voice, bow their heads in prayer and gratitude for their safe deliverance from the land of bondage."

An unexpected visitor to the Brith Sholom convention followed Gil to the podium. Kurt Peiser had never attended a Brith Sholom convention even though he had worked for Jewish community groups for many years. Still, he was widely known to many Brith Sholom members because of his position as the executive director of Philadelphia's Federation of Jewish Charities. But only a few in the room were aware that Peiser had been among the city's Jewish leaders who had tried to talk Gil out of the rescue mission. He certainly had no intention of reminding anyone on this day of his earlier opposition. Instead he took to the podium to "pay my tribute to your grand master and to Mr. Kraus and his wife and to Doctor Schless for their accomplishment. It is truly an incentive to all those [other] organizations that are engaged in refugee work." Peiser referred to the rescue of the fifty children as a "symbol" that hopefully would lead to "future accomplishments . . . that you have never dreamed of before."

A few days before the Brith Sholom convention, the *Philadelphia Jewish Exponent* published an editorial about the successful rescue of the fifty children from Vienna. Under a headline that read "A 'Now It Can Be Told' Story," the sharply worded piece began with an acknowledgment that the newspaper's editors had known about the rescue plan for months but had kept quiet so as not to potentially jeopardize its success. Now that the children were safely lodged at Brith Sholom's summer camp, "this intriguing story may—indeed should—be told." The editorial cast a critical eye on other Jewish leaders and groups that had attempted for months to block the Brith Sholom project. "The question is asked," the editorial concluded. "Why did German-Jewish Children's Aid try to dissuade Brith Sholom? Was it merely a case of poor judgment or worse? An explanation is in order."

Other newspaper articles, meanwhile, that reported on the arrival of the fifty children and their temporary custody at the Brith Sholom house in Collegeville served to further sharpen the original criticism other groups had leveled against the enterprise. On June 12, Jacob Kepecs, the Jewish children's advocate from Chicago, sent another letter to Clarence Pickett, the Quaker official, which reiterated his earlier concerns. "To my knowledge, neither Mr. and Mrs. Kraus nor Brith Sholom have had any experience in the foster care of children," Kepecs tartly noted. "Undoubtedly similar individuals and organizations will attempt the same thing. In my opinion, this is a risky procedure all around, and the welfare of the children is jeopardized."

Two days later, Razovsky wrote again to A. M. Warren, the State Department's head of the visa division, this time in direct response to the stinging editorial in the *Jewish Exponent*. "The effect of this editorial and the success of Brith Sholom's plan," she wrote, "is likely to start an avalanche of similar organizations." To be sure, Razovsky had been working tirelessly since 1934 to bring Jewish refugees—adults and children—to the United States. But in the immediate aftermath of Gil's triumph, Razovsky clearly feared that her own efforts had been eclipsed.

While the success of the Brith Sholom project captured the attention of others who likewise hoped to rescue European Jews, it also raised eyebrows in Washington, particularly among members of Congress who opposed any attempts to ease America's immigration laws. "My attention has been called to a newspaper article which describes the arrival in the United States of fifty Jewish refugee children aboard the United States Liner *President Harding*

en route to foster homes awaiting them in Philadelphia," Senator
Rufus Holman wrote to Secretary of State Cordell Hull on June 8.
"I will be obliged if you will furnish me with a detailed statement of
the manner in which these immigrants were admitted to the United
States under existing immigration laws." A conservative Republican
from Oregon, Holman had recently joined several other senators in
sponsoring legislation to reduce the immigration quotas by 90 percent. He was not happy to hear that fifty Jewish children had somehow managed to make their way into the country. In his two-page
reply, Hull assured Holman that the children had properly received
visas because their "turns on the waiting list had been reached in
the regular order" and that they were all legally admissible under
the immigration laws. Hull also told the senator that the children
had been "selected abroad by representatives of the Brith Sholom
Lodge of Philadelphia, which has undertaken to place the children in
a home where they will be supported in the United States."*

Within a few weeks of the children's arrival, the earlier spec-
ulation over the details of Gil's mission had given way to a series
of critical—and largely inaccurate—conclusions about how he had
carried it out. On the afternoon of June 27, leaders of the National
Coordinating Committee, a coalition of organizations that had been
working to bring Jewish refugees into America, met at the New York
City home of Marion Kenworthy, a prominent New York psychia-
trist and social worker who had become a passionate advocate for
Jewish refugees. The discussion at Kenworthy's Fifth Avenue apartment quickly turned into a critical investigation of the Brith Sholom
project. Kenworthy mentioned that committee members had told Gil
long before "there would be a great deal of damage done should he
go to Europe and take a group of children. He said he was going to

---

* In addition to his position against immigration, Holman held strong anti-Semitic
views. In 1941, he spoke glowingly of Adolf Hitler from the floor of the Senate: "At least
Hitler has broken the control of the international bankers and traders over the rewards
for the labor of the common people of Germany."

do this, and he was so annoyed at what he thought was an attempt to block him that he decided he would prove it could be done."

Given Gil's fierce streak of stubbornness, Kenworthy may well have been accurate, at least partly, in ascribing his original determination to fulfill the rescue mission despite the opposition of others. But she then veered off into a wholly imagined account of his actions, asserting that Gil had somehow managed to obtain fifty "preferential" visas for the children. Kenworthy also claimed another member of the National Coordinating Committee had heard that in advance of his own trip to Europe, Gil had "sent people abroad to search for children" and had obtained lists of Jewish children from orphanages in Vienna.

The committee's leaders reconvened at Kenworthy's apartment two days later, on June 29. Once again, the discussion turned to the still-vexing issue of how Gil had managed to bring a large group of children into the country at a time when other rescue efforts remained stalled. Committee members were perplexed in particular by Gil's success in satisfying the Labor Department's rigid affidavit requirements.

Throughout the summer of 1939, the rescue mission continued to receive scrutiny. "Just how the children were selected, just who selected them, and how it cleared with the consular service—all these things are part of a great mystery to folks in New York and Philadelphia," Robert Balderston, from the American Friends Service Committee, wrote in a July 16 memo apprising other Quaker officials of ongoing refugee efforts. "Apparently the Kraus children shipment [sic], arranged outside the regular coordinating committee created quite a commotion, for it was done apparently to show up the regular Jewish organizations." Balderston noted that Gil's plan had been "severely criticized because the children [were] placed in a home or orphanage in Philadelphia and not in private homes as is the regular practice."

Was it envy that prompted others to criticize what had clearly been a stunningly unique and successful rescue? Whatever their motivation, some of these same people now wondered if they might simply duplicate Gil's strategy. In his letter accusing Brith Sholom of jeopardizing the rescued children's welfare, Jacob Kepecs enthusiastically suggested that German-Jewish Children's Aid and the American Friends Service Committee search for other unused visas that could be reserved for additional children. "I think it would be worth exploring the possibility of using unused quota numbers for children," replied Clarence Pickett in a June 20 letter to Kepecs in Chicago. "However, at the present time I doubt very much whether there would be a single unused quota number."

The historical record, unfortunately, is silent on whether anyone from these groups ever spoke again with Gil about his rescue mission. But there is no doubt that he, along with Eleanor, forever remained convinced that he had done the right thing despite—or perhaps because of—the strenuous efforts to stand in his way.

In his stirring speech at the Brith Sholom convention, Gil spared no words in describing the sad fate of children left behind in Nazi Germany. "Little children—like the children that we brought to America—are not permitted to go to school. But worse than that, they're not permitted to play with other children on the streets. They are not permitted to be seen in public beyond a certain small distance from their homes," he told the audience. "These same children, these very children who are now in Collegeville, have—every one of them—suffered the same fate at the hands of the Nazi government. But at least these children now have a home and a roof over their head and a beautiful park to play in. And so temporarily—and everyone now lives only temporarily in Germany—they are better off than the children who are still there, who are not in their homes, and whose families have been chased out of their homes.

"And so, my friends, coming out of that fiendish existence, you have brought fifty souls to America," said Gil. "You have brought fifty children out of that inferno of hate and into America."

CHAPTER 24

Look at these children. It makes me wish we could bring thousands of them over.

—Louis Levine

COLLEGEVILLE, PENNSYLVANIA
AUGUST–SEPTEMBER 1939

As the end of summer approached, Gil and Eleanor turned their attention to finding suitable homes for every one of the children. Although many of them had relatives living in the United States, not all of them had the financial or practical means to take on the responsibility of caring for an extra family member or two. "Wherever the relatives were in a position financially and were interested in having a child, this request was granted," said Eleanor.

"Some of the people from Brith Sholom wanted foster children, and where this could be done, their requests were granted."

Irma Langberg and Ella Spiegler were the first two children to leave Collegeville. Their bittersweet departure the first week in August was noted in a mimeographed camp newsletter written in German by a couple of the children and translated into English by Brith Sholom volunteers. "Not only will we deeply miss them, it is much more," the newsletter reported. "We know that Irma and Ella [are] the first of us 50 children to leave the home and go into that America which we only know through our storybooks. Irma and Ella, do not cry about leaving us! You are entering into a life for which hundreds of thousands over there [in Germany] will envy you."

Throughout August, Gil spent hours interviewing relatives of the children as well as others who had volunteered to become foster parents. Gil and Eleanor sometimes received letters out of the blue from perfect strangers who had read about the children and hoped to adopt one. "Can we please have a little girl with blue eyes and yellow hair?" one couple wrote. Another woman, seeking to adopt a child, enclosed a photograph of her husband because she wanted the child "to look as much like him as possible."

But Gil refused to allow any of the children to be legally adopted. He had made a solemn promise to the parents in Vienna that their children would be cared for and looked after but only until such time as the parents themselves might be reunited with their children. He had no way of knowing, of course, how many parents would ultimately obtain their own visas. As Europe edged ever closer to war throughout the summer, the waiting list for American visas continued to grow as Jews who remained trapped in Nazi Germany sensed that time was running out. On the other hand, the fact that their children were already in the United States in some cases strengthened the parents' visa applications.

"All during that summer at the Brith Sholom camp, I remember thinking that pretty soon my parents would be with me, that I'd be reunited with them, and that's sort of as far as it went," recalled Helga Weisz. Her father, Emil, wrote that he was confident he would soon be joining her in the United States. But Helga's Hungarian-born mother, Rosa, had no immediate prospects for obtaining her own visa. By summer's end, Helga was sent to live with a foster couple in New York. She shared tearful good-byes with Inge Braunwasser, who had become her closest friend during their time together at the Brith Sholom camp. "I remember Inge crying, and I was comforting her, and I gave her a letter and a picture of me, and she gave me something of hers." The two would not see each other again for nearly fifty years.

Although Helga's foster parents, a childless couple, no doubt had the best of intentions, they turned out to be shockingly insensitive to what the young girl had experienced in Vienna. "Whenever I tried to tell them what had happened to my family in Europe, they told me that I was making up stories and that I should just forget about those times," said Helga. "They also said that if my parents were punished, it's probably because they did something bad against the government. They told me I shouldn't talk about it anymore and that I should concentrate on becoming an American."

All summer long, Henny Wenkart stubbornly proclaimed that she would not go live with a foster family. In fact, her parents and younger sister succeeded in coming to the United States in early August. But with no immediate prospects of making any sort of living, Hermann Wenkart knew he was in no position to adequately provide for the entire family. "My father came to see me at the camp," recalled Henny. "He said, 'We're going to be very poor, and I have been told that you could live for a while in the home of another lawyer. And it would ease my mind to know that at least you were living a normal life.'"

Fritzi and Elizabeth Zinger, unlike some of the other children, had relatives who were both willing and able to take care of the two girls. Toward the end of the summer, an aunt and uncle drove down from Utica, New York, to pick up nine-year-old Fritzi and six-year-old Elizabeth. "We combed our hair and washed our faces, and we came into this room to meet our relatives," Fritzi remembered. "My aunt cried out, 'Oh my goodness, they're blackies!' What she meant was that we had black eyes and black hair. I guess she expected two girls from Vienna to have blue eyes and blond hair." They soon settled into their new home in upstate New York with the relatives they knew as Uncle Max and Aunt Birdie. Elizabeth remembered that her uncle would tell them before bed each evening, "Now remember, I'm Papa and that's Mama. That is what you must call us now." After the lights in the room had darkened, Elizabeth would hear a soft, comforting voice just as she was drifting off to sleep. "*Er ist nicht dein Papa. Sie ist nicht deine Mama.*" It was Fritzi telling her younger sister, "He is not your father. She is not your mother." Uncle Max and Aunt Birdie were a wonderful couple who treated the Zinger sisters as if they were their own children. "But it was my sister who reminded me all of the time that we still had a mother and father," said Elizabeth. "I was always so grateful to her for that."

Some of Gil and Eleanor's closest friends offered to take in a child or two. Throughout the summer, Paul Beller assumed that he would be sent to live with an uncle in New York City. Instead, Philip and Emily Amram drove to Collegeville in late August and asked Paul if he would like to come live with them for a while. Philip was a well-heeled lawyer who traveled in the same Philadelphia professional and social circles as Gil. Eleanor and Emily also happened to be distantly related through marriage. At the time, Philip was leading the life of a gentleman farmer, having recently moved his family—which included a son, David, and a daughter, Marianne—to rural Feasterville, which was not too far from Collegeville. Coincidentally, the Amrams also employed a full-time nanny from Vienna who, of course, spoke fluent German.

By the end of the summer, Paul had taken to life on the farm,

riding the Amrams' big-wheeled tractor, eating loads of fresh vegetables, and enjoying hayrides and the other benefits of rural living.
His father, Leo, had succeeded by then in getting out of Vienna, only
to be detained by British authorities after trying to sneak by ship
into Palestine. He and others on the intercepted ship were sent to
a British detention camp on the Indian Ocean island of Mauritius.
Paul's mother, Mina, remained in Vienna, which became even more
dangerous for Jews once the war began in September. "She would
send me postcards that said everything was fine," Paul recollected.
"In reality, though, she was in tremendous danger all the time."

In mid-August, a reporter for the *New York Journal-American*
visited the Brith Sholom house and described the joyous atmosphere
in an article headlined "Little Refugees Proving Good As Americans." The reporter was accompanied during the visit by Louis
Levine, who smiled broadly as several children gathered around a
flagpole and sang "The Star-Spangled Banner," one of the songs
they had struggled so hard to learn while crossing the Atlantic
Ocean. "Look at these children," said Levine. "It makes me wish we
could bring thousands of them over. You can't doubt, seeing them
here so willing to stay and learn our ways, that every one of them
will develop into honest-to-goodness Americans." One of the boys,
twelve-year-old Herbert Vogel, came up to the reporter and proudly
showed off his slightly misshapen and discolored nose. "Already I
am a real American," he bragged. "See my nose? It was broken by a
baseball bat."

By the end of August, most of the children had left Collegeville.
"We were worried because people would come out on weekends to
look at the children, and more and more of the kids would disappear," remembered Robert Braun. As Labor Day approached, he and
his older sister, Johanna, were the only ones left. "My God, nobody
wants us!" Robert cried to his sister. What's going to happen to us?"

He did not discover until many years later that his fate, together with his sister's, had never been in doubt. Gil and Eleanor had decided—perhaps while they were still in Vienna—that Robert and Johanna would live with them and their children, Steven and Ellen.

By early September all fifty children were in their new homes and ready to begin their new lives. A few fortunate ones had already been reunited with their parents. Most of the others lived in hope—fleeting or otherwise—of seeing their mothers and fathers before too long.

In Europe, a war that would result in the deaths of millions had just begun. For fifty Jewish children, the nightmares that had robbed them of their innocent childhoods had come to an end. The Brith Sholom house in Collegeville once again stood silent and empty.

Epilogue

In June 1940—one year after the children arrived in America—the members of Brith Sholom gathered again at the Ritz-Carlton Hotel in Atlantic City for the group's annual convention. Once again, Louis Levine delivered a detailed "grand master's message" that focused on the ongoing threat to European Jewry. The war had been going on for more than nine months, and Adolf Hitler's relentless persecution inside the Third Reich now also imperiled millions more in Poland, Hungary, and elsewhere. The Final Solution had not yet been set into motion, but the blueprints for killing centers and death camps were not far off.

Levine, in his speech, continued to sound the call to come to the aid of Jewish refugees. "We of Brith Sholom have done our utmost to cooperate with all agencies in the effort to make available havens for refugees," he declared. "We have also endeavored to help refugees who have found their way to these shores. We have contributed large sums of money to other agencies devoted to this purpose. Above all, we in Brith Sholom are proud of the achievement we have accomplished. With your help, we brought last year to these shores fifty German-Jewish children. Who can forget the thrill we all experienced when we saw these little ones safe on our shores?"

Levine also noted that Brith Sholom had so far helped to bring thirty-one parents of the children into the United States. "We are also endeavoring to bring over the parents of the remaining children so that at least this part of the work will be completed." In his conclusion, he expressed the hope that Brith Sholom would soon embark on a new project to bring yet more children into the United States.

But there would be no more Brith Sholom rescue missions. The *Kindertransport* that had brought ten thousand children to England during 1938 and 1939 had come to an end with the outbreak of war. In the summer of 1940, Congressman Richard Hennings of Missouri introduced a bill allowing U.S. ships to evacuate British children endangered by the war and bring them to the United States, where they would be admitted outside of the normal immigration quotas. The so-called Mercy Ship bill swiftly sailed through Congress and was signed by President Roosevelt in August 1940. Although it turned out to be largely superfluous—British officials were not keen on risking children's lives at sea while a war was on—the bill's passage nonetheless stood in stark contrast with the ill-fated Wagner-Rogers measure to admit Jewish children from Germany. Shortly before Congress approved the Mercy Ship bill, a Gallup poll found that nearly two-thirds of the American public was in favor of allowing British refugee children to remain in the United States until the war was over.

Between 1933 and 1945, the United States admitted between 1,000 and 1,200 "unaccompanied" Jewish children—children traveling without their parents—into the country. The fifty children rescued by Gilbert and Eleanor Kraus accounted for the largest known single group to be admitted into America during the entirety of the Holocaust. And while the United States opened its doors to 200,000 European refugees—mostly Jews—during Hitler's murderous reign, the sad fact remains that hundreds of thousands of additional lives lost in the ashes of the Holocaust might well have been saved had America been more generous.

Among the victims of the Nazis' Final Solution were one and a half million children.

. . . .

AFTER THE BRITH Sholom rescue mission was completed, Gil returned to his law practice in Philadelphia. From time to time, he and Eleanor corresponded with some of the children and their families. "It was nice to hear from you and your family, and Mrs. Kraus joins me in wishing you all a very happy New Year," Gil wrote in September 1941, during the Jewish high holidays, to Hugo Zulawski, who had gone to live with relatives in Brooklyn after his summer in Collegeville. Hugo's parents, who had made their way from Vienna to England, obtained visas for America earlier that spring. "It is nice to know that you are together with your family and have your own home. You are very fortunate indeed, as so many of our children have not yet been reunited with their parents." The letter was signed "Uncle Gilbert."

Eleanor immersed herself in other wartime work shortly after the United States entered the war in December 1941. On April 9, 1942, the Philadelphia *Evening Bulletin* published an article about a group of local women who had volunteered for the army's "Interceptor Service"—helping to monitor possible air raids by enemy planes. Eleanor was a "filterer"—someone who would track authorized flights in the area and alert army authorities to any irregularities. "Mrs. Kraus is a good filterer," the newspaper reported, "though men are supposed to be better filterers—more imaginative and resourceful than women. Mrs. K. should really be called an analyst." The reporter also noted that Eleanor only a week earlier had boarded up the family's New Jersey beach house after spending weekends and summers there for the past fourteen years. "She can't go now because she has pledged every other day to the army," the newspaper reported.

During the war, Gil closed down his practice and became vice president and general counsel of the *Philadelphia Record*. The feisty, liberal-voiced daily newspaper, which had begun publication in 1870, had been bought in 1928 by J. David Stern, a maverick publisher who was also closely connected to Albert Greenfield, Gil's former brother-in-law and client. By the time the newspaper went out of business in 1947, Gil was no longer interested in practicing law. Instead he inexplicably decided to take up farming. He and Eleanor—who was decidedly not thrilled about becoming a farmer's wife—moved to nearby rural Bucks County, where Gil bred Guernsey cows at his Sugar Bottom Farm. Sometime in the 1950s, he gave up on farming and returned to practicing law, this time in suburban Doylestown. By the early 1960s, Gil had become active in local Democratic Party politics and had founded the Doylestown Legal Aid Society. He also served as president of the Bucks County Mental Health Society.

Gil and Eleanor by this time had four grandchildren. Their daughter, Ellen, died in 1964, a victim of cancer at the age of thirty-three. "One of the great tragedies for my grandparents is that they could save fifty kids but were unable to save their own daughter," noted their granddaughter Liz Perle. "I think it broke a part of them. Even though they were able to look back and know they had kept fifty children from certain death, in the end they couldn't keep my mother—their own daughter—from one."

As the years passed, Gil and Eleanor moved back to Philadelphia and into an elegant apartment across the street from Rittenhouse Square. Gil died in August 1975 at the age of seventy-seven. Eleanor remained for a time in Philadelphia and later moved to Westchester County, New York, closer to her son, Steven, his wife, Suzanne, and their three children, Peter, Ginger, and Dan. Eleanor died in April 1989 at the age of eighty-five. Steven Kraus died in 2012.

BOB SCHLESS, WITHIN weeks of arriving in America with the fifty children, sailed back to Europe and returned to Vienna, where he and Hedy Neufeld were married in July 1939. The couple returned to the United States aboard the SS *Washington*—the same ship that had brought Eleanor to Europe in April—arriving in New York on August 3, 1939. Bob resumed his career in pediatric medicine and, after the war, brought Hedy's mother and sister to the United States. After he retired, Bob and Hedy moved to Berne, Switzerland, where he died in June 1972 at the age of seventy-seven. Hedy soon after returned to Philadelphia, where she lived for the rest of her life. She died in February 1989 at the age of seventy-four.

LOUIS LEVINE, BRITH Sholom's grand master during the 1939 rescue mission, continued to work for a variety of Jewish causes during and after World War II. He served as chairman of the American Committee for the Relief and Rehabilitation of Jewish War-Orphaned Children and also led the Jewish Council of Russian Relief. For two years beginning in 1946, he was a member of a World Jewish Congress committee that provided relief to children who had survived the Holocaust. Levine also served for twenty years as a member of the board of trustees of Yeshiva University in New York City. He died in February 1958 at the age of sixty-nine.

LEON SACKS, THE Philadelphia congressman who assisted in the Brith Sholom rescue mission, left Congress in 1943 to enlist in the U.S. Army Air Force. After the war, he became active in veterans affairs and was twice elected as a national judge advocate for the Jewish War Veterans organization. In 1965, President Lyndon B. Johnson appointed Sacks as chief counsel for the U.S. Customs Office. He died in March 1972 at the age of sixty-nine.

GEORGE MESSERSMITH LEFT his position as assistant secretary of state after President Roosevelt appointed him U.S. ambassador to

Cuba in 1940. The following year he was chosen as ambassador to Mexico, where he served until 1946. President Harry Truman that year selected Messersmith to be ambassador to Argentina, where he remained until he retired from the Foreign Service the following year. Messersmith died in Mexico in January 1960 at the age of seventy-six.

The Fifty Children

While researching this book and a related documentary film, I was eventually able to account for thirty-seven out of the fifty children rescued by Gil and Eleanor Kraus. Among that group, eighteen were living as of January 2015, and nineteen were deceased. I was unable to find any information about the remaining thirteen. To help in the ongoing effort to account for all fifty children, I would welcome hearing from any of these remaining men and women or their relatives.

The following are brief updated sketches of the children for whom I was able to account, following their arrival in the United States in June 1939. They are listed according to their original given and family names in Vienna. Names that appear in parentheses reflect Americanized given names and married names.

PAUL BELLER lived with the Amram family in Feasterville, Pennsylvania, for about a year. His mother, Mina, obtained a visa for the United States, arrived in February 1940, and settled in New York City. His father, Leo, waited out the war in a British detention facility in Mauritius, where he had been sent after being caught trying to enter Palestine illegally. After the war, he was allowed to immigrate to the United States, sailing on a freighter that arrived in Baltimore in July 1946. Paul attended City College of New York and later obtained a master's degree in public administration from New York University. He spent two years in the U.S. Army, after which he began a forty-year career with the federal government, most of it working for the national Medicare office in Maryland. He and his wife, Glenda, have three children, seven grandchildren, and three great-grandchildren. They live in New Jersey.

ALFRED (FREDDY) BERG and his younger sister, Charlotte, lived with distant relatives in Jersey City, New Jersey, until they were re-united with their parents in December 1939 and moved to Brooklyn, New York. Freddy entered the navy toward the end of World War II and was deployed to Okinawa, Japan, where he served until the war came to a close in August 1945. He later studied business and worked for many years as a stockbroker. He and his wife, Marianne, had two children and three grandchildren and lived for many years in New Jersey. He died in 2013.

CHARLOTTE BERG (HOFFMAN) remained in Brooklyn with her parents until getting married. She and her husband raised two children and lived for many years on Long Island, New York, and in Boca Raton, Florida. Charlotte passed away in 1999.

ROBERT BRAUN and his older sister, Johanna (always known as Hanni), lived with Gil and Eleanor and their children in Philadelphia for two years. During that time, Robert and Hanni attended Friends Select, the Quaker school in Philadelphia where the Krauses' daughter, Ellen, was enrolled. "Once a month or so, Mr. Kraus would give all of us a whole handful of nickels, and we'd take them to the Automat where we could eat anything we wanted," Robert recalled. "I thought that was just the biggest thrill in the world, picking out your own food, even if it meant having nothing but cake or pie. It was great."

In 1941, Robert and Hanni went to live with a cousin, another Viennese emigré, in Bridgeport, Connecticut. Their parents, Max and Karoline, survived the war in Vienna thanks to Karoline's official Nazi certificate that, based on her ancestors' birth and marriage records, identified her as an Aryan, even though she had converted to Judaism at the time of her marriage. The couple obtained visas for the United States and arrived on Christmas Day 1947.

Robert studied dentistry and served in the U.S. Army during the Korean War. He later became an orthodontist in Fairfield, Connecticut. One of his patients was Gil and Eleanor's granddaughter Liz Perle, who grew up in nearby Rowayton. Robert and his wife, Nancy, raised six children, have six grandchildren, and continue to live in Fairfield.

JOHANNA BRAUN (GITLIN) studied at the University of Connecticut School of Pharmacy, where she met and married her husband. They moved to Bridgeport, where they owned a pharmacy and worked side by side for nearly thirty years. They had three daughters and seven grandchildren. Johanna died in 1997.

INGE BRAUNWASSER (STEINBERGER) lived with a great-uncle and great-aunt in Texas until she was reunited with her parents, Simon and Elsa, who arrived in the United States in December 1939. After getting married, she moved to Cincinnati, where she worked for many years as a teaching assistant. In 1995, she was reunited after fifty-six years with Helga Weisz, her bunk mate aboard the SS *Harding*, during a Brith Sholom anniversary celebration near Philadelphia. Inge and her husband had two children and six grandchildren. She died in 2003.

SIGMUND and EDMUND DEUTSCHER lived for a year with their grandparents in Oklahoma City before moving to Chicago and enrolling as yeshiva students at Hebrew Theological College. Their parents, who escaped from Vienna but were interned in Italy during the war, came to the United States in 1946. Sigmund spent thirty years in the U.S. Air Force, and he and his wife have three children and two grandchildren. He lives in Colorado Springs. Edmund served in the U.S. Army and lived in Cincinnati, where he died in 1956.

RELLY EISENBERG (KATZ) was taken in by Charles and Ollie Weyl, Gil and Eleanor's Philadelphia friends, and continued to live with Ollie for several years after the Weyls divorced in 1947. Relly's mother obtained a visa for the United States but her father perished at Auschwitz in 1942. Relly graduated from the University of Pennsylvania and later earned a master's degree at Temple University. Married with one son, she spent many years as an adjunct English professor at various East Coast community colleges. Relly died in 2002.

FRED FREUTHAL lived briefly with a distant relative in Brooklyn after leaving the Brith Sholom summer camp. Both of his parents obtained visas and arrived in the United States in September 1939. The family soon after moved to Pittsburgh, which was among the cities recommended to them by Jewish refugee aid groups in New York. Fred studied biology at the University of Pittsburgh and spent his career as a medical technologist, focusing on microbiology and related fields. He and his wife raised three children and live in suburban Maryland.

ERIKA GOLDSTEIN (MANSFIELD) lived for a few months with a foster family in Philadelphia until she was reunited with her parents and younger brother, all of whom arrived in the United States in October 1939. She grew up in New York City's Lower East Side and attended Brooklyn College, where she studied economics, psychology and sociology. Erika worked briefly on Wall Street for a mutual funds company before getting married in 1959 to Morris Mansfield and moving to Merrick, New York. She and her husband raised three children and had six grandchildren. She later returned to work as a secretary at a community college in New York and retired with her husband to Boynton Beach, Florida. Erika passed away in 2005.

FRITZ (FRED) HABER lived for a year with a foster family in Philadelphia and, after being reunited with his parents, moved to the Washington Heights section of New York City. He later enrolled at UCLA. After working for several summers as a hotel waiter in New York's Catskill Mountains, Fred and his older brother Henry (who escaped from Vienna to London only days after Fred left for the United States) bought a hotel in Fleischmanns, a resort town popular with European refugees. Fred and his brother also started an office supply business that grew into a national company with offices in Los Angeles, New York, Las Vegas, and Miami. Fred has two sons and three grandchildren, and lives in Riverdale, New York.

GERDA HALOTE (STEIN) lived with her grandmother and other relatives in New York City until she was reunited with her parents in 1941. She grew up in Queens, where she became the first female member of her high school's chess club—by beating the club president. She later studied economics at Brooklyn College and attended graduate school at New York University. After living briefly in Israel, Gerda and her Israeli husband returned to the United States and settled in Los Angeles, where she worked for many years as an accountant. She and her husband have three daughters and six grandchildren and live in the San Fernando Valley area of Los Angeles.

KURT HERMAN and another rescued child, Julius Wald, lived together with a foster family in Allentown, Pennsylvania, after their summer in Collegeville. Kurt's father, Heinrich, left Vienna in May 1939 with nearly one hundred other Jewish passengers aboard a French steamship, the *Flandre*, which sailed for Cuba around the time of the SS *St. Louis*. After being turned away in Havana, the *Flandre* returned to France, where Heinrich was sent to a displaced persons camp. Kurt's mother, Martha, obtained a visa and sailed to America on a ship that left from Genoa, Italy, in October 1939. Heinrich spent a year in the refugee camp and then obtained a visa for the United States, where he was reunited with his wife and son in April 1940. The family lived in Allentown.

Kurt received a business degree from Pennsylvania State University, after which he served for three years in the U.S. Coast Guard. He worked for many years as the chief financial officer of the Jewish Federation of Greater Philadelphia during which he learned about Brith Sholom's role in the children's rescue. After becoming a member of the group, he was elected president of its Kraus-Pearlstein Lodge—which was named partly in honor of Gil's father, Solomon. Kurt and his wife had three daughters and eight grandchildren. He passed away in 2014.

ROBERT KELLER was reunited with his parents, Viktor and Amalia, and his older brother about two years after his arrival in the United States. The family lived in Trenton, New Jersey. An accomplished musician, Robert entered the U.S. Army toward the end of World War II; he was sent to the Pacific where he performed in jazz bands that entertained in officers' clubs. He later studied at Champlain College in Illinois and the University of Denver before obtaining a Ph.D. in microbiology from the University of Pennsylvania. He became the associate director of microbiology and immunology at Michael Reese Hospital in Chicago and also served as the dean of the School of Allied Health Sciences operated in conjunction with the University of Chicago. He and his wife had one child. Robert passed away in 1982.

FRITZI KLEIN (NATKO) was reunited with her parents, who escaped from Vienna and arrived in America in November 1939, where they were taken in by a relative in Irvington, New Jersey. Fritzi's brother was part of the Kindertransport to England and rejoined the family in the United States in April 1940. Fritzi graduated from New York's Pratt Institute in 1949 and later worked as a dress designer in Manhattan. She and her husband had two sons, and Fritzi had two grandchildren years after her husband passed away. Fritzi died in 2014.

OSWALD LEWINTER, the mischievous little boy who tossed the children's suitcase keys into the ocean, lived with a foster family until he was reunited with his parents, who both obtained visas for America and settled in Brooklyn, New York. At the age of twenty, Oswald was arrested for illegally wearing a Marine Corps uniform—a federal offense—in an attempt to hitch a free ride on a Coast Guard plane. After graduating from college, he earned some acclaim as a published poet and taught literature for a few years at Marist College in Poughkeepsie, New York.

Oswald was arrested again in 1971, this time in London, after authorities accused him of unlawfully possessing a New York City police detective's badge and papers falsely identifying him as a foreign diplomat. Over the next several years, he had several more scrapes with the law, culminating in an incident in which he presented himself as a CIA operative who was allegedly involved in the release of American hostages held in Iran. His final hoax, which resulted in a prison sentence in Austria, involved his attempt to sell fabricated documents claiming that the British spy service MI6 was behind the 1997 car crash deaths of Princess Diana and Dodi Fayed. Oswald later moved to South Carolina, where he died in 2013.

FRIEDRICH (FRED) LIFSCHUTZ lived with his grandmother and aunt in the Bronx, New York, after spending the summer in Collegeville. To avoid arrest in Vienna, his father, Morris, tried to escape to Switzerland but was caught at the border and sent back to Vienna. Unable to obtain a visa for America, he returned to Podhajce, the town in Poland where he was born and where other relatives were still living. Just as Fred's mother, Bertha, was about to join him, Morris warned her not to come after hearing that the town was no longer safe for Jews. Bertha obtained a visa for America soon after and was reunited with her son in January 1940. Morris remained in Podhajce, which the Germans occupied in June 1941. He was killed two months later, though Fred and his mother did not learn of his death for several years. Fred attended City College of New York and has worked for years as a sales representative for various toy companies. He and his wife have two daughters and four grandchildren and live on Long Island, New York.

PETER LINHARD, whose father committed suicide in Vienna shortly before the children's departure, lived for several months with a foster family in New York. His mother, Regina, obtained a visa and came to America in November 1939. After living in Brooklyn, the family later moved to Philadelphia, where Peter spent much of his time in the city's pool halls. Following his discharge from the U.S. Army in 1955, he worked in a number of jobs before settling on a career as a semiprofessional pool player—and self-described compulsive gambler—who went by the nickname of "Peter Rabbit." He died in Philadelphia in 2005.

KLARA RATTNER (KAY LEE) lived in New York with a great-uncle and great-aunt while waiting for her parents to obtain their own visas for America. Her father, Jakob, was among the thousands of Jewish men from Nazi Germany who found temporary refuge at Camp Kitchener, a former British Army base. Her mother, Esther, also left Vienna for England, where she worked as a domestic servant in a Jewish household. After the family was reunited in May 1940, they moved to the San Francisco Bay Area, where another uncle was living. Klara graduated with a teaching credential from the University of California at Berkeley. She and her husband, who owned a commercial refrigeration business, raised three children and had four grandchildren. She has lived for many years in Atherton, California.

KURT ROSENBERG LIVED with cousins in Brooklyn and was reunited with his parents, Simon and Regina, who succeeded in escaping from Vienna in time to celebrate their son's bar mitzvah in December 1939. Kurt later attended City College of New York and had a long career in the retail business, starting out as a shoe salesman and winding up in executive management positions for companies in Los Angeles and San Diego. He and his wife had three children and four grandchildren. Kurt passed away in 2007.

KURT ROTH (ADMON) lived briefly with a foster family in Albany, New York, before moving to another family on Long Island. After his father died at Buchenwald in October 1939, his mother obtained visas for herself and her younger son Herbert. She arrived in the United States, by way of Italy, in March 1940. After starting college in New York City, Kurt moved to the newly created state of Israel in 1948 where he joined a kibbutz and changed his last name from Roth to Admon (a name similar to the Hebrew word for *rot*—German for "red"). He later studied economics, specializing in kibbutz-related management issues.

During the 1980s, Kurt took a family trip to Vienna, where he went in search of his father's gravesite. "The Jewish part of the cemetery there had not yet been reconstructed. A lot of the gravestones were broken and thrown all around," he recalled. A woman who worked at the cemetery provided him with the precise location of his father's burial site. "You can destroy the graveyard. And you can kill everyone," he said. "But these people were very good at keeping order." Kurt has six children and eleven grandchildren and lives in Netanya, Israel.

ELLA SPIEGLER (GOLDSTEIN) lived in Hagerstown, Maryland, and later Newark, New Jersey, after leaving the Brith Sholom camp. Her parents escaped from Vienna to England in 1939, and her father served in the British army during World War II. Ella was reunited with her parents after they immigrated to the United States in 1948. She spent most of the rest of her life with her husband in West Orange, New Jersey, where she worked as an office secretary and raised two children. At the time of her death in 2004, she had four grandchildren and two great-grandchildren.

ROBERT SPIES lived with distant relatives in the Bronx and later moved to Brooklyn after his parents obtained visas and arrived in the United States in April 1940. He earned a degree in mechanical engineering from Cooper Union, after which he got married, moved to California, and enrolled in graduate school at the University of Southern California. After many years as a mechanical engineer, Robert obtained a law degree in 1975 and went into private law practice. He lives in Los Angeles.

KURT STEINBRECHER lived with relatives in the Bronx for a couple of years after his arrival in the United States. He later learned that his parents escaped from Germany to Russia before making their way to Vancouver and then Seattle. Kurt remained with his relatives in New York until shortly after his bar mitzvah in 1941, after which he joined his parents in Seattle. He attended the University of Washington, where he obtained undergraduate degrees in zoology and pharmacy. He served in the U.S. Army during the Korean War although he was deployed to Europe rather than to Asia. He later earned a Ph.D. in pharmaceutical chemistry and worked for many years in the Seattle office of the U.S. Food and Drug Administration. He has one son and continues to live in Seattle.

ERIKA TAMAR was the youngest of the fifty children, a week away from turning five when she arrived in the United States along with her older brother, Heinz. After living briefly with a foster family in Houston, Erika and Heinz were reunited with their parents, Julius and Pauline, who arrived in the United States in the fall of 1939 and settled in New York City. Erika later attended New York University, where she studied creative writing and film. After college, she worked as a production assistant and casting director for the daytime soap opera *Search for Tomorrow*. Years later, after she married and raised three children, Erika enjoyed a successful writing career as the author of several best-selling young adult novels. Her second novel, *Good-bye, Glamour Girl*, featured a young Jewish refugee from Vienna determined to abandon her European heritage in favor of becoming an all-American glamour queen along the lines of Rita Hayworth. Erika has lived for many years in New York City.

HEINZ (HENRY) TAMAR studied biology at New York University and later earned a Ph.D. in sensory physiology at Florida State University. He was a professor of physiology and anatomy at Indiana State University for many years. He and his wife had three children and five grandchildren. He passed away in 2014.

ERWIN TEPPER lived with an aunt and uncle in the Bronx after his summer in Collegeville. His parents, who had originally escaped to England from Vienna, obtained visas for the United States shortly before America entered the war in 1941. After being reunited with their son, the Teppers moved to Bridgeport, Connecticut. Coincidentally, Robert Braun's Viennese cousin was Erwin's doctor while he was growing up. "I remember going over to the doctor's office with my mother or father, and there was a young woman there who would occasionally help out. I knew she was a foreigner because she had a slight accent, and I thought it might've been the doctor's daughter." In fact, the young woman was Robert's sister, Hanni, though Erwin did not recognize her or realize until much later that she was one of the rescued children. He earned a degree in zoology at Yale University in 1953 and obtained a medical degree six years later at the University of Basel in Switzerland. After spending two years in the army, he practiced radiation oncology for many years at Monmouth Medical Center in New Jersey. Erwin has three children, two grandchildren, and five step-grandchildren, and continues to live in New Jersey.

JULIUS (JAY) WALD, along with Kurt Herman, temporarily lived with a foster family in Allentown, Pennsylvania. His father, who had been imprisoned by the Nazis at both the Dachau and Buchenwald concentration camps, did not survive the Holocaust. His mother obtained a visa for the United States about a year after her son arrived. Julius had two sisters, both of whom had been living with an aunt in Connecticut. He served in the U.S Army during World War II, after which he obtained a degree in business administration at Adelphia University in Garden City, New York. Throughout his career, Julius worked in various capacities in law enforcement and the insurance industry. He and his wife had two sons, and the couple currently lives in Palm Beach, Florida.

HEINZ WEINIGER was taken in by a couple from Chicago, who continued to raise and support him for several years. His parents escaped from Vienna to England, where they found work as domestic servants, and eventually immigrated to America after the war. Heinz, however, never again lived with his parents. He had an older brother who escaped to Palestine and an older sister who also found safe haven in England and later came to the United States. Although his foster parents never legally adopted Heinz, they officially changed his last name to match theirs when they enrolled him at school. He was known for the rest of his life as Harry Kirchheimer. He studied accounting in college, obtained an MBA from the University of Minnesota and spent his entire career at Arthur Young & Company, where he became one of the firm's first Jewish partners. He and his wife—she was one of the Kindertransport children sent from Germany to England—had three children and four grandchildren. Harry passed away in 2001.

INGE WEISS (MICHAELS) and her younger sister, Kitty, were reunited with their parents in August 1939 and raised in the Bronx. Inge later moved with her husband to Miami, where the couple owned a real estate company, during which time Inge obtained both a broker's license and an insurance license. After their daughter finished college, Inge fulfilled her own lifelong dream of earning an undergraduate degree in psychology from Barry University in Miami. She had two granddaughters and passed away in 2002.

KITTY WEISS (PENNER) attended Brooklyn College and transferred to Barnard College, where she studied art history. She has spent the past several decades working as an artist and an art teacher. Kitty has two children and four grandchildren, and lives in Maine.

HELGA WEISZ (MILBERG) was reunited with her father, Emil, who obtained a visa and arrived in the United States in 1940. They moved to Detroit, where Emil worked as a caretaker in a Jewish cemetery. He was not able to obtain a visa for his wife, Rosa, who remained in Vienna. Years later Helga learned that her mother had been among a group of one thousand Vienna Jews deported by the Nazis in June 1942. The train was originally destined for the Izbica concentration camp but was diverted at the last minute to Sobibor, an extermination camp in Poland. Other than fifty-one men who were diverted to a forced-labor camp, everyone else was killed immediately upon arrival. Rosa was on the same train as Heinrich Steinberger, the young boy who had to forfeit his spot on Gil and Eleanor's list when he fell ill.

Helga became a teacher and lived for many years in Tucson, Arizona. She and her husband had three children, four grandchildren, and one great-grandchild. She passed away in 2012.

HENNY WENKART'S parents arrived in America on September 1, 1939, the same day that Germany invaded Poland. The family lived with relatives in Brooklyn and later moved to Baltimore before eventually settling in Providence, Rhode Island. Henny attended Pembroke College, the women's branch of then all-male Brown University. She later obtained a master's degree in journalism at Columbia University and a doctorate in philosophy from Harvard University. Henny has published several books of poetry and founded the Jewish Women's Poetry Workshop. She and her husband raised three children and have five grandchildren. She lives in New York City.

FRITZI ZINGER (NOZIK) and ELIZABETH ZINGER (DAVIS) remained with relatives in Utica, New York, and were reunited with their parents, Benjamin and Rosa, who arrived in the United States in January 1940 on a ship that sailed from Trieste, Italy. Fritzi later went to college and became a registered nurse. She had three children and five grandchildren. Elizabeth attended college and worked in public relations, including a position at the American Federation for the Blind, where she met Helen Keller. She and her husband had two children, three grandchildren, and two step-grandchildren. Fritzi lives in Florida and Elizabeth lives in the Boston area.

HUGO ZULAWSKI lived with a cousin in Brooklyn and was reunited with his parents, who obtained visas for the United States about a year after he arrived. In the summer of 1944, Hugo was inducted into the U.S. Army, where he was assigned to the intelligence corps and deployed to Munich. He later attended City College of New York, where he received a degree in civil engineering. During his career he worked on various construction projects in the New York area, including the building of the Long Island Expressway.

He and his wife had three children and four grandchildren. Hugo passed away in 2003.

BELOW ARE THE names of the remaining children for whom I have not been able to account or locate biographical information:

Vera Auerbach
Marlit Beiler
Erwin Berkowitz
Felix Heilpern
Irma Langberg
Franzi Linhard
Paula Schneider
Bianca Siegmann (Kirstein)
Kurt Singer
Edith Sommer
Ruth Taub
Elfrida Toch
Herbert Vogel

Afterword

It is often the frightening statistics that come to mind when people hear the word "Holocaust." Six million Jews murdered in the course of a war that took the lives of between 50 and 80 million soldiers and civilians. Over 1.3 million people, including 1.1 million Jews, murdered in a single location, at Auschwitz-Birkenau. Over two million Jews executed at close range in towns and villages in Axis-occupied Soviet territory. The numbers are staggering. The killing was the work of a vast number of perpetrators—Nazi Party members, German soldiers and civilians of every sort and station, civilian and military authorities from countries that were allied with Germany, and local collaborators all across Europe. Those who stood silently by were also complicit in their way, giving full rein to the perpetrators, facilitating genocide, and proving that to be a "bystander" in the presence of evil is not a neutral act.

The sheer numbers are so daunting that despite decades-long efforts by memorial institutions, scholars, prosecutorial authorities, as well as humanitarian organizations, it has proven impossible to retrieve the names of all the victims of the Holocaust. It has been equally difficult to identify, let alone hold accountable, all the major perpetrators and their closest collaborators, not to speak of the innumerable others who failed to respond as their fellow countrymen, their neighbors and their families, including 1.5 million Jewish children, were targeted, marked, deprived of their possessions, and exterminated.

By contrast, the number of people who sought to blunt the perpetrators' actions and took risks to rescue their fellow man was
small. Rescue took an act of courage, generally born of a deep-
rooted moral sense and "inability to do anything else," as rescuers
have often responded when asked why they acted as they did. Their
willingness to stand against the tide, despite risks and disincentives,
is what makes every story of rescue worthy of special attention. It
is, after all, the behavior of the rescuers that reveals the most noble
of all human potentials.

The stories of the rescuers during the Holocaust are not always
easily known. People who became rescuers did not do so to gain
recognition, and few sought recognition after the fact. For reasons
ranging from fear to greed to shame, acquaintances and fellow
countrymen often looked with disapproval at rescuers, not only
during the war but after it as well. Being identified as a rescuer
could be risky. This was obvious while the Axis powers dominated
Europe. Risk remained after the war because rescuers punctured
the comforting myth that it had been impossible to help Jews, or in
some cases because successful rescues created the possibility that
survivors might return to declare the truth of what had happened
in a particular town or village, or simply seek to reoccupy a family
home or reclaim personal property appropriated by others during
their absence. Thus, for the most part, rescuers did not dwell on
what they had done. They resumed their normal lives and routines
when the war was over. Many did not share their stories even with
family. Rescuers generally had no ongoing contact with the individuals they saved. And most have now passed away, without ever
having shared publicly the full details of what they did.

For all of these reasons, discovering the details of rescue stories
can be difficult, as the decades-long effort by the State of Israel to
identify non-Jewish rescuers and honor them as Righteous Among

the Nations makes clear.* Yet each of these rare stories deserves to be individually remembered, studied, and taught, because it is the rescuers' behavior among all human potentials that most deserves emulation and holds out the greatest hope for the future.

The story of Gilbert and Eleanor Kraus, who rescued fifty Jewish children from Nazi Germany on the eve of the outbreak of a war that would unleash the systematic murder of millions, is one such story. It shares some characteristics with others, first and foremost that what was at stake was life and death. That filmmaker and author Steven Pressman was able to interview many of the children and meet their families a full seventy years after the event is ample proof. So is the fact that five-year-old Heinrich Steinberger, the child who became ill and was left behind in Vienna, was murdered at the Sobibor death camp three years later. The Krauses took personal risks and confronted numerous—from all appearances insurmountable—obstacles. Consider that they risked travel to Germany, where the Nazi regime had already proven itself ruthless, violent, and unpredictable. A State Department official sounded a clear danger signal, particularly for Jews. Yet the Krauses (and Dr. Schless) left their own children behind to attempt to save the children of others. Social contacts, leaders of the Philadelphia Jewish community, and national Jewish organizations all sought to dissuade them. The public mood in the United States and political will in the United States Congress were opposed to opening the country to Jewish refugees. American immigration laws were complicated and restrictive. The outcome was uncertain right up to the end. Despite all of this, the Krauses sought no recognition and lived in anonymity after the war.

---

* See Mordecai Paldiel, *The Righteous Among the Nations: Rescuers of Jews During the Holocaust* (New York, HarperCollins Publishers, 2007).

But the story of the Kraus rescue mission is also unique in quite startling ways.

First, while most rescues were the work of Europeans on their own continent, the Kraus rescue mission is quintessentially American. The Krauses were an American couple, spurred on by a quite typical American voluntary association—Brith Sholom—on whose help they knew they could rely if their mission was successful. Gilbert and Eleanor Kraus demonstrated the independence of thought, individual initiative, and persistence that Americans consider to be American national "virtues." For anyone who believes that the Holocaust was foreign and not American history, this story reveals multiple ways in which the United States was implicated in shaping the fate of European Jewry during the 1930s and 1940s. American isolationism and widespread anti-Semitism made it impossible to craft public policies that might have been more compassionate toward refugees and led the American Jewish community, fearing a backlash, to be exceedingly cautious in advocating on behalf of European Jewry. Racial and religious prejudice, though diminished in recent decades, controversy over immigration issues, and reliance on individual initiative all continue to characterize American society today, making the story of Gilbert and Eleanor Kraus more than simple "history" and powerfully relevant in the twenty-first century.

Additionally, while finding help from neighbors, clergy, and others of good will was often a determining factor in successful rescue attempts during the Holocaust, the Krauses received assistance from a totally unexpected quarter, which turned out to be critical. It is not overstatement to say that without the aid of George Messersmith and Raymond Geist, the Krauses' rescue mission would likely not have taken place. Despite his defense of the status quo when it came to American immigration law, Messersmith's personal experience with and deep disgust for the Nazi regime and his personal exposure to the plight of German Jews created a level of understanding which distinguished him among State Department officers of similar rank. Just as important, the fact that Messersmith and Raymond Geist had served together in Germany created a degree of mutual confidence and "intimacy" between the two men that made it possible for them to consult, through official and unofficial channels, and to proceed in a way that might otherwise have been impossible. Neither feared betrayal by the other, and each was convinced that the other would proceed carefully enough that they would be able to respond effectively to the inevitable after-the-fact inquiries that might—and did—materialize from members of Congress, Jewish organizations embarrassed by the Krauses' success, the Department of Labor, and the corridors of the State Department itself. Their "personal and confidential" letters to one another did not require the multiple clearances, and did not receive the wide distribution, that would have been typical for "official" diplomatic messages and cables. And it was not by chance that Geist shared with Messersmith via private letter his view that "The Jews of Germany are being condemned to death." Given the bureaucratic risk, it is not surprising either that Messersmith obtained in advance a letter ruling from the Immigration and Naturalization Service indicating hypothetical approval of the plan to bring in fifty children. Nor that on May 18–19, 1939, just three days before visas were issued to all fifty children by the American Mission in Berlin, Messersmith and Geist exchanged *official* telegrams mutually affirming to one another that they were acting in full conformity with immigration law. All of this provided bureaucratic cover for two seasoned diplomats who knew they might need it.

The Kraus rescue story extends beyond the power of the story itself to puncture some of the myths that have persisted for decades regarding the Holocaust. Many myths have survived because they make it easier to contemplate the Holocaust, though they make honest confrontation with the past more difficult. In the Netherlands, the myth was built around Anne Frank and left it to be understood that every Dutch family was hiding Jews. For decades the

French myth was that all Frenchmen were in the Resistance. In the United States, the most common myth, embraced to explain America's failure to act more compassionately toward refugees and more forcefully in the face of mass murder, is that we did not know what Nazi Germany, her allies and collaborators, were doing. But the Krauses were not intelligence agents privy to classified information. They were reading the newspapers after Kristallnacht and learning of the brutality with which Jews were being treated in Vienna and across Germany. What distinguished them from others is simply that they chose not to close their eyes to what they were reading. In 1938–1939 information regarding Germany's treatment of Jews was publicly available to all Americans. Recent research and the opening of formerly classified American wartime archival documentation have also made it clear how much information American policymakers had regarding the mass killing of Jews that began after the outbreak of war in September 1939.

Another surprisingly resilient myth is that no one could foresee that accelerating discrimination against the Jews might culminate in mass murder. It is true that the Holocaust exceeded in ferocity, magnitude and intent any mass killing that had taken place up to that time. Yet here, within the confines of this one story, we encounter an American diplomat who sees German Jewry "being condemned to death." Jews had been killed during Kristallnacht, and some of the thousands of Jewish men sent to concentration camps after Kristallnacht perished there. The Jews desperately seeking to leave Germany understood the potential danger. Parents were eager to hand their children over to Gilbert and Eleanor Kraus because they understood, to quote Klara Rattner's father, "We may die here." While the imminence and all-encompassing scale of the Holocaust was probably not understood, and while before war broke out only German Jews seemed immediately at risk, people did recognize that what was at stake for Jews was a matter of life and death.

Another misconception that, whether intentionally or not, has provided unwarranted durability to the portrayal of Jews as some-how "less than human"—a key aim of Nazi propaganda—is the notion that Jews went to their deaths during the Holocaust "like lambs to the slaughter," that is, without resisting, as "real" human beings surely would have done. The Kraus story counters this myth on multiple levels. Two American Jews, Gilbert and Eleanor Kraus, responded in a dramatic and courageous way to the imminent danger facing Jews in Germany. In Europe, the Jewish Community of Vienna (Israelitische Kultusgemeinde—IKG), which had mobi-lized after the *Anschluss* to assist Jews through complex emigration procedures imposed by the Nazis, provided essential assistance to the Krauses, helping to identify eligible children, communicate with their families, organize interviews, and obtain essential travel au-thorizations. Much of what happened in Vienna during the Krauses' time there is known through documents in the IKG archives, which remarkably survived the war and can be consulted today. It is also in those archives that one discovers the fate of children who could not emigrate before the mass deportations of Viennese Jewry began. The Union of Jews in Germany (Reichsvereinigung der Juden in Deutsch-land) fed and housed the fifty children overnight in Berlin. These Jews who assisted the Krauses did so because they were systemati-cally involved in helping others who were seeking to emigrate or in need of food and shelter. The Kraus story reveals the stark reality that they often paid for their courage with their lives. The Holocaust was indeed a slaughter. But the story Steven Pressman has given us makes it clear that Jews did not "go like lambs." They did what was possible to resist, despite the odds, and even though they knew that most often their efforts would be in vain.*

Finally, *50 Children* challenges the most self-comforting and widespread myth of all. The assertion that "there was nothing we

---

* See the monographic study on this topic by Bob Moore, *Survivors: Jewish Self-Help and Rescue in Nazi-Occupied Western Europe* (Oxford, Oxford University Press, 2010).

could do" transcends all borders and languages. It makes no difference whether one refers to Germany itself, an Axis allied state, an occupied country, or a member state of the United Nations. Officials and inhabitants of every country have made essentially this same assertion when confronted with the mass murder of European Jews—a genocide that we now call "The Holocaust," though neither of these words existed at the time. The United States is no exception. And yet, while Great Britain took in 10,000 unaccompanied German children in an organized effort collectively knows as Kindertransport, the United States took in a total of only about 1,000 unaccompanied children, of whom fifty—*or one of every twenty*—were saved by this one couple from Philadelphia. During the years when it was possible for Jews to leave Germany for the United States, American public opinion, government insensitivity, lack of interest, and a depressing failure of human compassion all worked against them. The Kraus rescue mission makes it crystal clear that there were things that America could have done to alleviate the suffering of Europe's Jews. What the United States could not do was overcome the prejudices of the day to do what was possible. Immigration quotas and restrictive visa practices prevented Jews who might have left Germany from finding a place to go . . . except for the ghettos, concentration camps, and killing centers where no immigration quotas barred their way.

TWO SURVIVORS AMONG the many who were permitted entry to the United States *after* World War II ended have had particular impact on the ways in which the legacy of the Holocaust has been addressed in our own country and internationally. Both born in 1928, each survived as a child, emerging from the catastrophe an adolescent at war's end. Each had lost most of his family. Barely older than the majority of the children saved by Gilbert and Eleanor Kraus, each became a leading advocate for Holocaust remembrance and human rights.

The first of these two survivors, Elie Wiesel, in 1986 would be awarded the Nobel Peace Prize for his contribution. Wiesel had survived Auschwitz and Buchenwald, and described the nadir of humanity during the Holocaust in his seminal work, *Night*. He captured the depravity of the concentration camp world and humanity's failure both inside and outside the camp when, in response to Wiesel's visible concern for his father, who was dying, a Kapo tells him:

> Here, every man has to fight for himself and not think of anyone else. Even of his father. Here, there are no fathers, no brothers, no friends. Everyone lives and dies for himself alone.*

The second of the two survivors, Tom Lantos, was the only Holocaust survivor ever elected to the United States Congress. Lantos was subjected to forced labor in his native Hungary, but found refuge in a safe house in Budapest under the protection of Swedish diplomat Raoul Wallenberg. As a result, he escaped deportation to Auschwitz, where over 450,000 fellow Hungarian Jews were being deported and gassed in mid-1944. Wallenberg, of course, put his own safety at risk to save Jews from a country not his own. Lantos served in Congress from 1981 until his death in 2008, founded and chaired the Congressional Human Rights Caucus, and for decades represented the strongest voice on behalf of human rights in the entire American national legislature. Tom Lantos, like Elie Wiesel, spoke and wrote with deep emotion and insight. In one of his favorite stories, he would ask, "How can one know the moment when the *night* has ended and dawn has come?" Then, attributing the answer to a sage rabbi, but in fact giving his own personal response, he would reply, "The moment when you know that the night has turned to day is when you see the face of a stranger and recognize him as your brother."

---

* Elie Wiesel, *Night* (New York, Hill and Wang, 1960), p.111.

Night and Day. . . . Failure or Compassion. . . . Impotence or Courage. . . . Death or Life. . . . These were the alternatives of the Holocaust. The choices people made in that frightening era made a difference, and it was often the difference between life and death. Despite the obstacles and unfavorable odds, Gilbert and Eleanor Kraus chose compassion and courage, and saved the lives of fifty children in mortal danger. Their story brought light to a darkened landscape, sheds light on what is possible, and serves as a powerful reminder that the noblest of human potentials lives on in each and every human being. What each person does can make a world of difference.

Paul A. Shapiro
Director
Center for Advanced Holocaust Studies
United States Holocaust Memorial Museum
Washington, D.C.

Acknowledgments

The dramatic story of Gil and Eleanor Kraus's rescue of fifty children from Vienna would have been impossible to tell without unfettered access to Eleanor's private unpublished account. I am grateful to members of the Kraus family—in particular Gil and Eleanor's four grandchildren—for allowing me to draw freely from this remarkable document. In particular, I am indebted to Peter and Jill Kraus, Dan and Elaine Kraus, Ginger Kraus, and Liz Perle for their warm and gracious support. I also owe loving thanks to Suzanne Kraus, Gil and Eleanor's daughter-in-law, for sharing her memories and family photo albums in the service of recounting this wonderful story.

Beyond the blueprint provided by Eleanor's manuscript, I received copious amounts of support from several research institutions and historical archives. The United States Holocaust Memorial Museum in Washington, D.C., proved to be an indispensible partner throughout this project for whom a simple expression of thanks hardly seems sufficient. I especially want to acknowledge Paul Shapiro and Robert Williams at the museum's Center for Advanced Holocaust Studies. Without their generosity and encouragement, a complete and accurate account of Gil and Eleanor's mission could never have been told. At various stages throughout the project, several others at USHMM also provided extraordinarily helpful support and assistance: Aleisa Fishman, Anatol Steck, Bruce Levy, Judy Cohen, Caroline Waddell, Andrea Barchas, Elissa Schein, Dana Marine, Raye Farr, Lorna

Miles, and Sara Bloomfield. I cannot speak highly enough of this incredible institution, and it has been an immense honor to work closely with everyone there these past few years.

I relied heavily on the National Archives and Records Administration (NARA) for historical records and documents pertaining directly to Gil and Eleanor's rescue mission and to the general period in which it took place. In particular, I wish to thank NARA's Rodney Ross and Katherine Mollan for their kind assistance. Special thanks go to Lisa Hemmer and Polly Pettit for helping me to further navigate through reams of archival materials.

In Philadelphia, my research benefited immensely from archival documents located at the Pennsylvania Historical Society, American Friends Service Committee, Temple University's Urban Archives, and the National Museum of American Jewish History. In addition, I want to thank Colleen Puckett and Dick Hoffman for welcoming me at Friends Select School and digging through the school's records and yearbooks. Similarly, Nancy Miller at the University of Pennsylvania helped to unearth fascinating materials that illuminated Gil's undergraduate years there. I am hugely indebted to Myrna Wolman, who gave me free rein to rummage through a thick pile of materials in her office at Brith Sholom's headquarters. I am grateful to Beryl Kravetz and Lance Zeaman for leading me on a delightful and memorable tour of the site of the Brith Sholom summer camp along the banks of Perkiomen Creek in Collegeville, Pennsylvania. Kenneth Milano helped to unearth some key Kraus family records, and Jean Brubaker graciously welcomed me into the very same home from which Gil and Eleanor's mission first unfolded.

In New York City, I wish to thank the Center for Jewish History, which houses both the American Jewish Historical Society and YIVO Institute for Jewish Research. Not only is the Center one of the most pleasant places to conduct research, but its holdings proved to be enormously useful when it came to documenting the social and political background that existed in the United States during the time of Gil and Eleanor's mission. Along the same lines, I offer thanks to Kevin Proffitt, senior archivist at the American Jewish Archives at Cincinnati's Hebrew Union College, for helping to make my research trip there so productive.

In Vienna, the staff of the Israelitische Kultusgemeinde Wien (IKG), Vienna's official Jewish community organization, enthusiastically opened its doors (and its historic file cabinets) in support of my research. I owe specific thanks to Susanne Uslu-Pauer, the archives manager, and Wolf-Erich Eckstein, who patiently presides over the Vienna Jewish Records Office. Elsewhere in Vienna, I am grateful to Astrid Peterle and Christa Prokisch at the Jewish Museum, Susanne Trauneck at the Jewish Welcome Service, and Helmut Pflügl at Filmarchiv Austria. During two extended research trips, I also received invaluable advice and counsel from Lothar Hölbling, Ingo Zechner, Doron Rabinovici, Mara Kraus, Thera Khan and Edward Serotta. Jakob-Moritz Eberl deserves special recognition for his expert services as a city guide, translator, and research assistant. I owe a huge debt of gratitude and extend gracious thanks to Hannah Lessing and Evelina Merhaut at the Austrian National Fund for the Victims of National Socialism.

In Berlin, I thank Gudrun Maierhof for cheerfully escorting me around the city in an effort to retrace Gil and Eleanor's steps there nearly seventy-five years earlier. And in Jerusalem, Hadassah Assouline patiently tracked down records kept at the Central Archives for the History of the Jewish People, which are housed at Hebrew University.

Before writing this book, I had the privilege of making a documentary film titled *50 Children: The Rescue Mission of Mr. and Mrs. Kraus*, which premiered on HBO on Holocaust Remembrance Day in April 2013. I am eternally grateful to Sheila Nevins, HBO's president of documentary films, for embracing my film, helping to improve it, and providing a showcase on the single most prestigious platform for American documentaries. I also want to thank HBO's

Jacqueline Glover, who served as the film's supervising producer and who could not have been more supportive throughout its completion. Stephen Scheffer deserves my profound thanks for bringing the film to HBO's attention. Similarly, E. Gabriel Perle played a pivotal role, along with being a wonderfully supportive father-in-law.

This is not the place to thank all those who had a hand in the film's production; indeed, there's a long list in the closing credits. Instead, I will confine myself to acknowledging Ken Schneider for his superb editing talents and inspiring creativity, both of which were instrumental in transforming Gil and Eleanor's story into cinematic language. Peter Riegert deserves special mention for helping to guide a novice filmmaker through a daunting process. His sage counsel and warm friendship will be forever appreciated.

I could never have told the story—whether on-screen or on the printed page—without the enthusiastic cooperation of several of the surviving children rescued by Gil and Eleanor. My heartfelt thanks go to Kurt Admon, Paul Beller, Alfred Berg, Robert Braun, Elizabeth Davis, Kurt Herman, Kay Lee, Fred Lifschutz, Fritzi Nozik, Kitty Penner, Robert Spies, Gerda Stein, Erwin Tepper, and Henny Wenkart. I also offer thanks, albeit posthumously, to Helga Milberg. I am delighted that she had a chance to see my film and was deeply saddened when I heard that she had passed away only a few months later. I am truly grateful for all of the help—including photographs, documents, scrapbooks, and other materials—provided by spouses, children, and other family members of the rescued children, both living and deceased. I'm afraid the names are too numerous to mention, so I will instead thank all of you, collectively, for your invaluable contributions. Similarly, I'd like to thank the descendants of Dr. Robert Schless for sharing memories, photographs, and other accounts of his extraordinary life and role in the rescue mission.

Elizabeth Kaplan is both a marvelous literary agent and a dear friend who deserves far more appreciation and gratitude than mere words can offer. This book would not have existed without her.

At HarperCollins, Jennifer Barth is the sort of editor every writer should wish for—intelligent, thoughtful, insightful, and then some. I'm grateful that she shared my vision for this book from the very outset, while also helping to improve it in ways both large and small. I also wish to thank David Watson at HarperCollins for his diligence and patience in helping to see the book through to completion.

While making the film and writing the book, I've continued to be blessed with close friendships that have long nurtured and inspired me. Thanks to Peter Allen, Eric Effron, Tema Goodwin, Mark Schapiro, Spencer Sherman, and Peretz and Becki Wolf-Prusan for everything you've all done to enrich my life.

I'm very fortunate to count on the continued love and support of my parents, Jerry and Allie Pressman, along with my brother, Harold, and my sister, Lauren. We are a lucky lot who never take for granted the profound value and treasured benefits of close family bonds. I am also proud to acknowledge my two wonderful children, Roshann and David, who wound up hearing far more about Nazis and Jewish refugees during these past few years than they had ever bargained for.

Finally, nothing in these preceding pages could ever have been written were it not for Liz Perle. Her role extends far beyond her willingness to entrust me with her grandparents' story. Almost from the moment we met several years ago, Liz has provided me with a raison d'être for just about every aspect of my daily existence. I don't know precisely what I did (or didn't do) to deserve her arrival in my life. But hardly a day goes by without my shuddering to think what life would be like without her.

Notes

All quotations from Eleanor Kraus come from her private unpublished memoir and are included throughout the book with the kind permission of Liz Perle and the Estate of Steven Kraus. All quotations and recollections from the rescued children are from interviews conducted with the author. The following archives also yielded a variety of documents that are cited in the notes.

American Friends Service Committee Archives, Philadelphia (AFSC)

American Jewish Historical Society, Center for Jewish History, New York City (AJHS)

Central Archive for the History of the Jewish People, Jerusalem (CAHJP)

George S. Messersmith papers, Special Collections, University of Delaware Library, Newark, Delaware (Messersmith Papers)

Jacob Rader Marcus Center of the American Jewish Archives, Hebrew Union College, Cincinnati (AJA)

National Archives and Records Administration, Washington, D.C. (NARA)

CHAPTER 1

5   Coincidentally, three prominent Philadelphia Quakers: "Friends' Society Sends Mission to Intercede for German

Jews," *Philadelphia Record*, December 5, 1938, in Quaker & Special Collections, Haverford College.

7 On January 2: "Solution of the Jewish Problem Seen by Goebbels as World's Task," *Montreal Gazette*, January 2, 1939.

7 A week later: "Nazis Arrest Jews As Spur to Bargaining," *Pittsburgh Post-Gazette*, January 9, 1939.

8 "In this hour I can report": Weyr, *The Setting of the Pearl*, 37.

CHAPTER 2

13 "Miss Eleanor Shirley Jacobs": "Prosecutor's Aide Weds," *Evening Public Ledger*, October 9, 1924.

14 In 1892 he was chosen: "S. C. Kraus Dies; Charities Leader," *Philadelphia Inquirer*, July 30, 1928.

14 The gathering turned into: "Pattison Named for the Mayoralty," *Philadelphia Inquirer*, January 17, 1895.

15 "Greenfield and Kraus had similar": quoted in "The Rise of Albert M. Greenfield," an essay in *Jewish Life in Philadelphia: 1830–1940*, edited by Murray Friedman ISHI Publications, Philadelphia, 1983, 218, 219.

15 By the time that Gil began: Ibid, 219.

16 Solomon played a leading role: History of Eagleville Hospital—www.eaglevillehospital.org.

17 Without obtaining a formal diploma: " 'Buddies' Now Lawyers," *Philadelphia Bulletin*, October 14, 1921.

18 "Give her about a week": Albert M. Greenfield Papers, Pennsylvania Historical Society, Philadelphia.

19 A photograph accompanying: "Former U. of P. Grid Man Gets City Post," *Philadelphia North American*, February 5, 1924.

20 "To work for his people": "Solomon C. Kraus Dies Suddenly in Atlantic City," Philadelphia *Jewish Exponent*, August 3, 1928.

21 "Stokowski pioneered what later became": *New York Times*, September 13, 1987.

CHAPTER 4

36 "And so, I take leave": Schuschnigg's farewell radio broadcast quoted in *The Nazification of Vienna and the Response of Viennese Jews*, Ilana Fritz Offenberger, doctoral dissertation, Clark University, May 2010.

37 Three weeks earlier: *Setting of the Pearl*, 72.

37 By the end of April: *American Jewish Yearbook 5698*, Jewish Publication Society, Philadelphia 1938, 214.

38 "The Jew must know": *Washington Post* article, March 27, 1938, cited in *The Jewish Trail of Tears*, Dennis Ross Laffer, dissertation, University of South Florida, 2011, 30.

40 "Undesirable interruptions and delays": An English translation of Bürkel's memo can be found in the online Jewish Virtual Library, a project of the American-Israeli Cooperative Enterprise (www.jewishvirtuallibrary.org).

40 "This is like an automatic factory": Höttl's remark comes from his testimony in the trial of Adolf Eichmann, Session 17, Volume I, p. 269, found at the online Nizkor Project (www.nizkor.org).

42 During the previous twelve months: *American Jewish Year Book*, Ibid.

CHAPTER 5

46 "May God forgive me": *The Day the Holocaust Began*, Gerald Schwab, Praeger, 1990, 43.

46 Shortly after midnight: Heydrich's memo can be found in the Jewish Virtual Library.

47 "Anti-Jewish activities": "All Vienna's Synagogues Attacked; Fires and Bombs Wreck 18 of 21," *New York Times*, November 11, 1938.

47   "It is true": "Thousands Hopeless Amid Wreckage," Jewish Telegraphic Agency, November 13, 1938.

47   "The justified and understandable anger": "Bands Rove Cities," *New York Times*, November 11, 1938.

48   "All Jewish organizational": *New York Times*, Ibid.

48   A news brief: "Noted Leaders Among 35,000–50,000 Jews Arrested," Jewish Telegraphic Agency, November 14, 1938.

CHAPTER 6

53   "The members of Brith Sholom": Kraus to Messersmith, NARA 150.626 J/610.

53   In 1933, during Hitler's first year: *The Politics of Rescue*, Feingold, 16, 335.

53   "The Department of State": Morgenthau's diary entry is cited in *Bureaucratic Response to Human Tragedy*, Melissa Jane Taylor, Holocaust and Genocide Studies, Volume 21, Number 2, Fall 2007, 246.

56   As early as 1934: Wilkinson's memo cited in *Frances Perkins and the German-Jewish Refugees*, Bat-Ami Zucker, American Jewish History, Volume 89, Number 1, March 2001.

57   George Kennan, the veteran diplomat: *American Refugee Policy*, Breitman and Kraut, attributed to *George Kennan, Memoirs, 1925–1950*, Pantheon, 1969.

58   "The extreme brutality": Messersmith to Phillips, 0109_0312-00, Messersmith Papers.

58   In an earlier nine-page: Messersmith to Hull, 0109_0127-00, Messersmith Papers.

59   During his tenure: Messersmith, in notes he wrote for an unpublished memoir, attributed Hitler's comment about him to Gestapo chief Rudolf Diels; 0109_1971-00, Messersmith Papers.

59   in November 1936: Messersmith to Moore, 0109_0784-00, Messersmith Papers.

59   "The Jews in Germany": Geist to Messersmith, 0109_1087-
      00, Messersmith Papers.

59   Only a few days after: *Frances Perkins and the German-
      Jewish Refugees*, see footnote 90.

60   Despite Messersmith's strenuous: *Frances Perkins and the
      German-Jewish Refugees*, see footnote 94.

60   In a "personal and confidential" memo: Messersmith to Geist,
      0109_1093-00, Messersmith Papers.

62   "We will supply satisfactory": Kraus letter to Messersmith,
      NARA 150.626 J/610, February 3, 1939.

62   On the same day: Messersmith cable to Geist, NARA, Ibid.,
      February 3, 1939.

63   Three days later: Messersmith letter to Kraus, NARA, Ibid.,
      February 6, 1939.

63   "I believe that this group": Messersmith memo to Warren and
      Coulter, NARA, Ibid., February 7, 1939.

64   "They have approached this whole problem": Messersmith
      letter to Geist, NARA, Ibid., February 6, 1939.

64   Two weeks later: Geist telegram to Messersmith, NARA
      150.626 J/612, February 20, 1939.

CHAPTER 7

65   "What is American citizenship": The text of Reynolds's
      radio broadcast appears in 84 Congressional Record, p. 501,
      February 13, 1939.

66   "Millions of innocent and defenseless": 84 Congressional
      Record, p. 1278, February 9, 1939.

66   "In Germany you have": Rogers's testimony before the
      Committee on Immigration and Naturalization, U.S. House
      of Representatives, 76th Cong., First Session, p. 291.

67   "It is difficult to see": This and other newspaper editorials
      appear in 84 Congressional Record, p. 641, February 21, 1939.

68   "It is impossible to offer": 84 Congressional Record, p. 982,
      March 14, 1939.

68   A 1938 survey: *Jewish Trail of Tears*, Ibid, 83.

68   Even 20 percent of American Jews: Ibid, p. 84.

68   A series of public opinion polls: *Jews in the Mind of America*,
      Charles Herbert Stember et al., Basic Books, 1966.

69   "It is my opinion": *Anti-Semitism in America: 1879–1939*.
      Harold Quinley, ed., Arno Press, 1977.

69   "All Jews are enemies": "Kuhn Admits Aims Are Same As
      Nazis'," *New York Times*, June 24, 1938.

70   Rabbi Stephen Wise: *American Refugee Policy and European
      Jewry*, Breitman and Kraut, 229.

70   "As heartless as it may seem": *America, Its Jews and the Rise of
      Nazism*, Gulie Ne'eman Arad, Indiana University Press, 2000, 200.

71   Her actions, however, prompted: Fletcher memo to Hogdon,
      NARA 150/01 2168, January 8, 1934.

71   "My husband says": *Eleanor and Franklin*, Joseph P. Lash,
      Norton, 1971, 576. Eleanor Roosevelt's correspondence with
      Justine Wise Polier can also be found at the American Jewish
      Historical Society in New York City.

72   Agnes Waters, representing a group: Hearings on H.J. Res
      165 and H.J. Res 168, Committee on Immigration and
      Naturalization, House of Reps, 76th Congress, First Session
      (page number unknown).

72   "I know it must be difficult": Ibid.

72   "Shall we first take care of our own": 84 Congressional
      Record, p. 1011, March 16, 1939.

73   Instead, she casually remarked: *The Politics of Rescue*, 150.

74   "He says that personally" *Eleanor and Franklin*, 576; Polier
      papers at AJHS.

74   "Caroline O'Day asked me": Ibid., p. 577; the original copy
      of Watson's memo, with FDR's notation, is at the Franklin D.
      Roosevelt Presidential Library in Hyde Park, New York.

CHAPTER 8

76 Two days later: "Plans Penna. Home for Reich Children," *Evening Public Ledger*, March 1, 1939.

76 A slightly longer article: "Brith Sholom Brings 50 Refugee Children Here," Philadelphia *Jewish Times*, March 3, 1939.

76 "We had a telephone message": Goldman letter to Warren, NARA 150.626 J/604.

77 In his response: Warren letter to Goldman, NARA, Ibid.

77 In the fall of 1933: *Cecilia Razovsky and the American-Jewish Women's Rescue Operations in the Second World War*, Bat-Ami Zucker, Vallentine Mitchell, 2008, 31 et seq.

77 But news of their arrival: *Frances Perkins and the German-Jewish Refugees*, footnote 10.

78 only about one hundred children: *Frances Perkins and the German-Jewish Refugees*, footnote 71.

78 "We not only are not taking": Cecilia Razovsky papers, AJHS.

78 "Since the quota waiting list": Ibid.

78 "I am afraid there will not be": Ibid.

79 "Persons who received affidavits": Ibid.

81 "We saw Mr. Geist": Clarence E. Pickett's Journal, September–November 1938, AFSC.

82 "The Department desires you": Hull cable, NARA 150.626 J/609A.

83 "Visas have been withheld": Geist telegram to Hull, NARA 150.626 J/621.

83 One day later: Warren memo to Messersmith, NARA, Ibid.

CHAPTER 9

89 A few months earlier: "Wilson to Depart from Reich Today," *New York Times*, November 16, 1938.

93 "They are sailing, I believe": Messersmith cable to Geist, NARA 150.626 J/625A.

CHAPTER 10

97 The dinner service began: I am grateful to Robert Braun for
providing an original dinner menu from the *Queen Mary*,
dated April 9, 1939.

99 Billikopf for many years: Billikopf Papers, AJA.

100 Its popular bar: *In the Garden of Beasts*, Larson, 225.

101 Geist was a man of imposing: *The Virginia Plan*, Robert
Gillette, The History Press, 2011, 30, et seq.

101 "Now that I cannot work": Cecilia Razovsky papers, AJHS.

101 Julius Seligsohn's wife: "Dr. Seligsohn, Outstanding Jewish
Leader in Germany, Dies in Concentration Camp," Jewish
Telegraphic Agency, April 30, 1942.

103 "You must walk past": *Report of Thirty-Fourth Annual
National Convention*, Independent Order of Brith Sholom,
June 1939.

104 "The visa section is in a state": Wiley memo, NARA
124.63/98, March 22, 1938.

104 "We hear constantly": Wiley cable to Messersmith, NARA
124.633/261, March 19, 1938.

104 "The object is not": Messersmith memo to Hull, NARA
150.01/2458, November 13, 1936.

CHAPTER 11

113 "Never before had Chancellor Hitler": "Hitler Becomes
Citizen of Danzig," *New York Times*, April 21, 1939.

115 "France is not the only place": "Parisians Blame It All on
Hitler," *New York Times*, April 23, 1939.

CHAPTER 13

134 Hammond was later accused: *Bureaucratic Response to
Human Tragedy*, Taylor, 255 et seq.

135 "We can delay": *No Ordinary Time*, Doris Kearns Goodwin,
Simon & Schuster, 1994, 173.

137 "You will remember": Geist letter to Messersmith, NARA
     150.626 J/649, May 4, 1939.

137 "I pointed out that": Geist letter to Messersmith, NARA
     150.626 J/649, May 4, 1939.

137 Two days after Geist: Morris cable to Geist, NARA 150.626
     J/649, May 6, 1939.

CHAPTER 14

143 About 50,000 Jews: *In the Garden of Beasts,* Larson, 57–58.

CHAPTER 15

146 "I am genuinely delighted": I am grateful to Steven Zulawski
     for providing me with a copy of Gil's letter to the parents.

149 The letter outlined: CAHJP, A/W 2003, Box 566.

CHAPTER 16

159 The memo, written by: R. C. Alexander memorandum,
     NARA 150.626 J/649, May 16, 1939.

160 "Referring fifty non-preference": Hull memo to Morris,
     NARA, Ibid.

160 "This plan, as carried out:" Razovsky letter to Warren,
     NARA 150.626 J/648, May 15, 1939.

160 In his matter-of-fact reply: Warren letter to Razovsky, NARA, Ibid.

161 "It seems to me quite hazardous": Kepecs letter to Pickett,
     May 29, 1939, Marion Kenworthy Papers, AJHS.

CHAPTER 17

168 Richard Friedmann never made it: Central Database of Shoah
     Victims' Names, Yad Vashem, Jerusalem.

170 Five years earlier: "Dollfuss Sends Greeting with His Trade
     Mission," *New York Times,* February 13, 1934.

170 Kuffler's business career: "Refugee Aid Group Resumes in
     Vienna," *New York Times,* November 20, 1938.

CHAPTER 18

174 Hitler himself lavishly praised: *Degenerate Art: The Fate of the Avant-Garde in Nazi Germany*, Stephanie Barron, Harry N. Abrams, 1991.

CHAPTER 19

182 "To those . . . who have not": "Reich Future Closed, Jewish Leaders Warn Berlin Meeting," Jewish Telegraphic Agency, January 30, 1938.

182 In the spring of 1940: "Heinrich Stahl, Former Head of Berlin Jewish Community, Dies in Exile," Jewish Telegraphic Agency, November 29, 1942.

183 "The route over which": "Reich Hails Ciano; Pact Signing Today," *New York Times*, May 22, 1939.

CHAPTER 21

199 "The persons responsible": "50 Child Refugees Here from Vienna," *New York Times*, June 4, 1939.

CHAPTER 22

209 "An after-dinner discussion": "50 Child Refugees Here from Vienna," *Philadelphia Inquirer*, June 4, 1939.

210 The Associated Press dispatch: "Cuba Changes Mind, May Let Refugees Land," *Philadelphia Inquirer*, June 4, 1939.

210 "Most urgently repeat plea": NARA 837.55.

210 A telegram from the State Department: NARA, Ibid.

211 Of the 937 passengers: "The Search for St. Louis Passengers," online exhibit, United States Holocaust Memorial Museum (www.ushmm.org).

211 "No doubt you received": Kraus letter to Engel provided by Steven Zulawski.

212 "It is a great comfort": Ibid.

212 "It was my intention": Kraus letter to Messersmith, NARA 150.626 J/657, June 8, 1939.

212 "I know that you must feel": Messersmith letter to Kraus, NARA, Ibid., June 8, 1939.

CHAPTER 23

217 "While the number fifty": *Report of Thirty-Fourth Annual National Convention*, Independent Order Brith Sholom, June 1939.

218 "As I stand before": Ibid.

221 "The question is asked": "Fifty German-Jewish Refugee Children (A 'Now It Can Be Told' Story)," *Philadelphia Jewish Exponent*, June 9, 1939.

221 "To my knowledge": YIVO archives, Center for Jewish History, New York City.

221 "The effect of this editorial": Razovsky letter to Warren, NARA 150.626 J/658, June 14, 1939.

221 "My attention has been called": Holman letter to Hull, NARA 150.626 J/656, June 8, 1939.

222 In his two-page reply: Hull letter to Holman, NARA, Ibid, June 17, 1939.

222 "At least Hitler has broken": "Private Citizens and American Rescue: Gilbert and Eleanor Kraus and the 50 Children of Vienna," Robert Williams, Center for Advanced Holocaust Studies, United States Holocaust Memorial Museum (see footnote 38).

222 On the afternoon of June 27: A stenographer's transcript of this and other meetings of the National Coordinating Committee can be found at the AFSC Archives in Philadelphia.

222 Kenworthy mentioned that committee members: Marion Kenworthy Papers, AJHS.

223 "Just how the children": Balderston memo, July 16, 1939, AFSC.

224 "I think it would be worth exploring": Pickett letter to
     Kepecs, July 20, 1939, AFSC.

CHAPTER 24

225 "Look at these children": "Little Refugees Proving Good As
     Americans," *New York Journal-American*, publication date
     unknown.

229 "Already I am a real American": Ibid.

EPILOGUE

232 In the summer of 1940: *Who Will Take Our Children?*,
     Carlton Jackson, McFarland (revised edition), 2008.

232 Shortly before Congress approved: " 'Mercy' Ship Bill Backed
     by Public," *New York Times*, August 17, 1940.

233 "Mrs. Kraus is a good filterer": "Women's Watchful Eyes Scan
     City Skies for Enemy Planes," *Philadelphia Evening Bulletin*,
     April 9, 1942.

Bibliography

American Refugee Policy and European Jewry 1933–45, Richard Breitman and Alan M. Kraut, Indiana University Press, 1987.

Beyond Belief: The American Press and the Coming of the Holocaust 1933–1945, Deborah E. Lipstadt, The Free Press, 1986.

Cecilia Razofsky and the American-Jewish Women's Rescue Operations in the Second World War, Vallentine Mitchell, 2008.

Challenging Years, Stephen Wise, G. P. Putnam's Sons, 1940.

Eichmann's Jews: The Jewish Administration of Holocaust Vienna 1938–1945, Doron Rabinovici, Polity Press, 2011 (first published in German as *Instanzen der Ohnmacht* Jüdischer Verlag Frankfurt am Main, 2000).

The Eichmann Trial, Deborah E. Lipstadt, Schocken Books, 2011.

Eleanor and Franklin, Joseph P. Lash, W. W. Norton and Company, 1971.

FDR and the Jews, Richard Breitman and Allan J. Lichtman, Harvard University Press, 2013.

George S. Messersmith: Diplomat of Democracy, Jesse H. Stiller, University of North Carolina Press, 1987.

In the Garden of Beasts: Love, Terror and an American Family in Hitler's Berlin, Erik Larson, Crown Publishers, 2011.

Jewish Life in Philadelphia 1830–1940, Edited by Murray Friedman, Ishi Publications, 1983.

The Jews of Vienna 1867–1914: Assimilation and Identity, Marsha

L. Rozenblit, State University of New York Press, 1983.

Memoirs of a Maverick Publisher, J. David Stern, Simon & Schuster, 1962.

The Politics of Rescue, Henry L. Feingold, Rutgers University Press, 1970.

Refugees and Rescue: The Diaries and Papers of James G. McDonald 1935–1945, edited by Richard Breitman, Barbara McDonald Stewart, and Severin Hochberg, Indiana University Press, 2009.

The Setting of the Pearl: Vienna under Hitler, Thomas Weyr, Oxford University Press, 2005.

Unfulfilled Promise: Rescue & Resettlement of Jewish Refugee Children in the United States 1934–1945, Judith Tydor Baumel, Denali Press, 1990.

Vienna and the Jews 1867–1938: A Cultural History, Steven Beller, Cambridge University Press, 1989.

The Vienna Paradox: A Memoir, Marjorie Perloff, New Directions Books, 2004.

List of Illustrations

Index

About the Author

S teven Pressman worked as a journalist for more than thirty years, writing and editing for newspapers, magazines, and other publications in Los Angeles, Washington, D.C., and San Francisco. He is the author of a previous nonfiction book, *Outrageous Betrayal: The Dark Journey of Werner Erhard from est to Exile* (St. Martin's Press, 1993). He is the writer, director and producer of the HBO documentary film *50 Children: The Rescue Mission of Mr. and Mrs. Kraus.* He and his wife, Liz Perle, have two children and live in San Francisco.